Revolutions in Sorrow

U.S. History in International Perspective

Editors: Peter N. Stearns and Thomas W. Zeiler

NOW AVAILABLE

Revolutions in Sorrow: The American Experience of Death in Global Perspective,
by Peter N. Stearns

Revolutions in Sorrow

The American Experience of Death in Global Perspective

by Peter N. Stearns

Paradigm Publishers

Boulder • London

Paradigm Publishers is committed to preserving ancient forests and natural resources. We elected to print *Revolutions In Sorrow* on 50% post consumer recycled paper, processed chlorine free. As a result, for this printing, we have saved:

10 Trees (40' tall and 6-8" diameter)
4,353 Gallons of Wastewater
1,751 Kilowatt Hours of Electricity
480 Pounds of Solid Waste
943 Pounds of Greenhouse Gases

Paradigm Publishers made this paper choice because our printer, Thomson-Shore, Inc., is a member of Green Press Initiative, a nonprofit program dedicated to supporting authors, publishers, and suppliers in their efforts to reduce their use of fiber obtained from endangered forests.

For more information, visit www.greenpressinitiative.org

Copyright © 2007 Paradigm Publishers

Published in the United States by Paradigm Publishers, 3360 Mitchell Lane, Suite E, Boulder, CO 80301 USA.

Paradigm Publishers is the trade name of Birkenkamp & Company, LLC, Dean Birkenkamp, President and Publisher.

Library of Congress Cataloging-in-Publication Data

Stearns, Peter N.
   Revolutions in sorrow : the American experience of death in global perspective / by Peter N. Stearns.
      p. cm.
   Includes bibliographical references and index.
   ISBN 978-1-59451-454-8 (hc)
   ISBN 978-1-59451-455-5 (pbk)
1. Death—Social aspects.   2. Death—Social aspects—United States   3. Death—Social aspects—Cross-cultural studies.   4. Social change   I. Title.
   HQ1073.S74 2007
   306.90973—dc22

2007015264

Printed and bound in the United States of America on acid free paper that meets the standards of the American National Standard for Permanence of Paper for Printed Library Materials.

Designed and Typeset by Straight Creek Bookmakers.

11 10 09 08 07   1 2 3 4 5

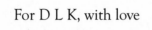

For D L K, with love

Contents

Acknowledgments

A number of research assistants contributed to this project: My thanks to Veronica Fletcher, Clio Stearns, Leah Lehman, and Mahati Gollamudi. Brian Platt provided useful suggestions. A reader of the manuscript offered valuable comments as well as encouraging enthusiasm, and Leslie Lomas, of Paradigm Publishers, was unusually helpful. Alicia Smallbrock rendered vital assistance in manuscript preparation.

Series Preface
U.S. History in International Perspective

This series offers a new approach to key topics in American history by connecting them with developments in other parts of the world and with larger global processes. Its goal is to present national patterns in mutual interaction with wider trends.

The United States has functioned in international context throughout its history. It was shaped by people who came from other countries. It drew political and cultural inspiration from other places as well. Soon, the nation began to contribute a variety of influences to other parts of the world, from new trade patterns to the impact of successful political institutions.

It is increasingly clear, however, that the field of U.S. history has not usually captured this perspective. National developments have been treated as significant but relatively isolated events. Distinctive American characteristics—sometimes systematized into a larger pattern called American exceptionalism—have been assumed but not tested through real comparison. Even the nation's growing role in world affairs has sometimes taken a back seat to domestic concerns. This kind of narrowness is inaccurate and unnecessary; it feeds a parochialism that is out of keeping with the global presence of the United States. A nation cannot be understood without placement in the perspective of other nations and transnational factors.

At a time when international developments play an increasing and incontestable role in any nation's affairs, the need for a new approach to national history becomes inescapable. This certainly applies to the United States. Calls for "internationalizing" the U.S. history survey course reflect this realization. The calls are welcome, but we need to translate them into accessible treatments of key topics in U.S. history—from obvious diplomatic and military initiatives to less obvious themes that in fact involve global interactions as well, themes that go deeply into the nation's social and cultural experience.

The project of internationalizing American history involves drawing a variety of connections. This series will compare American developments to patterns elsewhere to see what is really distinctive, and why, and what is more widely shared. Influences from other places, from technological innovations to human rights standards, factor in as well. The U.S. impact on other parts of the world, whether in the form of new work systems, consumer culture, or outright military intervention, constitutes a third kind of interconnection.

The result—and the central goal of this series—is to see American history in a revealing new light, as part of a network of global interactions. Wider world history gains from this approach as well, as comparisons are sharpened by the active inclusion of the United States, and American influences and involvements are probed more carefully.

Overall, a global window on the domestic interiors of U.S. history complicates conventional understandings, challenges established analyses, and brings fresh insights. A nation inextricably bound up with developments in every part of the world, shaping much of contemporary world history as well, demands a global framework. This series, as it explores a variety of topics and vantage points, aims to fill this need.

CHAPTER 1

Introduction:
Why Death?
Why the United States?

In his novel *No Longer at Ease*, the Nigerian author Chinua Achebe describes the following crisis: Obi, raised in a village but now prospering as a white-collar worker in the city of Lagos in the 1920s, has come to enjoy his work routine and lifestyle, including regular dances and a fair amount of womanizing. Then his mother dies. He sends money back for the funeral, but, due to his job and his dating schedule, he just does not have time to go himself. To the villagers, his behavior is a "thing of shame"—for he should have gone home not just for the funeral but for an extended period of mourning. As one old man put it: "This boy that we are all talking about, what has he done? He was told that his mother died and he did not care. It is a strange and surprising thing."[1]

In the United States, books on manners and etiquette from the late nineteenth to the early twentieth centuries had elaborate sections designed to show the proper courtesy toward a family that had just suffered a death. Visits, leaving cards to show concern, and assurances of sympathy were vital in a society in which death remained common and in which carefully prescribed etiquette was an important part of respectable life. By the 1940s, however, etiquette books changed dramatically: The emphasis changed to assert that a grieving individual must not impose on others. Extensive discussion of a loss through death was considered rude, and friends and acquaintances were not expected to put up with too much. By this point, psychologists were increasingly identifying part of their practice as "grief work," in which individuals who could not easily get over a death gained professional help to get their emotions under control. The social context for death had been virtually stood on its head. The issues were not the same as those in Africa, although there was some connection; the larger point was the apparent necessity, in otherwise very different contemporary societies, to reconsider basic aspects of the ways death should be approached. Fundamental changes were occurring in accepted encounters with death, from urban Nigeria to the suburban United States.[2]

Death is a human constant, happening eventually to everyone and figuring prominently in every human culture. But response to death can be organized very differently, depending on social values. Its incidence varies greatly as well, by social class, sometimes by gender, and certainly by historical time. So death is also a historical topic, important in itself and revealing a great deal about the nature and impact of social change. Basic developments like urbanization or redefinitions of manners change the reception of death—and Africa and the United States are hardly the only societies to experience this kind of impact in recent decades.

This book focuses on the modern experience of death, and particularly on crucial changes that occurred after 1880, comparing American developments with patterns in Western Europe and a few other societies. It does not offer a comprehensive survey of all the interesting variations and changes concerning death, in all times, all places. But, building from a brief discussion of some characteristic premodern beliefs and practices, it does convey the important modern challenges and tensions that continue to affect the treatment of death today. Fundamental changes have occurred in encounters with death, from urban Nigeria to suburban Russia.[3]

The United States has participated strongly in many of the major changes surrounding death over the past two centuries. It has seen the death rate retreat massively for key groups such as children. Causes of death have changed, moving away from communicable toward degenerative diseases. Rituals have been transformed, from death as a domestic experience to an initial transition toward elaborate mourning and then to a contemporary effort to reduce emotionality.

Some of these changes have been shared with other regions, particularly of course other urban, industrial societies like Western Europe or Japan. But the United States also has put its own stamp on the modern evolution of death—among other things, showing a somewhat unexpected conservatism when it came to alterations of ritual, while tolerating unusually high cost levels, where efforts both to fight death and to deal with its aftermath were involved. Looking at the United States in a global context helps pinpoint not only some important developments in modern history but also some particular national features that demand explanation—and in the eyes of some social critics, also cry out for reform.

Death is not only a personal and social experience, involving physical facts and cultural beliefs. It is also something that societies administer, through such practices as infanticide, punishment, and war. It is interesting that existing studies of death, often quite good, rarely go beyond discussing single societies to make more global comparisons and linkages, and they almost never consider these extensions of the subject. Yet ideas about death, and changes in ideas, have significant bearing on these wider reaches of the topic. Here, too, comparison is vital, and global consequences are very real.

Changes in the experience and attitudes toward death form the central part of the modern story, and of the comparisons between U.S. and global evolutions, but there is more. As the modern culture concerning death shifted, ideas about using death as a punishment for crime altered as well—moving away from patterns human societies had emphasized for thousands of years. The United States participated in this process and sometimes took a lead in developing new global standards. But here, too, the national course showed some distinctive features, and by the later twentieth century, the nation seemed to be moving away from dominant global standards. This is another anomaly to be explained, and a significant one; here, too, is an important component of the relationship between the United States and the rest of the contemporary world.

Unquestionably, American death expectations have had an impact well beyond the nation's borders. Associated with the steady rise of U.S. power in the world, and the frequent military involvements that seem to come along with world power, U.S. attitudes toward death have helped reshape both the nature and the impact of contemporary warfare, for example, by generating truly extraordinary efforts to recover casualties long after conflicts have ended. Reaction to U.S. deaths has become part of the military and diplomatic interactions of the contemporary world.

A final category in which there have been significant changes in the experience of and attitudes toward death involves issues of birth control, and particularly abortion, where the United States has differed on occasion—particularly, on recent occasion—from standards of many other societies. Here, too, finally, the United States and its distinctiveness have affected global patterns.

This book looks at changes and continuities in the various manifestations of death and their spillovers into military policy, punishment, and birth control. The changes have been substantial, a true indication of how different the modern experience is from that of the past, despite the inevitability of death in all times and all places. The United States has both participated in and resisted some of the larger global trends: Comparison is vital to establish how and why the nation stands out in some respects as well as to determine what the global framework has become. Aspects of U.S. reactions to death—particularly its reliance on the death penalty—now draw substantial international criticism. However, the United States has also influenced the global scene, particularly in the military strategies designed to minimize U.S. deaths, but also in arenas such as birth control and even funeral practices. The interplay between the nation and the larger trends is both complex and intriguing.

Death might seem an odd subject for a history—although in fact, because modern transformations have been so significant, there is a rich literature on key features of the phenomenon. It also might seem gloomy or starkly unpleasant—one of the frequent current comments on death in places like the United States is that it has become so removed from normal experience that many people shy away from discussing it. Although we will see that this judgment is oversimplistic, it is probably true that greater attention to death's history can contribute to some personal as well as social perspective. The obvious fact is that death is not just a part of life; attitudes toward it form a key component of the way societies function. It affects policy as well as personality. It influences global relationships, sometimes in unexpected ways. Death has always inspired awe and fear, and it still does. It should inspire interest and understanding as well.

Death also, perhaps unexpectedly, provides insight into some key questions about the United States in a world history context. Is the United States a separate civilization—an approach often known as U.S. exceptionalism—or is it part of a wider Western orbit? How much has the United States been influenced by global trends, not just today but in the past? How has the United States contributed to world history in turn, as the nation has attained increased power, and how does it approach the wider world? An analysis of death is not the only way to answer these questions, but its history does offer some telling specifics.

Death, though not a familiar historical topic, in fact has participated in some of the great changes of modern times. It also contributes toward answering basic comparative questions about the relationships among major societies and about the consequences of international power.

Beginning roughly two centuries ago, major changes in attitudes and practices associated with death began to take shape in a number of countries, including the United States. Earlier forms of death acceptance were rethought, in favor of a new emotionalism associated with death and a new desire to find ways to reduce death's incidence and impact. Ultimately, the raw facts of death changed as well, as mortality rates dropped first in the most advanced industrial societies, then globally. Death and modern society mixed less easily than had been the case in prior tradition.

A new emphasis on fighting or downplaying death had a number of advantages. Virtually no one living today would wish to go back to the experiences of and approaches to death that occurred even in the nineteenth century. Yet the fundamental shifts had drawbacks as well, which must be explored as part of understanding the modern condition. Some of the drawbacks are economic:

Fighting death can be extremely costly. But the more interesting qualifications are psychological, where the effort to combat death creates unexpected new vulnerabilities.

Furthermore, the current dominant trend toward mounting new resistance to death and its hold on the imagination was not always straightforward. For example, even as many societies recalibrated their stance on death, modern military technology created unparalleled opportunities to cause death: It has been hard to reconcile the two trends. Other practices—such as the punishment of criminals—might compete with the dominant trend toward reducing the number of deaths. In many cases, including the United States, the enjoyment of fictional accounts of death seems to have increased, even as actual death rates decline—another incongruence that must be addressed. The complexities of death trends, and their consequences, provide ample challenge for analysis.

The United States has been a leader in many modern changes in ways of looking at death, but it has also resisted some. U.S. wealth and space have created some distinctive twists on the basic modern story: No other major society has been able to afford the types of cemeteries Americans began to develop more than a century and a half ago. More recently, the U.S. impulse to find ways to resist death has paralleled the equally compelling increase in the nation's power to deliver death through the most advanced military armaments. The nation's inconsistencies on death—not necessarily greater than those of other societies, but distinctive—have become unusually influential in the world at large.

Notes

1. Chinua Achebe, *No Longer at Ease* (New York, 1961).

2. Amy Vanderbilt, *Amy Vanderbilt's Complete Book of Etiquette: A Guide to Gracious Living* (New York, 1966).

3. For a fascinating discussion of the growing modern discomfort with death, see Arthur Erwin Imhof, *Lost Worlds: How Our European Ancestors Coped with Everyday Life and Why Life Is So Hard Today* (Charlottesville, VA, 1996). The classic study, although much disputed, is Philippe Ariès, *The Hour of Our Death* (New York, 1981).

CHAPTER 2

Traditional Patterns of Death

Gilgamesh answered her, "And why should not my cheeks be starved and my face drawn? Despair is in my heart and my face is the face of one who has made a long journey, it was burned with heat and with cold. Why should I not wander over the pastures in search of the wind? My friend, my younger brother, he who hunted the wild ass of the wilderness and the panther of the plains, my friend, my younger brother who seized and killed the Bull of Heaven and overthrew Humbaba in the cedar forest, my friend who was very dear to me and who endured dangers beside me, Enkidu my brother, whom I loved, the end of mortality has overtaken him. I wept for him seven days and nights until the worm fastened on him. Because of my brother I am afraid of death, because of my brother I stray through the wilderness and cannot rest. His fate lies heavy upon me. How can I be silent, how can I rest? He is dust and I too shall die and be laid in the earth forever. But now, young woman, maker of wine, since I have seen your face, do not let me see the face of death which I dread so much."

She answered, "Gilgamesh, where are you hurrying to? You will never find that life for which you are searching. When the gods created man they allotted to him death, but life they retained in their own keeping. As for you, Gilgamesh, fill your belly with good things ... dance and be merry, feast and rejoice. Let your clothes be fresh, bathe yourself in water, cherish the little child that holds your hand, and make your wife happy in your embrace; for this too is the lot of man."

—*The Epic of Gilgamesh*[1]

The members of the human species are, as far as we know, the only living creatures aware at some level, from a fairly early age, that they will die, and the only creatures as well who are organized into societies that spend a good bit of time dealing with death in one form or another—organizing beliefs about it, trying to prevent it, developing rituals to accommodate its impact, even deliberately using it in punishment. Members of other species sometimes develop a perception that they are dying—sometimes, as with elephants, wandering away from the group to

7

complete the process. Some seem to react with sadness when death occurs—dogs even lamenting the death of a master or mistress—across species lines. But the generalized awareness, the consciousness of death even when it is not immediately present, and the deep need to explain and ritualize the experience, seem to be distinctly human. It is not surprising that debates over death figure strongly in the world's first known piece of literature, the Mesopotamian Gilgamesh epic of the third millennium BCE.

A serious practical issue also confronts human society, further contributing to the awareness of death: the need to dispose of dead bodies. Quite apart from the offensive sights and smells of corpses—which might vary a bit among different cultures but surely display some overall commonalities—bodies pose a health risk, as breeding grounds for bacteria and disease. Since humans have always been social—gathered in groups, which raises the potentiality for group exposure to contamination—it became clear well before recorded history that some means of disposing of corpses was essential. This need, combined with fearful awareness of death, further contributed to death beliefs and rituals, however varied their specific forms.

There is debate about when the awareness of death developed in species history. Humans in China (Peking man, about 500,000 BCE) might have buried tribe members—there are sites where bones were deliberately accumulated. But whether this was a sign of organized cannibalism or represented a desire to honor memory and enlist the aid of departed ancestors, we cannot be sure. By the time we reach *homo sapiens sapiens*, however, and the clear capacity for speech—60,000 years ago or more—there is no doubt: Human societies were devoting a good bit of energy to dealing with death and its anticipation. By this point many groups almost certainly believed that there was some kind of existence after death, for which the dead should be prepared. Bodies were placed in graves, often in a fetal position—either to prepare them for rebirth or to hinder their ability to return to the world of the living. Shells and other ornaments were placed around the body, presumably to indicate proper respect, perhaps to provide currency for the afterlife. Early on, death and social status were closely associated, even for children: Many graves of hunter-gatherers have been found in places like Russia, with beads and tools, suggesting relative wealth and power along with some belief that possessions might be needed in the afterlife. Even adolescents might be buried with rings, beads, and dozens of weapons. All of this began to be organized tens of thousands of years before we have signs of any other kind of human art or other types of ritual, suggesting the early and ongoing importance of death in human life and history.

Not surprisingly, given their separation in space, various hunting and gathering groups developed quite different approaches to death. Some warrior societies claimed to approach death without fear. Many American Indian tribes urged awareness of death but a sense that it was part of a cycle of life that should there-fore be greeted with acceptance. In contrast, Australian aborigines saw death as unnatural and frequently attributed it to the forces of evil and the magical powers of enemies.

Many societies worried about the dead returning to bother the living. Careful rituals partly reflected the need to conciliate the spirits of the dead to convince them that things were being done just right. Many African peoples developed a custom of cutting a special hole in the wall of the home to remove the corpse, then patching it immediately so the dead would have a harder time remember-ing the way back.

Early civilizations, beginning with Mesopotamia, generally furthered a com-mitment to elaborate rituals for death, while also displaying wide variance in belief. Civilizations certainly enhanced one of the key variables in human ap-proaches to death, by emphasizing social inequality. Many civilizations devoted great expense to death monuments for the ruling classes, assuming that this would aid a transition to an afterlife but also using pomp and monuments to solidify the power structure itself. It is not always clear where worldly show ended and sincere concern about death began. At the other end of the spectrum, the very poor in many societies struggled constantly to find means for some dignity in death, and they often failed. Common, unmarked grave sites—with the dead sometimes coated with lime to encourage rapid decay—protected society against the corpses of the poor, but they enhanced the sting of poverty by preventing access to death practices available to better-off peasants and workers, not to mention the wealthy. Many authorities noted that death was a great equalizer, but civilizations worked hard to mask this conclusion.

The range of civilized responses was important as well, in addition to varieties in social conditions. The first two civilizations to emerge in human history, near neighbors geographically, generated strikingly different approaches to death, revealing how the phenomenon both organized and reflected fundamental features of a society's worldview. Mesopotamians tended to emphasize gloomy aspects of death—the dead lived on in darkness, with dust for food, according to the great Gilgamesh epic. Mesopotamians also emphasized the way death leveled social ranks. Bodies were simply put in the earth, and there was no full idea of an afterlife. The Egyptian contrast was striking, generating monuments, rituals, and beliefs that survived for more than 6,000 years, until the conversion to Islam. Early Egyptian civilization produced the famous beliefs about the need to organize the dead for the afterlife while carefully maintaining hierarchy by producing far more elaborate monuments and accoutrements for the wealthy. Considerable expense went into death practices even for relatively ordinary folks, and a large professional labor force resulted. Egyptians might also have developed the first notion that the dead would be judged according to their performance in life, their sins weighed up in determining their later fate. This added to apprehension about death, but could relieve the Mesopotamian emphasis on wretchedness and the simple cessation of earthly existence: Most Egyptians seem to have believed that they would be judged favorably, although sinners might be eaten by the crocodile-headed monster, Ammit. The massive Egyptian pyramids for the very powerful—the largest tombs in the world—the widespread practice of mummification, and the placement of bodies with implements and jewelry, suggested both an obsession with death and a sense of some continuity between life in this world and the afterlife. Egypt's *Book of Death* is the earliest surviving sacred literature, again demonstrating the importance of the subject in Egyptian culture and the tight links between belief in the gods and assurances for the afterlife.

Obviously, marked differences among societies about how to treat death, including how to handle dead bodies, and what to believe about after-death planes of existence would continue to mark human history. A common and burdensome need to acknowledge death and deal with the fears attached to it—fears for one's own future and often fears of what the dead might do if improperly treated—generated a tremendous variety of specific reactions; even the intensified interactions associated with contemporary globalization have not produced homogeneity in this basic human response. An issue as simple as the consistent need to dispose of bodies produced an amazingly wide range of solutions.

Death in Agricultural Societies

After the early civilization period—from about 1000 BCE onward—a number of agricultural societies generated characteristic responses to death that would continue to influence both ritual and belief into the present day. The role of the major religions, beginning with Judaism, was crucial here, in formalizing ideas about death and any afterlife and in organizing ceremonies. Again, the theme of variety will emerge quickly, for different religions handled the emotions associated with death in very different ways.

At the same time, it is important not to lose sight of common elements of the death experience, which included both timeless features—true of any human society at any place and date—and characteristics particularly associated with agriculture as a way of life. Agriculture presented new issues concerning death—for example, how to handle the disposal of bodies now that people lived in durable settled communities—that differentiated farming societies from hunters and gatherers. Agricultural societies also faced physical realities that were different from those that would prove characteristic of industrial societies later on. Mortality levels provide a starting point, producing a context with which all agricultural societies had to contend.

The overwhelming fact of agricultural societies—the kinds of societies that dominated world history until about two centuries ago—was a high rate of death—by more modern standards, of course. Particularly striking was the level of infant mortality. In most societies, between a third and a half of all children would die by the age of two from chronic diarrhea, infectious diseases, and periodic epidemics of the sort that raced through whole regions every few years. Diseases like measles and smallpox swept many children away. This was why average life expectancy was so low. People who survived infancy had a decent chance of living to fifty or sixty, although it was true that women suffered from significant risks of death in childbirth. This was why societies had to generate rituals and beliefs that would help people cope with frequent death, because virtually every family would experience the deaths of one or more children.

Many agricultural societies seem, understandably enough, to have generated considerable callousness about children's deaths, although this does not mean that individual parents did not mourn extensively. A Roman author, Epitectus, noted, "When you kiss your child, you say to yourself, 'Perhaps it will be dead in the morning.'" The Roman writer Plutarch noted that when infants died, "people do not stand around long at their funerals or keep watch at their tombs." Traditional Chinese society, similarly, urged against much emotion at the deaths of children. Some societies—this would be true in Ireland up to the eighteenth century—often refrained from naming young children, until they reached the age of two and so demonstrated that they were likely to survive. Names of dead children were often reused, as well, another indication that death was both expected and accepted. Many agricultural societies went still further, deliberately killing some newborns as a means of birth control, a practice long regarded as neither illegal nor immoral. Daughters were particularly vulnerable, because they were not viewed as being as useful as sons and because their deaths would particularly limit the potential for excessive reproduction. Infanticide has been widely practiced in China even into modern times. Classical Greece and Rome depended on infanticide: Estimates suggest that as many as 20 percent of all girls in ancient Athens were put to death—usually by abandonment in woods or hills, where, although they had not been actually killed, they were unlikely to survive. Early governments usually legislated against this practice after about 200 BCE—as was true both in China and Rome—but the laws had little effect and were not vigorously implemented. This was yet another sign that death and childhood went hand in hand. Older children, of course, were far less likely to die and might be elaborately mourned if they did. But this only slightly modified the strong link between death and the young. And of course the impact of frequent death of siblings on the outlooks of people who did reach adulthood influenced the overall reaction toward the phenomenon in all the traditional civilizations and reinforced the inescapable presence of death.[2]

Beyond the distinctive age structure of death, agricultural societies also generated certain settings that were particular crucibles for mortality. Preindustrial cities routinely displayed higher death than birthrates, with populations that had to be replenished by in-migration from the countryside. Cities presented greater risk of contagion than rural areas as well as problems with spoiled food, sewage-polluted water, and other contaminants. The attractions of city life might outweigh the dangers, but the risks were quite real. Hospitals were also closely linked with death. The institutions existed in many societies—although they would only slowly emerge in colonial America—but they were uniformly places where people without other resources would go to die—typically, older people who for whatever reason lacked family support. Again, contagion, the diseases already contracted, and the lack of significant medical remedies for most life-threatening conditions explained why hospitals offered refuge but not cure.

Death was familiar in another sense in traditional societies: It normally occurred in or near the home. Although in many cases, religious advisers were available to help deal with death, families themselves had many direct responsibilities, including appropriately disposing of the corpse. This reinforced the most general commonality among agricultural civilizations in dealing with death: the universality of the experience—the frequency and propinquity of deaths of others and, through this, the almost inescapable need to contemplate one's own death, even amid the other demands and distractions of daily life.

The familiarity with death probably accounts for one final feature in the approach to death developed in most agricultural societies: an interesting combination of solemnity and sometimes crass relief. Rituals allowed expression of reverence for the dead, sometimes suggesting fears and uncertainties about one's own death or about repercussions if the dead themselves were not properly honored. But this might be joined by family and community feasting and, in some cultures, no small amount of drinking. On a single occasion, an individual could display several moods almost simultaneously. In imperial Rome, and some other traditional societies, death even figured strongly as a popular entertainment. On spectacle days, at the Roman Coliseum, mornings were devoted to the hunt, afternoons to gladiatorial contests, and lunchtime to the public execution of criminals, sometimes by animals.

Cultures of Death

Despite a number of common realities and shared impulses, agricultural societies did not necessarily generate uniform responses to death.[3] Different cultures continued to exhibit very diverse death practices and beliefs about what happened after death. Classical Greece and Rome, for example, developed only vague notions about existence after death, although there was a definite belief in Hades as a painful destination for at least some of the deceased. Greek philosophers like Socrates urged a calm acceptance of death, without undue fear or grief, but it is not clear how widely this approach penetrated. Funeral ceremonies could be elaborate, and in Rome professional funeral directors emerged, possibly for the first time in human history. Perhaps the most noteworthy feature of Greek and Roman management of death involves the widespread use of cremation: This was a practical solution to battlefield deaths in highly militaristic societies, allowing ashes to be returned to family members for funerals. The practice of cremation spread in Greece after about 1000 BCE, at least for elite families, and to Rome, until it began to subside by 100 CE, probably under the strongly disapproving influence of Christianity. Responses to death were clearly significant in classical Greek and Roman society, and some notions emerged that would be taken up in later systems (as in the transition from the Greek concept of Hades to the Christian concept of Hell), but there was no durable overall approach.

Chinese civilization did not develop a single approach to death—there were many regional and ethnic practices, with influences from Daoism and Buddhism as well. The culture placed great value on longevity and widely displayed a number of symbols for long life, including turtles and cranes. Death was acknowledged of course, and white was the color designated for proper mourning. Chinese rulers placed great emphasis on death monuments. When the Ming dynasty decided to relocate the capital to Beijing in the fifteenth century, an early concern involved identifying suitable dynastic burial grounds. A large acreage was reserved north of the city, and individual emperors spent considerable time planning their monuments. The thirteenth emperor, for example, who devoted little attention to the actual affairs of state, invested in a substantial tower (larger than that of his father, which was against precedent), in which he and his wife were to be interred. The ensuing dynasty, the Qing, not to be outdone, picked yet another spot near Beijing and constructed even more elaborate burial buildings.

With all this, the most characteristic feature of the overall Chinese approach to death involved the reverence paid to ancestors, whose spirits presumably continued to exist after death and to whom family members devoted regular rituals. Annual visits to cemeteries were part of this process, where many people believed they could talk with departed relatives directly. Customs developed whereby relatives would bring a deceased person's favorite treats to the grave—certain kinds of nuts, for example, or beer—in hopes that they could still enjoy them. Choice of burial plots depended of course on a given family's available funds; where possible, plots were located according to the most favorable natural alignment, according to the principles of feng shui. It was preferable to have mountains and water in view: The belief that ancestral spirits lived on dictated the same kind of concerns about arrangements that would apply to the living family itself.

Assurance of showing appropriate respect for ancestors might have promoted a relatively low level of anxiety about death in Chinese culture, at least in principle. Confucianism discouraged elaborate speculation about individual death or the afterlife, urging calm acceptance. This helped focus attention on remembrance and affection for the family ancestors.

Chinese culture, forming over many centuries, was unusual in not depending primarily on an otherworldly orientation to shape its approach to death; in this, it resembled the classical Mediterranean approach, but with far greater staying power beyond the classical period itself. In most major civilizations, by the classical or at least the postclassical periods, formal religion took on the main assignment of explaining the relationship between death and life, defining existence after death, and providing the rituals and religious personnel primarily responsible for dealing with death itself. The leading religions typically offered reassurance, including prayers that might support a dying person through invocations of divine guidance and community services that would guarantee remembrance and support even after death had occurred. Many religions, emphasizing a life to come, officially downplayed the significance of death in favor of ongoing spiritual growth, whether in a heaven or through progressive reincarnations. Some even sought to guarantee salvation for people who died for a religious cause: Thus Christian leaders offered this pledge to crusaders who died in attempts to conquer the Holy Land, and Muslims promised similar rewards for people who died in defense of the faith. At the same time, the major religions also characteristically resisted unnatural deaths: Most of them strongly disapproved of suicide. They also disapproved of infanticide, which Muhammad attacked directly in the Quran. And formal infanticide did tend to decline in regions where the more elaborate religions gained ground, as with Islam or Christianity.

But each religion also contributed particular beliefs and practices, increasing the variety of approaches to death available in world history as a whole. Judaism developed special prayers and ritual dress for the dead, including white shrouds, signifying the equality of every person before God. Coffins and gravestones were characteristically simple, with burial occurring as quickly as possible after death. Families sat in mourning after a funeral, greeting other friends of the deceased. Temple services to remember relatives allowed, but also helped control, expressions of grief, as they unfolded over specified intervals after a death.

Hinduism's emphasis on reincarnation and the basic meaninglessness of material existence shaped the approach to death of India's majority. An individual did not face a judgment after life ended, but rather participation in many further cycles of existence until he or she achieved ultimate spiritual liberation. But the direction of reincarnation—upward or downward in spiritual level—depended on fulfillment of caste obligations in this life. A dying person should be surrounded by friends and family, who would perform certain rituals and say Vedic chants.

Cremation should occur as quickly as possible, to facilitate release of the spirit (*athuna*) from the material body. Only young children were not cremated. The family accompanied the body to the cremation site, chanting verses and asking for divine help; and the body was washed and dressed with new clothes. Once the body was placed in the funeral pyre, the eldest son circled the pyre three times, pouring sacred water on the body and then lighting the wood with a torch that had been blessed. Mourners chanted Vedic mantras throughout to hasten the soul's liberation. Ashes were to be scattered on a sacred river. After this ceremony, the family was to mourn for several days, the first ten in isolation. The house also had to be purified through elaborate cleansing against the contamination of the death that had occurred there.[4]

Like many religions, Islam generated many portrayals of death, often likening it to sleep. Burials were community affairs, with plain coffins and modest cemetery markers. Even royalty did not build massive monuments, in a religion that emphasized the equality of souls. The afterlife—a vivid heaven and vivid hell—received great attention. The Quran was filled with admonitions about the dangers of ignoring one's mortality and not preparing for death. For example:

> And spend something [in charity] out of the
> substance which we have bestowed on you before death
> should come to any of you and he should say, "Oh my
> Lord! Why didst Thou not give me a respite for a little
> while? I should then have given (largely) in charity, and I
> should have been one of the doers of good." But to no soul
> will Allah grant respite when the time appointed (for it) has
> come; and Allah is well-acquainted with (all) that ye do.

On the other hand, Islam also stressed Allah's mercy and the steps needed to achieve salvation, including regular prayer and the pilgrimage to Mecca, despite humankind's sinful frailty: Death was a doorway into a vastly superior stage of existence. By the same token, the religion urged restraint in dealing with the death of loved ones, in recognition that the dead were returning to God. Crying and sorrow were recognized—indeed, Muslim writers discussed grief quite poignantly, including grief over the deaths of children—but loud wailing or the tearing of clothing in grief were discouraged. Prayer at the funeral ceremony in the mosque asked God to forgive the deceased; then the body was carried to the graveyard, where Quranic verses were read. Although coffins were allowed, it was viewed as religiously preferable to use no container, so the body would be reabsorbed into the earth as quickly as possible. Tombstones were discouraged, but many Muslims disregarded this. Families of the deceased were provided with gifts of food and visits by other members of the community for many days after the funeral. Obviously, Islam offered a distinctive mix of beliefs and community rituals around the subject of death.

Cultural diversities crisscrossed in intriguing fashion. The division between strongly religious and somewhat more secular approaches is obvious. Confucianism, although largely secular, shared with Judaism a strong emphasis on family and community rituals and on remembrance of the dead, in contrast to Christianity and Islam, which placed more emphasis on the individual facing death. Religions that predicated a later, more spiritual existence on one's behavior in life, or on some prejudgment by God, obviously could set up tensions in the contemplation of death that differed from systems that proffered neither judgment nor the idea of a specific afterlife. Some systems obviously placed great emphasis on surrounding the dead with material objects (varying of course with social station), whereas others—either not committed to an afterlife, or more purely immaterial in nature—held out for simpler accoutrements. And of course treatment of the body itself varied greatly. Finally, until modern times at least, there is little indication that societies copied each other significantly when it came to something as deeply personal as the arrangements for death; only the spread of a major religion, like Islam, prompted change through contact. Different systems flourished, not without change—for example, in response to devastating epidemics—but with impressive durability in basic approach, despite the widely shared practical realities of death in agricultural economies. Each system undoubtedly had distinctive strengths and weaknesses—some providing more comfort to families, perhaps, others aiding the individual to better adjust to an imminent prospect of death—but each proved clearly serviceable, demonstrating the extent to which a common challenge in human existence could be variously handled. It was within this pattern of diversity that Christian approaches to death—the approaches that would most clearly inform American practices from the seventeenth century onward—must be assessed.

The Christian Approach

Christian beliefs, borrowing from Egypt as well as from Middle Eastern and Greek beliefs and practices, emphasized the idea of judgment after death and a vivid distinction between bliss and punishment in the afterlife. Christian churches devoted great energy to rituals, such as baptism or services like the requiem mass devoted to the spiritual advancement of the dead, which might provide some reassurance that salvation was more likely than damnation in Hell. But fears ran high alongside these beliefs, partly of course because death remained so common. Christian clergy often used death as a warning to the living, including children, emphasizing the terrible fate of sinners more prominently than the rewards that awaited the saved. Russian Orthodox churches usually had icons of the last judgment, including images of sinners' condemnation to Hell, on the west wall as a spur to good behavior. The Christian approach to death was also strongly colored by the belief that the body would be reconstituted in the final judgment. Traditionalists long contended that the bodies of saints did not decay, that this exception from normal deterioration was a mark of holiness. More generally, the commitment to the body led to unusually strong efforts to identify and preserve bodies after death and, often, an unusual fascination with the natural processes of decay. Here was a marked contrast with the Hindu approach, where the body was irrelevant to spiritual progression after death.

The theme of death in traditional Christianity was in one sense unusually prominent. The death of Christ was a central feature in art and theology alike, contemplation of this death a sacred obligation for the faithful.

Later medieval Europe, afflicted by devastating plagues, generated a wider overall preoccupation with death alongside official overall Christian beliefs. Representations of the sufferings of the damned were common. Artists also stressed the decomposition of dead bodies and the decayed and insect-ridden flesh of corpses. The putrefaction of dead bodies provided obvious opportunity to comment on the transience of life, but it seems to have developed a fascination in its own right. Poets, like François Villon, used death as their major literary theme, highlighting death to remind people of the folly of earthly pleasures and social distinctions.

> Death trembles him and bleeds him pale,
> The nostrils pinch, the veins distend,
> The neck is gorged, skin limp and frail,
> Joints knot and sinews draw and rend,
> O Woman's body, so suave and tender,
> So trim and fair, must you arrive
> At such an agony in the end?
> Oh yes, or rise to Heaven live.[5]

Medieval commentary also emphasized the pain of dying itself. A common story cited the agonies of Lazarus, whom Christ had called from the dead, because he knew he would have to face death a second time. Christians of course continued to believe that their souls might live on in glory, but the medieval legacy concerning the body was grim. Graveyards, similarly, became places for bitter reflection, along with fears about ghosts and other manifestations of death gone wrong.

Christian and Western approaches to death underwent important changes well before the modern era, even aside from the panic that surges of plague could cause. It is important to realize that "traditional" takes on death were not static. The Renaissance, for example, encouraged much more elaborate funerals, as a means of worldly display that could accompany death and perhaps ease fear at its prospect. By the eighteenth century, in planning for death, many people reduced their focus on religious rewards and comforts in favor of thinking about decidedly this-worldly arrangements: Wills, most notably, began to be increasingly precise and elaborate concerning the disposition of property. Protestantism introduced other changes in some parts of Europe, for example, reducing religious rituals around death, notably eliminating the Catholic last rite as a sacrament. In some regions, Protestants retained some of the older customs like sprinkling holy water on the body of the deceased. Protestantism could encourage a great deal of thinking about death, but it lacked some of the spiritual props that older Christian tradition offered. Changes of this sort were important in their own right, although they pointed in varied directions; some of them helped prepare later cultural shifts associated more directly with modern times, as when U.S. Protestants, for example, attempted to embellish death with new kinds of monuments and settings in contrast with earlier starkness.[6]

Certainly the grim medieval mood, although it persisted as one strain of Western thought concerning death, changed considerably with the Renaissance and early Protestant Reformation, when emphasis was once again placed on immortality. Catholics placed increased hope in the idea of Purgatory, a place or state through which sinners might pass on their way to ultimate redemption. Early Protestants were confident in Christ's assistance in vanquishing sin and death. Thus an English poet wrote, in 1554:

> Death is a porte whereby we pass to joye:
> Lyfe is a lake that drowneth all in payne;
> Death is so dear, it killeth all annoye;
> Lyfe is so lewd, that all it yields is veyne.
> For, as by lyfe to bondage man was brought,
> Even so by deathe all freedom too was wrought.[7]

But Protestantism, in some of its versions, most notably Calvinism, also revived other strains in Christianity that were less optimistic about death and less rejecting of earthly life. Many Calvinists believed that earthly commitment was an important part of a religious life—one reason, it has been argued, that many worked so hard in business pursuits. They still looked forward to Heaven, but might as a practical matter be somewhat hesitant about abandoning accomplishments in this life. More important, Calvin and his followers also emphasized the select quality of salvation: Most individuals would be condemned to punishment for the original human sin as well as their own sins. Only a minority would achieve heavenly bliss. Furthermore, the idea of predestination emphasized that God chose the saved in advance; they weren't saved because of their own beliefs or acts. The implications were clear: Most people should fear death, because it would lead them to Hell, and everyone should fear death to the extent that they had no influence over what fate awaited them. Of course, in practice, many Calvinists developed some sense of confidence that they were among the saved—why else would they pray so hard or work so hard? Even so, there remained a stark shadow of doubt.

Overall, the Christian tradition offered an ambiguous legacy concerning death. It nourished hope. It developed rituals to comfort people in the prospect of death; like most religions, through prayers for the departed, it promised that the living would try to help the dead and that the connection was not fully broken in death. Because of beliefs that, as with Christ's body, human bodies would be resurrected in the final judgment, Christians also paid great attention to proper care of corpses and their interment. Correspondingly, the direst punishments, for example, for witches, involved denial of proper funerals and use of grave-yards as well as mutilation of their bodies after death. But the most important tradition involved questions and doubts about the afterlife—whether it should be anticipated with fear and dread, these emotions perhaps compounded by the traditional fascination with the deterioration of the body after death, or whether it could be anticipated with some confidence and joy. Individual reactions varied, not only because of the range of possibilities put forth, but also because alternate beliefs were emphasized in different periods. Always, however, there might be uncertainty, which was virtually built into the idea of a final judgment and which fluctuations in Christian beliefs compounded.[8]

Western Transmissions and New Contexts in North America

Colonial America provided another instance in which traditional patterns played out, borrowing beliefs and ideas from Western Europe and Africa. There was an additional variable: Because of the small cities and relative lack of crowding, plus abundant land and (usually) food, death rates were actually somewhat lower in the colonies than in most agricultural societies. This, plus a pressing need for labor, might have influenced a greater discomfort with death than was standard—a characteristic that might be passed on to later periods when the facts of death otherwise began to change more rapidly. Even so, death was a common topic in the colonies, and with greater urbanization and trade in the eighteenth century, mortality rates began to creep closer to more standard agricultural patterns.

From Western Europe, American colonials imported several beliefs and practices, modifying them slightly to fit the new resources available. In both societies, the Christian religion and religious authorities were fundamental in dealing with death. Although people consulted various practitioners to treat illness, including doctors, medical recourses had uncertain results. Some remedies, like bleeding patients to purge them of contaminants, might have even made things worse. In this situation, efforts to fight death could easily take a backseat to measures to prepare the soul for the possible afterlife. At the same time, death loomed large in popular religion. Ministers and priests maintained the long tradition of using death as a central feature in religious discourse, and of employing the fear of death as a disciplinary device. New England sermons thus deliberately reminded children of the imminence of death and the certainty of God's punishment for sin. One aspect of Christian belief, highly emphasized in much American Protestantism, made death seem particularly menacing with the idea of original sin, such that children who died would suffer punishment for the taint of humanity's earlier rift with God, because they didn't live long enough to have a chance to make good with acts of charity or devotion. This Christian tenet—which contrasted, for example, with the Islamic belief in children's innocence—might well have exacerbated fears associated with death.[9]

Western society—and again, the colonies initially participated fully in this tradition—was also accustomed to daily reminders of death in another sense. Burial grounds were located in the midst of the community. Tombs were placed either within churches or in grounds right around them, where people would pass by on a regular basis. The proximity might of course have modified fears of death, by simple habituation, but it certainly offered no separation between the inevitability of death and the other concerns of life.

Traditional society did offer the opportunity of what some historians have called the "good death," and this remained true in the colonies. When a person was dying in later age, of a respiratory disease, for example, he (or less commonly, she) might have had several weeks of gradual decline in which to set his or her affairs in order. Old feuds could have been resolved and final arrangements made for the transmission of property. At the same time, family members, most of whom lived in the same community, could gather to pay their respects. All of this occurred, of course, within the home. The dying person—or a person contemplating his or her own death in later adulthood—would have a sense that everything had been attended to and that the passing left no loose ends. Those observing the death could express their feelings and have similar comfort that they had paid due regard to the person who was passing. As a result, subsequent grief and guilt were less prominent than they would become in other, more modern settings.

Many deaths, however, were not good deaths. Families also had to handle the deaths of children or of mothers in childbirth. Periodic epidemics brought stark fear, when death rates soared over normal levels—sometimes carrying off as much as a third of the population of colonial cities—and took victims from all age groups, who were often suffering real misery. Heightened religious intensity might have accompanied these moments, amid fears that society had strayed and was reaping some divine punishment.

It has also been suggested that, in a frontier society with scant organization, death might seem particularly fearsome because of its destabilizing effects. Deaths of leaders were undoubtedly unsettling, and they might have mitigated any benefits realized from the comparatively low overall death rate. Colonists were also acutely aware that death deprived them of needed labor, in an already labor-short society, and this might have affected emotional responses as well.

Historians have tried to interpret reactions to the deaths of children, where issues in colonial America resembled those in Western Europe in the same period.[10] On the one hand, children's deaths were so common that people—even parents—must have had some sense of fatalism. We know that families were much less likely to call for medical help for young children's illnesses (deaths from infectious disease or diarrhea were particularly common), presumably on the grounds that there was little to be done. There was also surprisingly scant attention devoted to protecting children from accidents. Many water wells, for example, were left uncovered, and more than a few drownings resulted—again suggesting a sense that there were not many ways to protect children from death. We have seen that there were groups in Western society who carried this fatalism to even greater lengths, not bothering even to name children before they reached a certain age, because it was so likely they would die. The reuse of names of children who had died for later offspring offered another sign of resignation in the face of high mortality. On the other hand, we know that parents often suffered greatly when their children died, recording their sorrow in diaries, these passings marking key stages in their lives. This applied even to parents, like the Puritans, who believed that children had been poisoned by original sin and who used the threat of death as an active disciplinary tool. It is possible that parental grief was greater in the colonies than in Western Europe, because in the colonies, childhood mortality rates were a bit lower—bringing some comfort in the fact that the inevitability of death was slightly less certain—and because children's work was so vital in a labor-short society. The tension between resignation and high emotion was very real.

At the other end of the age spectrum, emotions might have also been mixed. In much of Western Europe, adult children could not establish full economic independence until their fathers died. Their futures depended on inheritance of land or family business. While the father still lived, he might have kept his sons as assistants, unable to make independent decisions. This was a situation rife with resentment, in which an older man's death might well have been a matter for quiet rejoicing. A French peasant in the eighteenth century noted, casually, "My father died today, and I was able to plow the back field." Older fathers were indeed the most common murder victims in eighteenth-century France.[11] Here again, the situation in North America might have been slightly different. More abundant land allowed many fathers to distribute some portions in advance of their death, allowing their sons to marry and establish independence. Even so, particularly when land resources tightened in the eighteenth century along the Atlantic seaboard, there were many instances of massive quarrels between fathers and sons, in which the deaths of the former were clearly welcomed.

Western traditions, even as adapted in American circumstances, thus provided diverse components for death and reactions to death. Fear was prominent, and the ubiquity of death was inescapable, but good deaths, as judged both by the dying and by those around him, might occur, and resignation and nonchalance were possible as well, particularly regarding the deaths of the very young and the fairly old—the two groups realizing the highest death rates in traditional societies. A rural funeral around 1800 emphasized nonchalance: Men entered, removed their hats, looked at the body, "made a crooked face," then sat down to talk politics or crops or horses until it was time to hoist the body to the cemetery. And death provided opportunities for outright escapist celebration as well. Funerals allowed communities to gather, amid considerable feasting. Callie Dawes's 1787 funeral in Boston cost the family $844, no small sum at the time, to provide beef, ham, poultry, fish, oysters, eggs, potatoes, peas, onions, cheese, and fruit. Novelist Nathaniel Hawthorne, just a bit later, wrote that funerals were "the only class of scenes ... in which our ancestors were wont to steep their tough old hearts in wine and strong drink and indulge in an outbreak of grisly jollity." Still another account noted the effects of drinking at funerals: "Fathers have been known to stagger to the grave, husbands to fall down and sons to be drunken at the burial of all that is dear."[12]

Christianity had long provided some standard measures in dealing with death, some of them dating back to the ninth century but many continuing in U.S. practice well into the nineteenth century. Religious authorities would be called to the bedside of an ailing person when it seemed likely that effective remedies were impossible; the goals were penitence for past sins, resignation toward death itself, and reconciliation as necessary with church, family, and community—this last, obviously, a key component of the "good death." After death, the corpse would be prepared at home for burial, washed by women, and also displayed for visitors. Funeral services would occur at home and in church, and then a procession would lead the body to the gravesite, where another religious ceremony would commit it to the ground. These rituals completed, members of the family would be reintegrated with the community and normal life would resume. After this, churches would organize prayers and appropriate memorial services on behalf of the dead person, and individual family members might undertake graveside visits.

Abundant resources might have encouraged some modifications of traditional resignation, while retaining familiar ceremonies, although several versions of Protestantism also fanned the flames of fear. The American colonial setting provided one other component: the frequency of deaths of others. During the seventeenth century particularly, death rates among Native Americans who came in contact with white settlers were very high, the result of diseases like smallpox and measles for which the indigenous populations had no established immunities. Ultimately, more than 80 percent of Native Americans would die from these imported diseases. Not all white settlers noticed this, of course, and they certainly did not deliberately cause this dreadful downside of new contacts among societies. But they definitely benefited from the deaths of the Native Americans, which reduced the strength of Indian resistance to territorial expansion. And the results might have encouraged, among whites, a particularly acute sense that the deaths of others mattered less than the deaths of one's own people. Later on, in the eighteenth and nineteenth centuries, some whites deliberately spread disease, for example, by passing blankets of smallpox victims to Native American groups in the U.S. and Canadian West: Did this reflect a differential approach to death developed from earlier, colonial patterns?

The same potential applied to the high death rates among African slaves. North American slave owners were more careful than their Caribbean or Latin American counterparts in limiting slave mortality—after all, it was their property that was at stake. But slave deaths were common, nevertheless, beginning, of course, with the appallingly high rates on the slave ships coming from Africa. Race was an early component in the U.S. experience of death, and this influenced physical experience and attitudes alike.

Culture also had an effect on some particular U.S. death practices. New England Puritanism, particularly, revived or intensified some of the Christian heritage both from Calvinist Protestantism and from the Middle Ages. Puritan influence was felt in one region directly, but because of later expansion had some disproportionate effects on U.S. culture more widely.

Most striking of the Puritan ideas was the pronounced sense of children's sinfulness; they had been polluted by Adam and Eve's original sin. Discipline and protection from the devil were vital in this view, and warnings about death and damnation, directed explicitly toward young children, were central. Along with the frequency of children's deaths, even in the healthier atmosphere of the colonies, this made early involvement with death dramatically different from what most people, Americans or otherwise, expect today. With 10 to 30 percent of all children dying before age one, parents were warned not to become too attached to an individual child. Thus Puritan ministers might almost have welcomed a devastating plague or war because "then God opens (children's) ear to Discipline." Sermons reminded the young that "Death waits for you. There is now a Moral and Contagious Disease in many Houses; the Sword of the Lord is drawn, and young men fall down apace slain under it: do you not see the Arrows of Death come flying over your heads? ... Know for certain that if you dye in your sins, you will be the most miserable of any poor Creatures in the bottom of Hell."[13] The same ministers might warn children that their misbehavior could cause their parents to die. They had no hesitation, either, in describing the physical horrors of death and the lasting separation from family members. The ubiquity of death was a less surprising theme, given the conditions of the time, but it, too, was driven home with great vigor: "[Y]ou may be at Play one Hour; Dead, Dead the next."[14] Small wonder that Puritan children are often described as terrified, bursting into tears as they contemplated their fate. Or that, grown to adults, the thought of death "would make the flesh tremble."[15]

For adults, furthermore, ministers continued to stress that salvation was uncertain: The Puritan world was one of predestination and anxiety, even for many of those who believed themselves righteous. There might have been hope of Heaven—the Puritan view stressed ambivalence about whether to welcome release from this life—but there was always doubt about one's own fate. Lack of fear of death might indeed have been a sign that one was not taking Christian doctrine seriously. Although many Puritans greeted their deathbeds with courage, it was not surprising that death itself earned the label "King of Terrors." The notion of a good death might have been modified, even erased, by an awareness of the magnitude of the sins one had committed and the little time available for repentance.

Puritan funeral services were largely devoid of ceremony; certainly, there was no intention to offer comfort to the survivors, and ministers might have used their words primarily to warn sinners of the torments of death. Burials occurred soon after death, within four days, because there was no attempt to preserve the condition of the body. Mourning clothes and symbols of death's-heads on the horse-drawn hearse added to the solemnity of the ceremony. The same symbols were used to mark many graves.

Puritanism was not the only cultural setting for reactions to death among the colonists. For a long time, in some places, like Virginia, ceremonies around death were almost nonexistent, perhaps because colonists had too much to do. Catholics in Maryland might have had the comfort of more elaborate rites, including opportunities to engage in sacraments and other religious acts that could provide considerable assurance of salvation—although not necessarily ever eliminating all of the uncertainty.

African Americans generated their own variants, even as they converted to Christianity. Slave funerals provided unusual opportunities for community gathering, without interference by masters; they were thus more social than those of their white counterparts at the outset. Funerals also allowed more open expressions of West African customs than were allowed in daily life, and this was displayed particularly in the music that accompanied slave funerals. Drumming on the way to the funeral site was mournful and filled with sorrow, but that played on the way back to the plantation was louder and more cheerful, in order not to antagonize the owners and also to prepare the slaves themselves to return to work—there was no day off for death in the plantation regimen. In New Orleans, this musical tradition ultimately transformed into the trumpet-filled parade that dominated funeral processions. More broadly still, African traditions and the fact that funerals involved not only death but community response amid repression, encouraged a level of emotionality and open grief that differed from the norms of whites. Here, obviously, was a cultural tradition that would persist even after slavery ended, and it served as a reminder that Puritanism was not the only cultural legacy on death that would shape United States practice.[16]

Even in New England, Puritan beliefs themselves began to moderate in the eighteenth century, toward less emphasis on fear and more on the assurance of salvation. But the earlier Puritan images of death and its relationship to human sin left an unquestionable legacy to a wider reach of Americans, with elements showing up, for example, in children's reading texts in the nineteenth century. This was a complex and, doubtless for some, difficult heritage. More modern ideas about death began to clash with Puritan staples very early, as we will see. Would it be harder to erase some of the traditions associated with fear of death in the U.S. context than in other Christian societies less affected by frontier conditions and unburdened by the particular zeal of the Puritans? The colonial heritage, with its strong doses of fear and racism, must be assessed in later, and superficially very different, American death practices.

Administering Death: Some Final Traditions

Attitudes toward death, and the larger context of death's familiarity, prepared several final features of death in traditional agricultural societies, where death affected larger social and political policies. All societies had to make some decisions about controlling or using the deliberate administration of death. In this category, although variety must again be noted, we return to some impressive commonalities among societies in world history's agricultural period, in a number of respects.

We have noted, for example, that many agricultural societies used infanticide as an explicit method of birth control. Even when religions opposed infanticide, it still might be practiced either illegally or by leaving unwanted babies on the doorsteps of churches or other charitable institutions—where in fact, despite good intentions, they would often die. A few societies, without practicing widespread infanticide, nevertheless killed certain kinds of children because they were thought to be harboring evil: Twins, in some parts of Nigeria, for example, were put to death on this basis. The commonness of mortality, in other words, although it did not produce uniform approaches to dealing with unwanted children, did tend to reduce the restrictions on the uses of death—at least when viewed in light of more contemporary standards.

Even more striking was the frequency with which death was employed as a punishment for crime. From the earliest recorded law codes in agricultural civilizations, from Mesopotamia, until at least the eighteenth century, not only murder, but in many cases various types of theft might be met with the death penalty: Hundreds of specific crimes could come within this purview, and major religions either concurred or protested feebly. Roman society used death freely, among other things to demonstrate the awesome power of the state. At most, religious authorities sometimes argued—both in Islam and in Christianity—that the death penalty might limit retribution. If a murderer were put to death, for example, the family or tribe of his victim might be satisfied and abandon even bloodier retaliation against not only the murderer but his kin. Religious authorities also sometimes argued that criminals might repent as they faced the death penalty, and thus, despite their sins, have a chance to gain divine salvation after death. These were interesting glosses on the death penalty, often sincerely intended, but they hardly conceal the fact that the penalty was, by modern standards, extremely common.

The most obvious reason for the frequency of death penalties involved the difficulties of policing premodern societies, which had few formal police resources and scattered populations.[17] Death seemed necessary not only to provide satisfactory retribution but also to intimidate potential criminals, for there might have been few other deterrents to their crimes. Join to this the eagerness of kings and emperors to put down potential protest, again by frequent use of capital punishment against rebels, and the basis for the policy is well established. Traditional societies not only used death penalties widely, but they insisted on their being public in nature. Hangings and beheadings drew huge crowds, sometimes sympathetic to the criminals, sometimes hostile, but always excited by the prospect of public punishment. Rebels might additionally have had their heads cut off and displayed on posts, as a further warning and deterrent. Russia's Peter the Great once displayed the heads of approximately two hundred executed rebels for a full four months, and this is just one of thousands of examples in the bloody history of human retaliation. But although crime prevention doubtless provided some of the motivation behind the frequency of capital punishment, the results coincided with the ubiquity of death in other respects. Here, too, people saw death widely, expected it; it would take a major recalculation for objections to the practice to emerge widely.[18]

War was a final area in which societies deliberately decided to administer death. Few leaders spent much time calculating deaths in war. Different cultures did develop distinctive approaches to war.[19] Chinese leaders, by the time of the Han dynasty, came to prefer peaceful strategies, viewing war as a sign of leadership failure. Even the great classical theorist of war, Sun Tzu, noted that war should be only one of several implements available to gain advantages over enemies, and surely it was the recognition of war's destructive power that caused this hesitation. Various religious leaders, including many Catholic popes, tried also to restrain war and the deaths that war caused. During the Middle Ages, church and royal leaders sponsored the Peace of God and Truce of God, to reduce warfare; these efforts, which met with limited success, were directed more at the general disorder frequent fighting caused, than at death itself. Indeed the Church was also capable, as in the Crusades, of sponsoring one kind of bloodshed outside Europe to help distract from internal conflict. And there was little sense, anywhere, once war was unleashed, that deaths could be curbed. Many leaders, from Mesopotamia onward, deliberately extended the slaughter of vanquished armies, continuing to kill even after battles were won, and sometimes subjecting the bodies of enemies to degrading defilement. It was also noteworthy that, with the advent of agricultural civilizations, wartime fatalities often increased—partly because larger armies could be fielded. Most hunting and gathering groups, even when touting military virtues, tended to threaten and bluster more than actually fight, which limited fatalities. It was true that, given the weaponry available before the nineteenth century—even including early guns—the numbers of actual fatalities in combat were not usually terribly great, at least by modern standards. Far more troops died from disease, and there seemed few means of remedying this pattern. But there were exceptions: In one battle in China, in the third century BCE, 240,000 soldiers perished on the field. And retaliations against not only opposing troops but civilian populations could be extensive as well, as leaders vented their emotions and, as with capital punishment, sought to use death to threaten and deter. Armies did not always inflict massive casualties on defenseless populations—situations and policies varied. But it was not hard to justify death in war, and certain situations—such as attacks on presumed religious heretics—prompted unbridled ferocity. Death and destruction in Germany's Thirty Years War (1618-1648), where Catholics and Protestants fought each other to a standstill, thus reached exceptionally high levels. With starvation and disease following the opposing armies, plus deliberate slaughter, as much as a third of the German population may have died. This was, to be sure, unusual, but it was another illustration of the omnipresence of death in traditional societies and the related assumptions that death, even when deliberately administered, could not readily be controlled.

Traditional societies did uniformly outlaw murder, and the major religions vigorously opposed suicide. The steady presence of death did not make private acts legitimate. Official policies, however, did not always have much effect, where death was so common in any event. Suicide rates varied greatly, depending on climate in large part; thus, northern Europe, burdened with dark, harsh winters, had much higher levels than the sunnier south. The incidence of murder was probably more revealing. Where governments had weak policing powers, as in Europe until modern times or in the American colonies, high rates of murder were standard, far higher than what would be experienced in more recent centuries in relation to the size of the population. Murders occurred for various reasons, of course, but in many traditional societies they often combined several settings and motivations. Family vendettas were one, particularly in cultures that placed a strong premium on honor; dueling, which not infrequently led to death, was one often fatal expression of honor common in certain times and places, including aristocratic Europe into the nineteenth century. Murders also reflected social hierarchy: The killing of a slave, serf, or family dependent might not be viewed as seriously as that of a social equal; in a few societies, murder of a disobedient child or a rebellious slave was completely legal. Finally, at least in premodern Europe, murders frequently accompanied robberies, not so much as an effort to avoid identification, in under-policed societies, as simply to use violence to complete the act. Murder rates were not constant; they increased in economic hard times, particularly through the linkage with robbery, and they were less common in some political and cultural structures than in others. Overall, however, they were high enough to call attention to the extent to which individuals could feel authorized to end life on their own. Again, the normalcy of death in many traditional societies seems to have reduced barriers to administering death—in what could easily become a vicious circle.

Conclusion

The tension between shared responses and sharp differentiations, in the long agricultural period of human history, marks the major features of death. Societies might have believed in a rich experience after death, or they might have remained largely silent on the point; but they all demonstrated a belief that death was an appropriate punishment for a variety of crimes. They might have sought to restrain grief or indulge it, but they would rarely display much public sentiment about the deaths of children.

The variety was undeniably important.[20] Death traditions, formed by different societies in the classical and postclassical periods and then carried forward into the eighteenth and nineteenth centuries, showed a host of responses to essentially common problems. The need to dispose of dead bodies, for the sake of the living, might have been handled through cremation and beliefs that the body was not an essential attribute of persistence after death, or through elaborate burials and beliefs that the body must be preserved as fully as possible, with attendant musings about decay and the ugliness of death. Fear might have been soothed by philosophical injunctions, by assurances of family remembrance, or by strong religious beliefs in a life after death. Funerals might have required loud lamentations, often with women playing special roles; but they might also have been occasions for community revelry. The wide range of traditions continues to provide different mechanisms for greeting death. Specific death practices might be one of the most durable badges of group identity, easily surviving the immigrant experience in countries such as the United States.

Yet death traditions were also dependent on some distinctive features of death itself that, although long lasting, would ultimately change considerably. Frequent deaths of children or the management of death in the home, to take two examples, no longer define death for the majority of people, not just in the United States but in urban societies around the world. When the patterns of death in agricultural settings gave way to the patterns in urban, industrial settings, what else would change? What would happen to some of the corollaries of the death experience, like capital punishment, when the normal context shifted? And, with due consideration for the persistence of specific traditional remnants, would age-old variety give way to greater uniformities when death began to command less attention? The history of death in premodern societies, rich and instructive in its own right, sets up an obvious battery of questions for modern history: we no longer die like that, and this means we need to explore a variety of aspects of change.

Notes

1. Epigraph: N. K. Sandars, *The Epic of Gilgamesh: An English Version with an Introduction*, rev. ed. (London: Penguin Books, 1972), pp. 101–102. The order of several lines has been slightly modified.

2. Beryl Rawson, *Children and Childhood in Roman Italy* (Oxford, 2003); see also Peter N. Stearns, *Childhood in World History* (London, 2005).

3. For a good introduction to cultural variations in responding to death, see Robert Kastenbaum, ed., *The Macmillan Encyclopedia of Death* (New York, 2003).

4. Kastenbaum, ed., *The Macmillan Encyclopedia of Death*; Hasmuk Rava and John L. Safford, *Bhagavad Gita: A Philosophical System* (St. Louis, MO, 1990). Vital treatments of traditional practices and beliefs also include Philippe Ariès, *Hour of Our Death* (New York, 1991); David Stannard, *The Puritan Way of Death* (New York, 1979), and on death

fears, Jean Delumeau, *Sin and Fear: The Emergence of the Western Guilt Culture, 13th–18th Centuries* (New York, 1990).

5. François Villon, *The Legacy, The Testament, and Other Poems* (London, 1973), p. 51.

6. Michelle Vovelle, *La mort en Occident: De 1300 à nos jours* (Paris, 1983).

7. Henry Harrington and Thomas Park, eds., *Nugae Antiquae: A Miscellaneous Collection of Original Papers ... by Sir John Harrington* (London, 1804), II, pp. 332–333.

8. Constance Jones, *R.I.P.: The Complete Book of Death and Dying* (New York, 1997), p. 14 and passim.

9. Stannard, *The Puritan Way of Death*.

10. Philip Greven, *The Protestant Temperament* (New York, 1977).

11. Peter N. Stearns, *Old Age in European Society: The Case of France* (London, 1976).

12. Jones, *R.I.P.*, p. 14.

13. Stannard, *The Puritan Way of Death*; Increase Mather, *Pray for the Rising Generation* (Boston, 1678), p. 22.

14. Cotton Mather, *Perswasions for the Terror of the Lord* (Boston, 1711), pp. 31, 36. See also the *New England Primer* (1727; reprinted New York, 1962).

15. James Fitch, *Peace–The End of the Perfect and Upright* (Boston, 1673), p. 6.

16. Donald Irish, F. Kathleen Lundquist, and Vivian Jenkins, eds., *Ethnic Variations in Dying, Death, and Grief: Diversity and Universality* (Washington, DC, 1993), pp. 51–66.

17. Pieter Spierenberg, *The Spectacle of Suffering: Execution and the Evolution of Repression* (Cambridge, 1984).

18. Stanley E. Grupp, ed., *Theories of Punishment* (Bloomington, IN, 1971); see also Michel Foucault, *Discipline and Punish* (Harmondsworth, 1977).

19. Michael Neiberg, *War in World History* (London, 2001).

20. Again, work on premodern Europe is especially rich in dealing with variety and change. See, especially, Vovelle, *La mort en Occident*; Ralph Houlbrooke, *Death, Religion and the Family in England, 1480–1750* (Oxford, 1981); and David Cressy, *Birth, Marriage, and Death: Ritual, Religion, and the Life-Cycle in Tudor and Stuart England* (Oxford, 1997).

CHAPTER 3

New Emotions
and Rituals in Death:
The United States
and Western Society

Signs of change were unmistakable by the 1820s, and by 1900 they had accumulated substantially. One specific example sums up larger cultural shifts. In 1820, a dead person would be laid out in the home, often showing the ravages of the fatal disease, and of course deteriorating further in the few days before burial, even when ice was used to slow decay. In 1900, an increasingly typical scenario involved a dead person embalmed, the traces of illness magically removed and deterioration prevented during viewing—and often not at home but in what was revealingly called a funeral parlor. (Parlors had emerged as the fancy visitor's room in middle-class houses earlier in the century; they were actually declining by 1900 in favor of the more informal "living room," but the respectability of the reference long preserved it in the new funeral business.) Obviously, the change toward a more removed and a more cosmetic treatment of a dead body reflected new commercial zeal and significant new or revived technology, including the use of chemicals and makeup. But there was more: The sight of death, routine in 1820, was becoming less acceptable, the emotions it aroused less welcome. Commerce and technology supported a major shift in cultural standards.

Unexpectedly, the first major moves away from traditional death traditions involved attitudes, more than the reality of death itself, with important public health measures alone suggesting a relationship between attitudes and desired standards during the first decades of the transformation. For a time, death became surrounded with high emotions, grief most obviously, but also guilt. New practices followed the emotional curve, with efforts to sweeten as well as to lament death. Gradually, the incidence of death itself began to follow the emotional waves, with new possibilities of limiting mortality rates below any levels thus far achieved in human history.

The basic developments were Western-wide, embracing the United States and western Europe alike. But there were distinctive American features from the outset, particularly in some of the new symbols, like garden cemeteries. The tension between shared fundamentals and evolving national frills would only grow with time.

In the United States, the period from about the 1820s to the early twentieth century was both unique and formative. New emotional emphases reached levels not seen either before or since—here was the most obviously distinctive feature. At the same time, however, a clear distaste for death emerged that would prove quite durable, a characteristic of modern American death attitudes still visible today. One historian has claimed, with some exaggeration, that the nineteenth century saw the origins of a U.S. "death of death"—a desire to push death as far away from normal consciousness as possible.[1] The relationship between this trend, which showed up most obviously in new funeral practices, and the unprecedented visibility of grief, was complex. We must lay out first the emotion, then the new rituals, and then turn to the assessment of how these developments fit together and how they compare to changes and continuities in other parts of the world.

A Century of Grief

At one level, until late in the nineteenth century, nothing greatly changed: Death remained ubiquitous. Even in 1900, when death was actually beginning a rapid retreat from groups prior to old age, U.S. life expectancy stood at only forty-seven years—up from the levels of 1800 but still reflecting a high mortality rate particularly in childhood. The family stories of U.S. writers show the frequent sorrow. Nathaniel Hawthorne lost his father when he was a young boy. Ralph Waldo Emerson's father died when the boy was eight; his first wife passed away when he was twenty-eight; and a beloved brother died soon thereafter. Herman Melville's father died when Melville was twelve. Edgar Allan Poe's mother perished when he was two, and his wife suffered from a lingering, ultimately fatal illness, while he was writing some of his most famous works. Catharine Sedgwick lost her mother at the age of seventeen. Lydia Child's mother died when she was twelve, after which she was sent to live with a married sister. Susan Warner, another novelist, was born after the death of her parents' first child, and two other siblings born later also died. Warner's mother passed away when Warner was nine. Sara Parton lost her mother, first child, and husband during a two-year stretch in the 1840s. Margaret Fuller's childhood and youth were marked by the deaths of an infant sister (when Fuller was three) and a baby brother (who died in her arms when she was nineteen).

Family deaths of this sort often involved more than loss. When a father died, the remaining family frequently suffered severe financial hardship, and not infrequently the family had to break up at least for a time, with children going to other relatives who could afford to take care of them, or even (in the working classes) to orphanages. Death of a mother could also lead to family dissolution, when children had to be farmed out to other caretakers—sometimes an aunt or an adult sibling. Ramifications of this sort understandably compounded the effect of the death itself.[2]

But these situations had always been routine in traditional societies. Infants often died. Accidents or contagious diseases or infections during childbirth frequently carried off parents when their own children were young. There was admittedly an increase in epidemics during the middle decades of the nineteenth century, compared with earlier experiences in white America. A huge cholera epidemic hit the cities at the end of the 1830s, for example, causing some affluent families to flee to new suburbs like the optimistically named Mt. Healthy, near Cincinnati. The epidemic surge followed from growing urbanization and increasing levels of international trade, with cholera spreading from Europe. Epidemics continued to challenge individual U.S. cities into the 1880s, but these developments largely highlighted the established patterns of frequent death.

What was most obviously novel was the level of emotional reaction. We have seen that family members felt the loss of parents or children keenly in traditional societies, but were usually able to combine appropriate ritual with private anguish, keeping public signs of grief at modest levels. Not so in the nineteenth century; grief and mourning almost literally exploded. Women became the chief agents for emotions at death, with men's responses more variable, but whole families were frequently engulfed in sorrow. Images of mourning abounded in popular art. Some girls' schools taught their students to emphasize figures of women draped over the tombstones of husbands or sons as they practiced their needlework. The theme of grief, like death itself, seemed increasingly ubiquitous.[3]

The emotion was often hauled out for discussion and praise in nineteenth-century family manuals. Grief was held to be the counterpart of love, which in turn was now urged as the foundation for proper family life. A marriage based on intense love, or the fervent bonds between parent (particularly mother) and child naturally established the basis for grief when a family member died or disappeared. Even the temporary absence of a loved one might be compared to death: Nathaniel Hawthorne wrote Sarah Peabody in 1840, "Where thou are not, there it is a sort of death." But it was real death that seized emotional center stage. It was the frequent subject of novels, which, like Louisa May Alcott's Little Women, focused on the tragedy of family loss through wasting disease. It peppered materials prepared for children, who needed not only to be exposed to death—a traditional staple—but also prepared for the elaborate emotions of contemporary grief. In its intensity and its link to great love, grief could have a bittersweet quality in the nineteenth-century emotional arsenal—deeply painful but almost welcome as part of a full emotional experience. In a family manual of 1882, a Protestant minister put it this way: "It may truly be said that no home ever reaches its highest blessedness and sweetness of love and its richest fullness of joy till sorrow enters its life in some way."[4]

The Civil War obviously challenged the new focus on grief, because of the unprecedented level of slaughter. Northern soldiers often wrote of the need for restraint on their part and on that of families back home. "Do not grieve too much" was a common theme. But grief ran high even so, and there was ample sorrow among soldiers at the death of comrades in arms. Profound grief was also suggested in Lincoln's moving address at Gettysburg, an interesting contrast to the dominant official U.S. posture in the two twentieth-century world wars, where emphasis on bravery and a stiff upper lip back home reflected clear departures from nineteenth-century norms. Victorian grief culture certainly reasserted itself, after the Civil War, until the early years of the twentieth century.[5]

The recalibration of grief allowed some significant changes in the presentation of death to children, with a fairly explicit shift resulting from active debates in Protestant circles during the first decades of the twentieth century. At issue was the relationship of death to fear and discipline. When children were seen as tainted with original sin, it was logical to use the threat of death and ensuing divine punishment as a disciplinary tool. However, in reform circles of Protestantism, these connections were now disputed. Children were increasingly regarded as innocent, corruptible only when mistreated by adults. The doctrine of original sin was not so much refuted as ignored, in a dramatic new vision of childhood. By the same token, the use of the threat of death to terrify children was vigorously disputed. Children should not have to fear. But this did not mean, at this point, that childhood and death could be separated, if only because the fact of high mortality rates required a continued connection. Here, benign sorrow could take the place of fear, training children to associate death with deep emotion but to stop short of terror.[6] In the ever-popular *McGuffy's Reader*, used widely in early schooling, sixteen of twenty-nine "poetical lessons" in the 1866 edition dealt with death and grief, including one entitled "What Is Death?":

> Child, Mother, how still the baby lies.
> I cannot hear his breath;
> I cannot see his laughing eyes;
> They tell me this is death.
> They say that he again will rise,

> More beautiful than now;
> That God will bless him in the skies;
> O mother, tell me how.

In this case, the mother replies with the image of a butterfly emerging from a lifeless chrysalis. In other poems, again in school readers, the dominant theme was the rejoining of loved ones in Heaven, after death had claimed them all.

> Oh, we pray to meet our darling
> For a long, long, sweet embrace.
> Where the little feet are waiting—
> And we meet her face to face.

Along with the emphasis on sorrow in death, the clear innovation here was the image of future refuge and the decidedly untraditional claim that Heaven would be the scene of massive family reunions. Again, the effort to get away from fearfulness was obvious, as was the association of death with great love: Celestial connections provided the way for people to express grief but to accompany it with some ultimate hope. It's important to note that this fervent belief in reunion had some additional side effects characteristic of the nineteenth century, particularly the many efforts to establish communication between living and dead. This was a common literary theme and supported the efforts of mediums to organize séances where links between the here and the hereafter could be developed directly.

But despite some mitigating hopes, the tragedy itself was real, at least for the moment of death itself, and death scenes remained commonplace in stories for children, calling them into the sorrows of illness and passing amid assurances that an outpouring of emotion was valid and ultimately healthy—although with implicit emphasis on the particularly female responsibility for mourning. A typical passage on the death of a friend: "Elsie's grief was deep and lasting. She sorrowed as she might have done for the loss of a very dear brother ... a half remorseful feeling which reason could not control or entirely relieve; and it was long ere she was quite her own bright, gladsome sunny self again." Louisa May Alcott wrote of a sister's "bitter cry of an unsubmissive sorrow," of "sacred moments, when heart talked to heart in the silence of the night, turning affliction to a blessing, which chastened grief and strengthened love."[7] Mother's assurances, repeated references to protecting angels (another popular innovation in U.S. Protestantism called up to help shape and cushion the new emotions surrounding death), and the heightened theme of familial reunion in Heaven all linked the power of grief to hope and love, but the power was not evaded. Intense emotion—now freed in principle from fear—was a desirable part of life, both suitable and inescapable for children, and ultimately an enhancement of the human ties of family and friendship. The starkness of death disappeared under sentimental overlays in these portrayals, but the inescapability, even the benefits, of a period of deep grief found confirmation.

The same themes pervaded popular parlor songs in the Victorian decades. The 1839 song "Near the Lake Where Droop'd the Willow" became an immense success in U.S. concerts and inspired imitations for several decades. The song focused on a girl loved in youth, who had died long ago:[8]

> Mingled were our hearts forever, long time ago;
> Can I now forget her? Never. No, lost one, no.
> To her grave these tears are given, ever to flow,
> She's the star I missed from heaven, long time ago.

Songs about death in the nineteenth century were personal and immediate, providing expression for emotional explorations. Minstrel shows dealt with the emotions of death, often without much reference to plot or character. Deathbed scenes, the emotional ties between dead and living, and the idea of ultimate reunion in Heaven all figured prominently. Literally hundreds of songs about dying girls were published, particularly in the 1860s when they clearly served to focus on, but also to distract from, the terrors of the Civil War: "Wait for me at heaven's gate, Sweet Belle Mahone;" "Though we may meet no more on earth, Thou shalt be mine above;" "Angels guard her with your wings . . . Bid her dream love-dreams of me—Till I come, sleep, Eulalie." But along with sentimentalized Heaven came real sorrow on earth, with frequent emotion-laden visits to the cemetery: "I'm kneeling by thy grave, Katy Darling; This world is all a bleak place to me;" "All night I sat upon her grave, And sorely I did cry."[9]

> Oh, a huge great grief I'm bearing,
> Though I scarce can heave a sigh,
> And I'll ever be dreaming, Katy Darling,
> Of thy love ev'ry day till I die.[10]

Poems echoed the motif of sorrow around the inescapability of death. Thus a line by Abraham Lincoln in 1846 about his childhood home: "Till every sound appears a knell,/And every spot a grave."[11] Etiquette books contained substantial sections on respecting the grief of others.

Open grief and pathos became a vital part of Victorian emotional culture, making the sorrow of bereavement seem natural, even desirable, although also to some degree consolable. Grief could soar, as love did. At the risk of trivializing grief (and certainly at real cost to Christian traditions concerning the afterlife, where images were now often filled more with repaired earthly grief than with spirituality), middle-class popularizations embraced sorrow openly, returning to the subject with endless fascination until the final decades of the nineteenth century.

Emotional Realities

Literature, songs, and manners recommendations, of course, are hardly the whole of reality. It is difficult to prove that real emotions escalated in the same fashion, because sorrow at loss was hardly a Victorian invention. Generally, however, changes in emotional culture—which clearly occurred in the case of grief—help shape and define actual emotional response, in this case making many feel freer to express deep feeling (and somewhat confused if the feelings did not arise). Letters and diaries from the period, predominantly middle class, certainly suggest that the emotional guidelines bore fruit in felt experience.[12] Under the spur of popular Romanticism, crying became more popular, initially for men and women alike, then increasingly just for women. References in letters, and insofar as we know, in actual personal experience to "bitter, bitter tears" abounded. The deaths of children produced almost overwhelming emotion, as an 1897 diary entry reported: "Jacob is dead. Tears blind my eyes as I write ... now he is at rest, my darling Jacob. Hope to meet you in heaven. God help me to bear my sorrow." Here, clearly, not only the pain of grief but also the conscious handling of the emotion with references to reunion and divine support reflect the currency of the larger culture. Men as well as women expressed their sorrow. Civil War soldiers often noted their tears at the deaths of comrades, as well as at partings from family. A minister in 1863 asks Jesus to "support me under this crushing blow"—his brother's death. Another man, recording in 1845 the death of a brother-in-law, ended his diary entry: "Oh! What sorrow burst in upon us at the melancholy news of his death ... All is sorrow and weeping." The new grief culture also encouraged sadness in recollection: Sarah Huntington thus remembered a loss of two years earlier, "Reading these letters revived all the exclusiveness and intenseness of my love for him I once called husband."[13]

Reactions varied, of course, depending on personality as well as specific circumstances, with the gender factor often relevant as well. New ideas about death and grief could actually enhance the older comforts of a "good death." An adult woman in Schenectady, New York, Mary Palmer, contracted tuberculosis in 1845. Her health fairly steadily declined, over a period of roughly two years. During these months, she was able to attend church occasionally, and her family had time to adjust to the inevitability of her death. She herself felt prepared and made it clear that she realized her family had done the right things in caring for her. Both she and her family commented on their ultimate reunion in Heaven. "She told us not to mourn for her, for she would be happy and hope and trusted that we should all meet in heaven and be a happy Family there," her father recorded. Capped by a widely attended funeral, the family does not seem to have grieved extensively after her death. In contrast, about a decade later, another Schenectady resident, a sixteen-year-old boy, died suddenly when he drowned after his boat capsized on a river. His father—for whom, unusually, this was the first direct experience with death—reported that God "in his wise Providence ... has filled our hearts with desolation." Of course there was every belief that the boy would be rejoined in Heaven, and a huge outpouring of community support occurred at the funeral, but the sorrow was almost unbearable, even so. The boy's father could barely go about normal activities, clearly falling into depression: "How does the world recede ... when death enters our dwellings. All the vain things that please us most lose their interest." And in this case the memory lingered, reviving periodically, even years later, "with crushing effect." Frequent visits to the gravesite brought some consolation, in a grief that became a lifelong companion.[14]

Despite important variations, there is every reason to believe that the need to record both grief and its intensity became more prominent among many nineteenth-century Americans. As the sense of loss deepened, the dependence on consoling beliefs in later encounters increased.

Indeed, the culture deliberately prepared many people for strong emotion, not only in stories but in items for play. By the 1870s and 1880s many girls were given mourning kits for their dolls, complete with black clothing and appropriate coffins, in order to train them in the emotional reactions and rituals they would experience in later life.

The Causes of New Intensity

Why did grief receive new attention? We have seen that the focus on grief was part of a larger emotional redefinition of the family, in which the rewards of love began to take precedence over more traditional economic functions. Middle-class children, for example, no longer worked; they stopped serving as economic assets. What, then, was the purpose of having children? The dominant cultural response was clear: Because they were so innocent, so emotionally precious. Respectable middle-class women also stopped working outside the home. They depended heavily on husbands for their economic support, but what was the purpose of marriage for men? The response, aside from unstated advantages in the convenience of having household help, was of course the strength of mutual love. Both for parenthood and for marriage, then, new definitions and justifications increasingly involved intense emotional ideals. Never before had U.S. culture placed such emphasis on fervent, almost religious-like affection within the family. In this context, loss of a loved one inevitably itself took on new emotional overtones, at least in principle. Here was a key part of the new grief equation. Not everyone actually approached the emotional fulfillment Victorian culture called for, but few disputed the expectations, or their implications for death.[15]

Another angle, however, is also suggestive. Many middle-class people began to think that certain kinds of death should be preventable in a well-ordered, progressive society. Middle-class culture emphasized increasing faith in science, as a means of providing new explanations but also new remedies for traditional ills. They believed that, under the aegis of modern enlightenment and the values of their own class, progress in this world should be expected. They increasingly saw the Christian God as benign, not punitive, another force for progress. Rhetoric surrounding the establishment of the U.S. republic emphasized progress as well: The United States had improved on the politics of the old world, and it was reasonable to assume it could also improve on traditional standards of health. Commerce and increasing wealth also supported the progressive theme. But death seemed less changeable than were science, politics, and the economy.

For, as we have seen, death remained pervasive. Middle-class people could and did begin to move to suburbs by the middle decades of the nineteenth century, seeking to get away from the pollution and filth of increasingly industrial cities and the physical and moral challenges of the urban lower classes. Middle-class health was undoubtedly superior to that of the poor, but death persisted. Science, including medical science, had as yet little to offer in the face of this fact. It was hard to reconcile the apparently unavoidable and unpredictability of death with the commitment to secular progress. Not surprisingly, deaths of children and young people seemed particularly contradictory to the growing commitment to advancement.

Heightened emotions around death thus reflected not only family intensity but also the frustrations of the clash between standards and reality. More than that: Particularly in the case of children, it reflected growing guilt. It was increasingly hard for parents to believe that there was not something they could or should have done that would have prevented the death of a child. The new genre of women's magazines, like *Godey's Lady's Book*, picked up this sense implicitly, along of course with stories that praised love and grief. Mothers came in for new admonitions. Many infant deaths, a new group of advice givers claimed, resulted from careless feeding or smothering a baby with excessive clothing. Even though there was as yet no breakthrough in infant mortality rates, a belief developed that careful, enlightened parenting would do the trick—which meant in turn that, when a child did die, mothers might easily wonder if they had failed in some fundamental way. Rising grief, in this sense, reflected a decline of fatalism, even though the levels of mortality improved slowly at best.[16]

Some of the same transformation could apply to reactions to the deaths of mothers in childbirth. A traditional sense—palpable in eighteenth-century

United States—that women should not complain about the possibility of death clearly began to yield to greater sympathy, from husbands and fathers as well as other women. In a progressive society, women should not have to face this level of risk in an act of such obvious importance to the family. But again, the risk remained: There was no major improvement in maternal mortality rates until late in the nineteenth century. At most—and a growing number of men agreed with their wives on this point—the birthrate might be reduced, in order to alleviate exposure to mortality by curtailing the occasions of childbirth. When death occurred nevertheless, however, a husband might well experience the same kind of guilt-enhanced grief that affected mothers when their children died.[17]

Death was becoming less palatable, because of new expectations about progress as well as new levels of claimed attachment to family members. But lack of acceptability did not, as yet, mean much change in life expectancy. Grief, openly, even ritually expressed, was the result of this gap—the emotional resolution for an otherwise agonizing disjuncture.

One other cultural staple of the middle decades of the nineteenth century suggests the new ambiguities about death, which a focus on grief alone might obscure. Fictional stories, on both sides of the Atlantic, featured burial alive as a frequent horror theme. Entombment of the living might reflect simple error on the part of caretakers, or murderous malice: The main point was that death spiraled out of control. This terror theme (obviously far less current after 1900, despite continued addiction to fictional fear) reflected changes in the actual practices of caring for the dead, discussed in what follows, that began to move the management of death outside full personal and family control. But it also symbolized death's new unacceptability and the new guilt and revulsion it aroused. The new discomfort with lack of control over mortality found expression in this dramatic representation of death both arbitrary and unfair. Here again was an abundant reservoir for grief, where new intensity in recommended standards could provide public acceptability for a greater mixture of emotion—guilt and fear, as well as grief itself—in fact.

Death and Empathy

This new emotionalism associated with death had a number of corollaries. Humanitarian revulsion was one, a significant new development. Beginning in the early nineteenth century, it began to become obvious that a key way to rouse public outrage was to highlight the deaths of innocent people, particularly children. The theme became a common ingredient in the antislavery movement. Some might be stirred by the idea of servitude and its violation of basic human rights, but unjustified death might offer a more emotional inducement. Thus

Harriet Beecher Stowe, in *Uncle Tom's Cabin*, linked the capacity to mourn for private losses to political support for those trapped in slavery:

> By the sick hour of your child; by those dying eyes, which you can never forget; by those last cries, that wrung your heart when you could neither help nor save; by the desolation of that empty cradle, that silent nursery—I beseech you, pity those mothers that are constantly made childless by the American slave trade! And say, mothers of America, is this a thing to be defended, sympathized with, passed over in silence?[18]

Stowe's phrases like "dying eyes" and "empty cradle" were repeated frequently in periodicals, making virtually every U.S. reader familiar with this dramatization of maternal sorrow.[19]

The linkage between the emotions of death and social causes was vital in the accelerating opposition to slavery, but it would continue into the later nineteenth century and beyond, stirring humanitarian sentiment for victims of various sorts. We are so familiar with the appeal today—the picture of a starving child as the basis for charity campaigns for Africa, for example—that it takes a specific exercise of historical thinking to remember that the assumption that one should empathize with deaths of distant people in distant places is actually quite modern. Although humanitarianism had other roots as well, it was unquestionably partly a fruit of the extension of the new level of grief in the face of death.

A Century of Growing Evasion? The New "American Way" of Death in Burial and Ritual

The more immediate results of nineteenth-century grief, however, involved massive changes in the arrangements for the handling of death itself within the family and community. One historian, plausibly enough, has labeled the century after 1820 the crucible of a special American approach to death, and although we need to test this against comparative data, it is certainly true that innovations accumulated on the Western shores of the Atlantic.[20]

The first shift involved the location and ambience of cemeteries. As cities grew throughout the Western world in the early nineteenth century, space considerations almost compelled some new attention to cemeteries. The old practice of burial near churches or village squares became impossible, given other demands on urban territory amid rapidly growing population. Furthermore, dominant theories of disease, which stressed contagious "miasmas" from swamps and other centers of infection, prompted new worry that undue proximity to dead bodies might also be unhealthy. European as well as U.S. cities closed down some older cemeteries—in Paris, a number of center-city graves were relocated to a buried catacomb in the southern part of town, where even today the bones can be visited by venturesome tourists—and even more generally halted the growth of remaining sites. This necessitated movement of cemeteries outside the cities, into more sparsely populated suburbs. To this extent, the redefinition of U.S. cemeteries was part of a larger Western trend that was only indirectly linked to ideas about death itself, although it did have the result of distancing death scenes and reminders from normal daily contacts. Because the United States preserved many open spaces and small towns in the countryside, in fact, informal burial locations near homes and churches continued longer than they did in Europe—lasting, in places like central Illinois, into the early twentieth century, complete with home-based funerals and other traditional trappings.

But in the American cities, like Boston, relocation did occur, and along with it an even more suggestive redefinition of what cemeteries were all about. The new idea was to make cemeteries look as much as possible like bountiful English gardens. Discussion focused first in the Boston area, in the late 1820s, where several reformers noted the deplorable state—the untidiness and unhealthiness—of existing urban facilities. A horticulturalist was involved, along with several people in the forefront of other urban improvements, as were real estate interests, as the decision was made to open a new cemetery in the rural suburb of Watertown—and the new Mt. Auburn cemetery became the first of many new garden enclaves in the United States. More was involved than simple urban improvement, although the coincidence of occurrence with other new measures, such as an underground water system for Boston, was obvious. Two further goals predominated, and they both related to a growing desire to tame and beautify the perception of death and to express a sentimental grief. In dedicating Mt. Auburn in 1831, a judge, Joseph Story, made it clear that opposition to the old types of facilities went beyond hygiene and land use concerns. The traditional cemetery was simply depressing, with "death's-heads and crossbones; scythes and hour glasses; angels, with rather a diabolical expression" and gloomy inscriptions.[21] In place of this approach, death should now be associated with the beauties of nature, with a sense of calmness and serenity rather than themes of decay. Mt. Auburn, accordingly, was equipped with all sorts of landscaping, several ponds, tidy paths, and impressive monuments. Caretakers, trained by gardening groups, took meticulous care of the grounds. All of this reflected the reigning atmosphere of cultural Romanticism, which ascribed all sorts of beneficent qualities to nature—and not just any nature, but one carefully improved by human planning. Boston already led the nation in formal gardens, and a cemetery that looked like these other facilities garnered high aesthetic marks. As another commentator noted, "when nature is permitted to take her course—when the dead are committed to the earth under the open sky, to become early and peacefully blended with their original dust, no unpleasant association remains. It would seem as if the forbidding and repulsive conditions which attend on decay were merged and lost in the surrounding harmonies of the creation." Bodies would dissolve in the "embrace of nature," in "the bosom of mother earth."[22]

The second element celebrated in the garden cemetery was the new theme of communion with loved ones. Traditional cemeteries were places of ugliness and fear; it was not pleasant to visit them. A garden, however, was another matter, and visits could be positively pleasant. Here was a setting in which family ties could be maintained after death. Of course garden plots themselves could be purchased to allow family members to be buried side by side. A young man, learning his father had bought a family allotment in Mt. Auburn, rejoiced that "as we have been united in life, we may not be separated in death." But gardens also encouraged links between living and dead. Judge Story again: by encouraging mourners to enjoy the garden's beauty, Mt. Auburn would promote visits that would allow the living to commune with the dead, "to hear the tones of their affection ... to listen to the voice of their wisdom ... and to return to the world purer, and better, and wiser from this communion with the dead." The garden cemetery, in other words, promoted the same themes of reunion that were being developed in the new apparatus of grief: Death confirmed family love and family ties and was softened by them in turn. Natural beauty would at the same time reduce the level of grief.[23]

As the garden cemetery movement expanded, many families introduced new types of monuments that complemented—or in the view of later observers, conflicted with—the natural setting. Building on changes in graveside markers that had begun in the later eighteenth century, many families now covered tombs with statues of cherubs, or mothers cradling children—implying confidence amid grief that the individual would ascend to Heaven. New emotionality about children's death also showed in popular tombstones depicting idyllic children asleep—a theme that reflected the widespread idea that the garden cemeteries themselves could be seen as "a vast and exquisitely beautiful dormitory." Weeping willows, fingers pointing heavenward, and butterflies emerging from cocoons were other popular motifs. These monuments contrasted with the old death's-head figures popular in traditional U.S. cemeteries, particularly in New England, which recalled medieval European emphasis on bodily decay. They helped portray the new popularity of grief amid the garden surroundings. And they also allowed families to celebrate their wealth and some degree of individuality, particularly when they were incorporated into imposing family vaults.

Garden cemeteries did more than reduce anguish and bind families. They also, in a society increasingly democratic in theory, set up barriers between the upper and middle classes, on the one hand, and the hoi polloi on the other. Expensive monuments pointed to these distinctions explicitly. Social differentiation was hardly a brand-new theme in burials, as the rich had often insisted on markers different from the poor, but it was actually a new emphasis in U.S. cemeteries. The garden—regular gardens as well as the new type of cemetery—also served as a counterthrust to the other trappings of modernity and urbanism, which many middle-class people, even as they eagerly participated in the rewards of business and the modern professions, also valued. Cemeteries became an alternative to the fast pace of normal life, thus serving the living as well as the dead. A New York observer commented on this aspect, after the Green-Wood Cemetery was opened as another garden haven, in 1838, "Ever since he [the weary and worn citizen] entered these greenwood shades, he has been sensibly getting farther and farther from strife, and business, and care … A short half-hour ago, he was in the midst of a discordant Babel, he was one of the hurrying, jostling crowd; he was encompassed by the whirl and fever of artificial life. Now he stands alone in Nature's inner court—in her silent, solemn sanctuary. Her holiest influences are all around him."[24]

But the key point was the garden's role in making death more palatable. It is vital to remember, among all the gracious words, that the rural or suburban cemetery segmented death from daily life in ways that differed markedly from Western, including colonial American, traditions. People might be lured to visit the garden site, but it would be an excursion, not part of regular routine. The association with nature not only appealed to dominant Romanticism, but lent an air of escape and nostalgia to the treatment of death. The dead were increasingly seen as resting, while also being transported to Heaven; the starkness of burial and decay was muted in this new vision. Cemetery names stressed pleasant imagery: Laurel Hill, Green-Wood, Greenmount, and Spring Grove—not coincidentally rather like the names of suburban subdivisions in the United States today.[25]

The phenomenon spread very quickly during the middle decades of the nineteenth century. One observer claimed in 1849 that "there is scarcely a city of note that has not its rural cemetery." Even smaller cities joined the parade.[26]

Fashions changed a bit with time. The garden cemetery began to seem too cluttered, particularly when individuals set up fences and other borders to mark their plots. In particular, objections arose to the large, sentimental monuments, which were seen as too saccharine emotionally and too disruptive aesthetically. In this vein, new lawn cemeteries replaced the wooded terrain, with large open meadows over gently rolling hills, along with restrictions on individual constructions and personal sentimentality that might spoil the vista. Surface plaques, rather than more elaborate stonework, marked individual graves, the idea being that the view, not the death site, should really be the focal point. Regularity and coordination took precedence over individual vagaries, as death became more regimented as well as more remote. By the 1880s the movement had gone far enough that a professional organization of cemetery superintendents emerged, committed to this new park plan, now praised as "the most beautiful and best in every way." It was easy to assume that the landscaping took precedence over any particular attention to death: "[T]he superintendents of our leading cemeteries, generally, have for a long time recognized the fact that the requirements for the cemetery, apart from the burial of the dead, are very largely those of the park." Or again: "While there are some people who say a cemetery should be a cemetery, the great majority of people have come to believe in the idea of beauty."[27]

There was more than new design in this park emphasis: Cemeteries became big businesses, complete with plans not only to regulate individual families in their commemoration of death, but also to sell additional products such as "perpetual care" for the grave site. This kind of care had the double advantage of making money but also preserving the freshness of the site and avoiding reminders of deterioration or decay. Too much dwelling on death could be a deterrent to efficiency and commerce. A Kansas City professional noted, "Today cemetery making is an art, and gradually all things that suggest death, sorrow, or pain, are being eliminated."[28] The reduced visibility of gravestones and limitations on inscriptions formed part of this subordination. The editor of the *Ladies Home Journal* similarly praised the parks and their reduction of individual graves as an attack on what he called "grewsomeness": "there is nothing to suggest the presence of death."[29] Emphasis now was on the modernity of cemeteries, not their alternative to modern life: The reduction of attention to death was part of a larger commitment to efficiency. Grief was still assumed, but it should be restrained, not expressed lavishly. There should be no reminders of individual death, no caving in to anachronistic lines about remembering death; a name and dates were quite sufficient. As with the garden spots earlier, organizers hoped that people would visit cemeteries just for the beauty, with no special interest in the remains hidden underground. But even more than with the garden type, the emphasis on beauty and design should distract from death even for family members, "robbing death of the many terrors with which the ignorance and superstition of older times surrounded it." No "gloomy thoughts" here: Even weeping willows were banned because of their connotations. "Kill off every plant and remove everything you see that suggests sadness." Life, the cheerfulness and quick restoration of the living, should win out over death and the dead. One landscape architect even hoped to "put such smiles" into your cemeteries that they would become positively "cheerful places."[30]

Modern technology helped as well. More and more cemetery workers waited to cover the coffin with earth until the mourners were no longer present, using an automatic casket lowering device, bedecked with flowers. The idea was to make it seem that a "departed friend" had been gently lowered into a "curtained couch" rather than dropped into the ground. Other organizers replaced family and friends as pallbearers with uniformed attendants, who were obviously unlikely to break down with grief. As one onlooker noted, "everything that tends to remove the gloomy thoughts is done."[31]

Obviously, cemetery trends, particularly with the park approach of the later nineteenth century, partially conflicted with the highlighting of grief that ran through the century as well. The conflict was concealed to some extent, in the garden cemetery, by the sentimentality of the natural setting and by the construction of expressive monuments. But with the lawn movement, the tensions between a desire to discipline death and a desire to grieve emerged quite clearly. Many Americans were torn between the idea of a highly emotional reaction to death and a desire to override death with considerations of aesthetics and efficiency. Ultimately, as we will see, the "modern" de-emphasis on emotion would tend to win out, at least publicly. Yet the tension reminds us that the "modern" trends in American death were not simple, even aside from a wide range of personal reactions.

At the same time, it would be a mistake to dwell just on the tension here. Both approaches involved challenge to traditional treatments of death, though of course the new cemeteries were more explicit about their innovative qualities than were the grief advocates. New grief signaled a new level of discomfort with death, even on occasion a sense of guilt; it was accompanied by ideas of reunion in the afterlife that served to take some of the sting out of the emotion. Cemeteries more explicitly indulged a discomfort with death, in this case by downplaying it and seeking to distract. Both currents, certainly, tried hard to reduce the fear associated with death. The approaches were not easy to reconcile, until grief itself could be taken in hand. But they both defied tradition; they both moved away from too much focus on the process of death and decay; they both suggested a desire to distract from attention to morbid starkness with some combination of high emotion and aesthetic alternative.

The cemetery movement was not uniformly triumphant against more diverse, even traditional concerns. The park cemeteries often had to allow more grandiose grave markers than the landscapers preferred; families simply insisted on greater display and individuality. Different ethnic groups also maintained distinctive traditions, sometimes setting up enclaves within a garden or park site. Catholic cemeteries followed some of the park-like trends, but they were often somewhat less manicured, a bit starker than their mainstream Protestant counterparts—to some extent because there was less money involved. At an extreme, some Chinese Americans buried their dead in special sections of American cemeteries only temporarily, waiting to save money to return the bodies to China, where the spirits of the ancestors could be properly revered.

On the other hand, modern cemeteries alone were not the only sign of a desire to redefine death and reduce its impact. The "American way" of death harbored further innovations in mainstream practice and, often, official regulation as well.

By the later nineteenth century, novel cemeteries were joined by dramatic new trends in the care and preparation of the dead themselves. Embalming the dead body was the most striking late nineteenth-century change, along with increasing interest in using cosmetics to beautify the corpse as well. Prior to this period, embalming had been known by most Americans as a procedure used only in ancient Egypt—outside the scope of modern civilized practice. Traditionalists continued to argue that any pretense that human beauty could be restored was contrary to nature and to true respect for the dead. But traditionalists increasingly had to give way to yet another set of innovations for dealing with the dead. From the 1860s onward, a number of elements combined to encourage new artificial methods to preserve and decorate corpses. Geographic mobility contributed to the practice, and it is worth noting for comparative purposes that to this day Americans remain an unusually mobile people. Embalming was used for some of the dead in the Civil War, to permit them to be transported back to family members. Abraham Lincoln was embalmed, allowing his body to be taken on a funeral caravan lasting fourteen days, from Washington, D.C., to Springfield, Illinois, with the casket opened at every major stop along the way—more than 7 million people viewed his body in the process. By the 1880s, the utility of preservation of the bodies of people who were on travel or who had moved away from their primary family extended the benefit of embalming.

Embalming also responded to new concerns and perceptions about hygiene problems associated with the dead. Traditional layouts, with the corpse in the home—even when deterioration was retarded by the use of ice—undoubtedly left open the possibility of contagion, either from decay or from diseases, like diphtheria, that had caused death in the first place. Fears about hygiene were compounded by the special nineteenth-century anxiety about premature burial, though this literary theme was less popular in the United States than it was in Britain: There would be no question that an embalmed corpse was dead.[32]

Whatever the spur to embalming—and for a time undertakers combined this practice with continued icing, only after 1890 turning to embalming alone—it rapidly appealed to a growing interest in making the dead seem less dead—here clearly joining forces with the motivations that had earlier developed in cemetery redesign. One funeral director put it this way: Thanks to embalming and cosmetics, "when I come for the last time to look upon my dead, they will look to me as natural as though they were alive." Another spoke of "retaining and improving the complexion as one of the conditions of success." By the 1880s, one association was offering a $1,000 prize to the embalmer who made his subject look the most lifelike. As with cemeteries, human art should conceal the traces of death, often making a corpse look not only less fully dead, but noticeably younger than she or he had been for several years, particularly when a wasting illness had been involved. Relatedly, normal dress clothing began to be used for the final costume, rather than traditional shrouds. Bodies should be dressed and positioned, another expert noted, with "one idea ... always to be kept in mind, and that is to lay out the body so that there will be as little suggestion of death as possible." By the early twentieth century some funeral directors were even advertising services at different prices, ranging from the relatively cheap "composing the features" to the more expensive "giving the features the appearances of Christian hope and contentment." Even flowers could now be preserved, around the body, so their decay would not suggest unsavory aspects of the process of death.[33]

Here, clearly, were new ways to distance death, and the goals became even more explicit than with the cemetery movements. Similar invocations of science and modernity were attached. Embalming experts sometimes referred back to Egypt, advertising their "oriental wisdom." More commonly, however, embalming was linked to science and progress, including of course the improvements in hygiene. Funeral directors indeed aspired to a professional status comparable to that of doctors, but their subject was still gloomy enough that they never quite made the jump. Nevertheless, their standing did improve and their efforts to associate themselves with physicians, in fighting contagion and decay, seemed to make some sense. Like the cemetery managers also, they appealed to a beauty in nature—ignoring the fact that natural death is not lifelike.

Embalming could easily link with the new interest in grief, because family members had more time to view the body and to express emotion. On the other hand, most professionals in the field saw embalming as a means of cutting grief or at least reducing its pain, "by preserving the remains of those they love." Whatever the emotional calculus, embalming was portrayed as a progressive move, joining the modern fight against decay and deterioration.

Furthermore, the practice was part of a larger set of changes in handling the dead that offered further buffers between family and death. Most obviously, undertaking or funeral direction was becoming a clear occupation, even a profession, complete with associations, journals, and training; no longer was the family itself primarily responsible for handling the body. Caskets became steadily more elaborate, with companies rather than local carpenters providing the products by the 1870s. On the one hand, this change allowed people to demonstrate their wealth and status by buying fancy products. But elaborate, velvet-decked caskets could also reduce the sense that the dead were being pushed toward immediate dissolution with only the crudest protection against the elements; a fancy casket would keep agents of destruction out, aside from natural decay itself, and help family members preserve an active, living memory of the deceased. Here too, lavish aesthetic appeals might help disguise the meaning of death itself. However irrelevantly, modern caskets conveyed the impression of comfort—which might indeed have comforted the living in distancing them from the less pleasant aspects of death. Caskets, like other modern consumer items, also now featured novel designs periodically, another link, however superficial, to the reigning idea of progress.

Even more important was the shift of location of bodies between death and burial, from the home to the funeral home. The funeral home, gaining ground clearly by the early twentieth century, was not the only place a body could be prepared for viewing. Embalmers could work in individual residences, and funerals could be organized even in urban apartments, particularly once professionals developed special devices for moving corpses through narrow doorways. Funeral parlors did respond to the geographical mobility factor; when a dead person was transported from place of death to the old home town, local family might not actually be available for the ceremony. The new specialized locations filled that need quite clearly. Funeral homes played a vital role as well in preparing bodies for shipment, which was why, as early as the 1880s, there was a particular concentration of these institutions in California. The home also appealed to funeral directors because they could arrange the whole operation, thus gaining additional status and opportunities for profit.

Not surprisingly, the new establishments picked up the common trappings of the modern way to look at death. They were subdued but "as cheerful and pleasant as possible," with a businesslike atmosphere superseding grief or the trappings of death itself. The emphasis on flowers replaced more traditional use of black draperies. As one commentator noted, "Often the placement of the casket in the room, gracefully canopied by an attractive curtain, and banked against flowers artistically arranged, forms a picture so beautiful as to relieve the scene of death of some of its awfulness." Most of all, however, funeral homes freed the family home from any need to be available to display death—its rooms (which decreasingly included a formal, stiff parlor) could be devoted to the living and to acquisitive abundance. It's been argued that the parlor declined in part because it became too closely associated with death, although its formality and stiffness were factors as well in a society increasingly interested in casual consumerism. Families, further, were freed from the need to concentrate much on death arrangements. This might have been a double-edged sword, because it created more time for grief, but it certainly reduced inherent need to focus heavily on death. One could turn to the newly available professional for that.[34] Death became an occasional event, not an integral part of family life.

A final set of changes involved the funeral service itself, again developing from the late nineteenth century onward. The services became steadily shorter, after 1880. Reformers, including funeral home directors, urged ministers to avoid the old fear-and-damnation approach, in favor of offering comfort to the living. The sermon should not promote additional grief but should emphasize hope and comfort. Some ministers of course resisted taking this stance, in favor of more traditional theology; and some religions retained older rituals. But there was a trend toward more positive messages. Furthermore, ministers now shared roles with the undertakers, who definitely tried to limit emotional pain. Their responsibility for arrangements, including decor, transportation to the cemetery, music, and even the greeting of family friends, was undertaken to maximize consolation and soothing. All of this increased funeral costs, which rose 250 percent in the United States in the four decades after 1880, but the public was clearly willing to pay.

Many writers picked up on the overall theme of these various changes, that death and the funeral should become "less of a tragedy." People should be prepared to get back to the pleasures of life as quickly as possible. Funerals should stop being "like a funeral ... but more like some wonderful canvas representing a spring festival with lovely groups and garlands against the tender greenery of the dainty season." Death might still occasion grief—this tension was hardly eliminated—but emotion should be cushioned as dead bodies now were, and the worst sting should be removed from the whole experience.[35]

Interestingly, one final innovation, widely advocated by certain proponents in the late nineteenth century, did not take wide hold: the idea of cremation. Cremation had all sorts of potential appeals. It was far more sanitary than burial, it eliminated the problem of decay, it was efficient and arguably particularly modern. But although a few people chose cremation, the option was far too radical for the vast majority even to contemplate. Christian tradition, based on Christ's own rising from the dead, assumed the resurrection of the body, which cremation made hard to envision. All the progressive arguments were mustered, but at this point to no avail. Change was a dominant theme, but it was constrained by important remnants of custom.

Still, the transformation of U.S. death practices from about the 1830s onward was truly impressive. Despite continued high rates of mortality, at least until the 1880s, many Americans tried to reposition themselves with regard to death. Fear and horror gave way to sentimental grief and aesthetic distractions. What used to be regarded as the realities of death were heavily obscured. A society that was beginning to lead the world in indulgence of consumerism introduced new consumer forms and themes into one of the most fundamental ritual areas of the human experience.

"Modern" Versus "American" in the Nineteenth-Century Way of Death

We know that urbanizing Western societies in the nineteenth century shared with the United States the need to relocate cemeteries and consider new issues of hygiene. They also shared in cultural Romanticism, which could lend new emotionality to death. The key question is this: Did they, however, share the larger American impulses to distance and conceal death? How "American" were the overall changes in nineteenth-century beliefs and rituals?

To get beyond a narrowly national approach, the major changes in U.S. ways of looking at death need to be compared with those in other parts of the world, particularly western Europe. After all, western Europe and the United States shared not only Romanticism but also Christian heritage and the grow-ing influence of science. They were undergoing roughly common, fundamental processes of industrialization and urbanization, including the emergence of a growing urban middle class. We have seen that urban crowding forced some reconsideration of cemeteries on both sides of the Atlantic. New understanding of contagion and hygiene, even before the germ theory, also prompted revisions in thinking about the location of cemeteries and the treatment of dead bodies. New cultural themes also crisscrossed the Atlantic. The reverence for nature, such a fundamental expression of the Romanticism that supported the U.S. garden cemetery, was a common current. So, broadly speaking, was the new emphasis on family love, which could enter into the recalculation of grief. Changes in Christian tradition, through the emergence of new types of Protestantism in the United States, were paralleled in places like Britain at least to some extent, and in Europe an outright decline of religion proceeded more rapidly, spurred among other things by the spread of science: Although particulars varied, shared trends could and did lead to a reconsideration of fear and an attack on older Christian invocations of this emotion.

So the issue is this: Did so many common trends generate European changes in approach to death to match those in the United States? Or did the more ardent U.S. embrace of efficiency and consumerism, a frank delight in at least claiming to shake off traditions and too much European-ness in favor of stak-ing out a different national identity, generate greater differentiation? Ironically, though revealingly in terms of a national historical habit that likes to assume U.S. exceptionalism without going to the trouble of testing it, the good work on the "American way" of death has not been subjected to comparison. There's an obvious challenge and opportunity here to figure out more precisely what was going on. Did western Europeans take similar pains to try to distance death?

Several historians, certainly, have pointed to western European precedents, both in Enlightenment thinking and in Romanticism, for the attack on certain Christian traditions associated with death that would spread to the United States by the early nineteenth century. As early as the 1740s the French writer Charles Drélincourt had written *The Christian's Defense against the Fears of Death*, with directions on how to die well. The text was quickly translated into English and widely popular. The book explicitly opposed the practice of using death to scare children and began to develop the theme of beauty in death that became so pervasive in U.S. Romanticism and cemetery arrangements a hundred years later. The central theme was death as a form of sleep through which individuals would attain a better existence than could be found in this life. English literary work was also imported into the young United States, featuring conversations between the living and the dead—an important literary notion in the nineteenth-century United States that supported the idea of reunion in Heaven. Related practices, like the séances designed to establish communication directly with a departed friend or family member, were about equally popular on both sides of the Atlantic during the nineteenth century itself. Copious weeping at funerals was another emotional emphasis that was transatlantic, developing first in Europe around 1800 and then extending to the United States for a somewhat longer time. Shared Romanticism, from an initial European base, helps explain some of the key changes in U.S. ideas and practices about death and makes it clear that they were part of a wider movement. The intellectual foundations of the "American way" of death were thus not clearly American at all, but stemmed from a larger Western change in which Americans of various levels came to participate.

Yet, with this said, it seems clear that response to death in western Europe changed less, during the nineteenth and early twentieth centuries, than was true in the United States. Most notably, Europeans did not generate the rise of funeral homes or embalming, or the redefinitions of cemeteries, to the same extent as across the Atlantic. Changes did occur, as noted, even beyond the relocation of graveyards outside city centers. Growing hygiene concerns, combined with more crowded urban housing, created obvious tensions in places like Paris from the 1860s onward. Smaller apartments made the presence of a dead body less convenient, and Louis Pasteur's new germ theory created great anxiety about contagion. But the resolution of this dilemma—the relocation of death to hospitals—would not widely occur until the 1930s; the funeral home option, as a middle way, simply did not develop widely.

What was striking on the whole, however, was the greater persistence of tradition. Homes of the well to do in France assumed the domestic presence of death. In 1875 a priest wrote that the master bedroom should be considered a sanctuary, where people should expect some day to die; he recommended it should be equipped with a "soothing but instructive image of the death of St. Joseph," so that the ultimate purpose of the room would be signaled on a daily basis. Visits by friends and family after death also took place in the bedroom. Individuals ate in their own bedrooms, rather than at the dining table, while the body was in the house. Actual funerals were arranged by the priest, the town's funeral bureau, or, in Paris, funeral professionals who promised ceremonies "with tact and propriety." Funeral processions wound from home to the church and thence to the cemetery (with only close friends and relatives accompanying this final step). Expenses included the cemetery itself, mourning clothing, and black-bordered announcement of the death—but not the growing costs of U.S. funerals.[36]

The French worried that mourning periods grew shorter in the nineteenth century, but actually they lengthened—a sign of some participation in a greater culture of familial grief. Men mourned for six months in Paris, a year in the provinces; women, particularly widows, were held to twice those durations. In the 1850s, parents began to wear mourning clothes for children who died—another example of emotional change similar to that in the United States. Very complicated clothing and hairdressing arrangements accompanied each stage of mourning, particularly for women—although of course only the upper classes could afford full indulgence.

The Franco-American comparison, obviously, is mixed. Signs of new grief and certain new concerns suggest important parallels, based on emotional redefinitions and the new anxiety about disease. But French ceremonial aspects differed markedly, with far fewer innovations, far less challenge to traditional religious and domestic emphases, than in the United States—even though religion overall was declining far more rapidly in France than across the waters.

Death patterns changed more in Britain than in France during the nineteenth century, but even here the U.S. level of innovation was not matched. There was important overlap, between two countries that maintained active cultural links across the Atlantic. But British practices responded to some distinctive factors as well, and they did not seek to distance death as fully as was the case in the United States.

Some developments are familiar enough from U.S. patterns. Emphasis on grief increased. Mourning arrangements became steadily more elaborate during the middle decades of the nineteenth century, with special black clothing, markers on homes and carriages, and careful etiquette designed to respect the feelings of those who had experienced loss. The impact of Romanticism, which so obviously helped celebrate grief, showed on both sides of the ocean. References to families to be united in Heaven also increased, although at a somewhat less intense pace than in the United States. Similarly to the United States at this point as well, efforts to promote cremation, though framed in terms of modern science and maximum hygiene, made little headway among publics not ready to abandon traditional attachments to this extent.

Obviously, new issues arose in Britain about the location of cemeteries, given rapid urban growth and the emergence of greater concerns about hygiene and contagion. There was some movement toward graveyards on the outskirts of towns, with new levels of landscaping; but the full-fledged garden cemetery movement, so prominent in the United States, had no full British counterpart. Indeed some new or expanded cemeteries, in cities like Glasgow, remained in the center of the city and simply filled with a jumble of closely located tombstones;

this created greater pressure than in the United States to push for dramatic monuments that might stand out from the crowd and suggest both grief and social standing. Differences here were matters of degree, for wealthy American families also celebrated their achievements through monuments, but the escapism was less prominent.

By the early nineteenth century, Britain did develop a growing group of professional undertakers, who helped organize funerals and provided care for dead bodies outside the home. But for several decades the undertakers' main pitch, aside from new convenience, involved selling caskets, velvet-lined to be sure, with pillows, but above all carefully fortified. As one ad put it, with deliberate repetition, "A strong coffin . . . a very strong outside oak case." One historian has argued that the chief motivation for these innovations involved a great fear of body snatchers, criminals who in the early nineteenth century took new corpses from gravesites to sell to medical schools for use in anatomy lessons. Here may have been a spur to growing expense and to other innovations, including the construction of walls around cemeteries themselves—concerns and responses much less prominent in the United States in the same period. Only after 1832, with a new act of Parliament that provided the bodies of poor people who could not afford proper burial for use by the insatiable medical schools, did this anxiety abate—but by then the habit of elaborate paraphernalia and professional handling had already been established.

And what was missing at this point, aside from quite so much interest in bucolic cemetery settings, was the passion for embalming. Somehow, it can be suggested, the British, although participating in significant change, were less drawn to some of the innovations that would help distance and mask death.[37]

British approaches to death in the nineteenth century have been praised by historians who contend that elaborate mourning helped express inevitable grief in ways that would ultimately facilitate coping and by modern observers appalled at how the British have departed from Victorian conventions in more recent decades at the risk, they contend, of seriously shortchanging the impact of death.[38] Elements of this argument can be applied to the United States as well, although as we will see, recent innovations are less extensive on the U.S. side. To the extent, however, that the British seemed somewhat less interested in sanitizing bodies and removing death from the daily ritual, to the extent that they responded to a somewhat different set of problems, there is confirmation of some degree of U.S. distinctiveness at this point.

Americans were addressing some common needs—the issue of urban cemetery location, for example—and shared cultural signals, but in their own context. Prosaic factors provide part of the explanation for special U.S. trends: In a vast land, with ample space around cities, it was easier to found and afford escapist cemeteries than it was in Europe. Compared with Britain (though not with France), U.S.

commitment to lowering the birthrate began early, and with fewer children and a culture that increasingly celebrated children's delightful innocence, anxious concern about children's deaths might have stimulated a somewhat different approach, certainly to the linkage between children and mortality and perhaps toward death more generally. In a culture more unremittingly devoted to progress than even the British, Americans might have had a harder time accepting the fact of death, particularly before later age, a sentiment that, as we will see, would be explicitly vented early in the twentieth century. If this is true, here was another reason to seek to distance and beautify death, to conceal its harsher realities. The "American way" of death that began to emerge in the nineteenth century was not exclusively national—emotional trappings and new kinds of memorials spread more widely. But there was a national flavor, important at the time and capable of shaping reactions even later on. In fact, the U.S. rituals associated with death that had been established by 1900 persist in many ways today, whereas other societies, including Britain, have changed more fundamentally. Here, too, comparative issues remain both intriguing and significant.

Notes

1. James Farrell, *Inventing the American Way of Death, 1830–1920* (Philadelphia, 1980), p. 6 and passim.

2. Jeffrey Steele, "The Gender and Racial Politics of Mourning in Antebellum America," in Peter N. Stearns and Jan Lewis, eds., *An Emotional History of the United States* (New York, 1998), pp. 91–92.

3. Paul Rosenblatt, *Bitter, Bitter Tears: Nineteenth-Century Diarists and Twentieth-Century Grief Theories* (Minneapolis, MN, 1983); Peter Stearns, *American Cool: Constructing a Twentieth-Century Emotional Style* (New York, 1996), chs. 2 and 3.

4. Nathaniel Hawthorne to Sarah Peabody, 15 March 1840, Hawthorn Collection, Harvard University; Karen Lystra, *Searching the Heart: Women, Men and Romantic Love in Nineteenth-Century America* (New York, 1989), p. 50; J. R. Miller, *Homemaking* (Philadelphia, 1882), p. 299.

5. Michael Barton, *Good Men: The Character of Civil War Soldiers* (University Park, PA, 1981). See also Gerald Linderman, *Embattled Courage: The Experience of Combat in the American Civil War* (New York, 1989).

6. Daniel Fiore, *Grandma's Through: Children and the Death Experience from the Nineteenth Century to the Present* (Honors Thesis, Carnegie Mellon University, 1992).

7. *McGuffey's Fourth Eclectic Reader* (1866); Richard Evans, "The Golden Stein," *Analytical Fourth Reader* (New York, 1888); Martha Finley, *Elsie's Girlhood* (New York, 1872), p. 156; Louisa May Alcott, *Little Women* (New York, 1868), pp. 472, 488.

8. Words by George P. Morris, music adapted from "Long Time Ago," a "blackface" song by Charles E. Horn, in William R. Ward, ed., *The American Bicentennial Songbook* (New York, 1975), 2, p. 155. In addition to songs and schoolbook references, a vast amount

of popular art, including school paintings as well as samplers, was devoted to mourning themes between 1820 and the late nineteenth century. See Teresa M. Flanagan, *Mourning on the Pejepscot* (Lanham, MD, 1992) and Steele, "Gender and Racial Politics."

9. Nicholas Tawa, *Sweet Songs from Gentle Americans: The Parlour Song in America 1790–1860* (Bowling Green, OH, 1980), p. 134; "Literacy publications developed a near obsession with the grave," writes Lewis Saum in "The Popular Mood of Pre-Civil War America," *Contributions in American Studies*, no. 46 (Westport, CT, 1980), p. 90. See also David Stannard, *Death in America* (Philadelphia, 1975); Charles Jackson, ed., *Passing: The Vision of Death in America* (Greenwood, CT, 1977); *Christy's Plantation Melodies #2* (Philadelphia, 1858); *Buckley's Ethiopian Melodies* (New York, 1853–1857).

10. *Buckley's Ethiopian Melodies.*

11. L. Covey, *American Pilgrimage: The Roots of American History, Religion, and Culture* (New York, 1961); Lincoln's poem was entitled "My Childhood Home I See Again."

12. Nancy Schrom Dye and Daniel Blake Smith, "Mother Love and Infant Death, 1750–1920," *Journal of American History* 73 (1986): 329–353; Laurel Thatcher Ulrich, *Good Wives: Images and Reality in the Lives of Women in Northern New England, 1650–1750* (New York, 1982); Jan Lewis, *Pursuit of Happiness: Family Values in Jefferson's Virginia* (New York, 1983), chs. 3 and 5; Sylvia Hoffert, "'A Very Peculiar Sorrow': Attitudes Toward Infant Death in the Urban Northeast, 1800–1860," *American Quarterly* 39 (1987): 601–616.

13. Rosenblatt, *Bitter, Bitter Tears*, pp. 21, 38, 93, and passim; *Diary of Nellie Wetherbee*, unpublished manuscript, Bancroft Library, University of California at Berkeley, 1860.

14. Robert V. Wells, "Taming the 'King of Terrors': Rituals and Death in Schenectady, New York, 1844–1860," *Journal of Social History* 27 (1994): 717–734.

15. Lynn Lofland, "The Social Shaping of Emotion: The Case of Grief," *Symbolic Interactions* 8 (1985): 171–190; Steven Seidman, *Romantic Longings: Love in America, 1830–1890* (New York, 1991); Ellen K. Rothman, *Hands and Hearts: A History of Courtship in America* (Cambridge, MA, 1987); E. Anthony Rotundo, "Romantic Friendship: Male Intimacy and Middle-Class Youth in the Northern United States, 1800–1900," *Journal of Social History* 23 (1989): 1–25.

16. Patricia Branca, *Silent Sisterhood: Middle-Class Women in the Victorian Home* (Pittsburgh, 1975).

17. Kenneth Lockridge and Jan Lewis, "Sally Has Been Sick: Pregnancy and Family Limitations among Virginia Gentry Women, 1780–1830," *Journal of Social History* 22 (1988): 5–19.

18. On Stowe and others, Ronald G. Walters, *American Reformers, 1815–1860* (New York, 1978), p. 100.

19. Steele, "Gender and Racial Politics," pp. 98–101.

20. Farrell, *Inventing the American Way of Death*, esp. chs. 4 and 5. I am deeply indebted to Farrell's work in the sections that follow.

21. Farrell, *Inventing the American Way of Death.*

22. Lucius Sargnet, *Dealings with the Dead by a Sexton of the Old School* (Boston, 1856), pp. 40–42.

23. Jacob Bigelow, "The Interment of the Dead," in Cornelia Walter, *Mt. Auburn Illustrated* (New York, 1850), pp. 28–35; see also *The Picturesque Pocket Companion, and Visitors Guide, through Mt. Auburn* (New York, 1850).

24. *Picturesque Mt. Auburn*, pp. 34, 119; Nehemiah Cleaveland, *Green-Wood Illustrated* (New York, 1847), p. viii; Walter, *Mt. Auburn*, p. 38.

25. Cleaveland, *Green-Wood Illustrated*, pp. 13–14.

26. Andrew Downing, *Landscape Illustrated* (New York, 1921), p. 371.

27. "Editorial," *Park and Cemetery* 5 (March 1895): 1; O. C. Simonds, "Review of Progress of Cemetery Design and Development," *Association of American Cemetery Superintendents (AACS)* 33 (1919): 59; William Falconer, "The Ideal Cemetery," AACS 26 (1912): 22; G. P. Burns, "The Application of Landscape Design to the Cemetery," AACS 31 (1917): 30.

28. Sidney Hare, "The Cemetery Beautiful," AACS 24 (1910): 41.

29. Cited in Bayley Smith, "An Outdoor Room on a Cemetery Lot," *Country Life in America* 17 (March 1910): 539.

30. Mrs. E. E. Hay, "Influence of Our Surroundings," AACS 14 (1900): 21; Farrell, *Inventing the American Way of Death*, pp. 132–133.

31. Hay, "Influence of Our Surroundings," p. 47.

32. Farrell, *Inventing the American Way of Death*, ch. 5.

33. National Funeral Directors' Association (NFDA) 2 (1883): 22; W. P. Hohenschuh, *The Modern Funeral: Its Management* (Chicago, n.d.), pp. 82–83; Robert Habenstein and William Lamers, *The History of American Funeral Directing* (Milwaukee, WI, 1955).

34. W. P. Hohenschuh, *The Modern Funeral*, pp. 17–18; A. P. Burton, "An Experience Hour," NFDA 27 (1908): 100–103; Farrell, *Inventing the American Way of Death*, ch. 5.

35. Stannard, *The Puritan Way of Death* (New York, 1977), pp. 147–149. "The Ideas of a Plain Country Woman," *Ladies Home Journal* 30 (April 1912): 42.

36. Michelle Perrot, ed., *A History of Private Life*, vol. IV (Cambridge, MA, 1990), pp. 332–334.

37. Ralph Houlbrooke, ed., *Death, Ritual and Bereavement* (New York, 1989).

38. Geoffrey Gorer, *Death, Grief and Mourning in Contemporary Britain* (London, 1965, repr. 1987).

CHAPTER 4

The Administration of Death in the Nineteenth Century

New attitudes toward personal death inevitably, in some cases quite strikingly, affected broader policies. This was most impressively true with regard to the death penalty. New concerns about death also affected reactions to suicide and policies toward abortion. Even death in war was reconsidered. In most of these areas, many factors complicated the application of the growing distaste for death: Sometimes attitudes toward death were partly window dressing for policies supported for other reasons, sometimes attitudes toward death simply could not prevail against other developments. But the scope of reconsideration, at least to some degree, was impressive. New thinking about death prompted serious innovations in a variety of policy areas, connecting personal changes in emotions and rituals to major new initiatives that might affect hosts of strangers.

Americans participated strongly in many of these currents, and their approach was not always unique. Again, a combination of Western and U.S. approaches shaped the new terrain. The power of the West in the nineteenth century—the century of imperialism—meant that policy changes prompted by Western innovations toward death could have some wider impact, although this extension would be more visible after 1900 than before.

The Death Penalty: Trends and Countercurrents

Beginning in the eighteenth century and accelerating clearly through the first half of the nineteenth, a variety of political leaders and intellectuals voiced unprecedented concerns about the application of the death penalty. Their statements were not directly couched in terms of the larger redefinitions of death, but they related to these redefinitions intimately. If death seemed increasingly unacceptable, if its horrors were best masked in personal life—by more bucolic cemeteries or more cosmetic treatment of corpses—this surely called for reconsideration of death as punishment, whether the topic heading was death itself or a more general humanitarianism.

Traditionally, as we have seen, most societies had administered death penalties for a variety of crimes and had publicized the punishments widely. Crowds gathering for public executions constituted one of the standard excitements of urban life in premodern times. The frequency of death penalties reflected not only a widespread acceptance of death itself, a degree of familiarity we would find surprising, but also the absence of many alternative penalties and indeed the rudimentary qualities of policing before recent times. In Western society prisons began to become common only from the early seventeenth century, and they were quite expensive; before their wide availability, it was difficult to develop alternatives to the death penalty in the case of even reasonably serious crimes. Lack of formal policing meant that societies depended heavily on intimidation and fear as a means of inhibiting crime; public displays of executions constituted a central feature of this approach. By the eighteenth century, however, innovations were emerging: Police forces were becoming less inadequate and began to be visible deterrents to crime, the expansion of prisons provided viable alternatives that had the merit (in reformers' eyes) of not only avoiding the harshness of death but providing opportunities for rehabilitation. This was the context in which death itself could be rethought in this arena as in others.

Rethinking took three main forms. First, the number of crimes that called for the death penalty was steadily scaled back. Death now seemed too horrible to inflict for most types of theft, for example. Second, the death penalty when administered might be withdrawn from public view; death was too dreadful, its implications too barbaric, to inflict on a civilized population. And finally, the whole idea of the death penalty might ultimately be rejected altogether.

Reform began on both sides of the Atlantic. The first systematic attempt to reduce the frequency of the death penalty occurred with the Great Law of the colony of Pennsylvania, in 1682—a fascinating example of Quaker influence. Here, capital punishment was applicable only in cases of first degree murder. Fines and imprisonment were now used to punish other crimes. English codes were reestablished in Pennsylvania after the death of William Penn, in 1718, which meant that fourteen kinds of crime plus religious offenses could be punishable by death. But Pennsylvania took the lead immediately after the signing of the U.S. Declaration of Independence—on September 28, 1776—in directing its legislature to cut back the use of the death penalty once again. Witchcraft was removed as a crime punishable by death in 1791—indeed, executions for witchcraft had virtually disappeared in the Western world by 1750, and Pennsylvania exempted all crimes save first degree murder in 1794. Many other U.S.

states followed suit, in an ongoing process lasting more than a century. By the 1950s, six states had no capital punishment at all; fourteen states had only one category, almost always for murder; eight had two; and only two states had as many as six. Well before this, all states had eliminated capital punishment for property crimes, reserving the designation for violent crimes of personal injury or assault. The only two really new crimes to be subjected to the death penalty in at least a few states were train wrecking (for which no one was actually ever executed) and the crime that gained new attention by the early twentieth century, kidnapping. Rape was also added to the capital list in some southern states after Reconstruction, because of real or imagined fear of African Americans and as a means of legally intimidating them.

The reduction in use of the death penalty developed vigorously in Great Britain, which in 1780 still had 350 crimes for which in principle the death penalty could be administered, most of them fairly trivial crimes against property. By 1825 reformers had whittled the list down to 220; more dramatic reform reduced the number to 17 in 1839 and a mere 4 in 1861. The attack on capital punishment in Britain began with juries: Here, property-owning men became increasingly reluctant to inflict death even on lower-class criminals. They either acquitted accused prisoners or reduced the crime to a level below the capital—for example, by claiming that only thirty-nine shillings' worth of goods had been stolen as against the forty shillings that would have made the death penalty mandatory. Juries also stopped convicting accused criminals of forgery, again because they found the death penalty inappropriate, to the point that banks urged that the penalty be abolished because forgers had essentially become unpunishable. By the later eighteenth century, politicians were picking up the charge, arguing that a long list of capital crimes had become uncivilized and that the list must be pared down.

Similar developments occurred elsewhere in western Europe. Leading Enlightenment thinkers like Cesare Beccaria argued against frequent death penalties, claiming that they were barbaric and that they did not in fact deter crimes. Lesser, more rehabilitative punishments were far more effective. The French Revolution did not of course abolish the death penalty, but its use of the guillotine was originally intended to make death quicker and less painful. Later legal reforms in France and elsewhere pared down the list of eligible crimes. A key move in Russia's reform period in the 1860s involved the reduction of capital crimes, along lines similar to Britain a few decades earlier. By this point a mark of societies seeking to demonstrate their progressive qualities, by Western standards, characteristically involved limiting the number of crimes for which death was the punishment and reducing the number of executions altogether.

There was some ebb and flow within this general movement. Austria abolished many death penalties in the late eighteenth century but later restored some, as a reaction to what was regarded as the liberal excess of the French Revolution. Germany and Russia also moved back and forth a bit in the limitation process. In general, however, there was a clear trend that, by the later nineteenth century, was becoming global: There were better, more humane ways to punish many crimes than by death.

A related change that gained ground in the later nineteenth and early twentieth centuries involved allowing juries to decide whether the death penalty fit a murder, instead of mandating a death sentence. Only seven American states had a mandatory death penalty by 1930 (and only one, Vermont, by 1951). This shift led to a rapid reduction in the number of deaths actually imposed—while increasing the conviction rate in murder cases, with juries that would have been reluctant to impose the death penalty but now had an alternative.[1]

Along with reducing the number of capital crimes and allowing greater flexibility in sentencing, many societies also began to limit the groups who could be subjected to capital punishment regardless of the crimes they might have committed. Traditionally, children had been put to death almost as readily as adults. During the nineteenth century, however, reformers protested that child criminals had not reached the age of reason and therefore should not be deprived of life whatever their offense. In Britain, a series of laws beginning with the Children Act in 1908 abolished the death penalty in all cases in which the murderer was under eighteen years of age at the time of the crime. In many Western societies also, judges and juries became increasingly unwilling to subject women to capital punishment. Women were less likely than men to commit violent crimes in any event, and now they were increasingly excused, at least from the direst punishment, even when convicted. In Britain in the early twentieth century, only 15 percent of all women accused of murder were sentenced to death and fewer than 10 percent of these in turn were actually executed. New ideas about the horrors of death and new ideas about the purity of women combined to produce a dramatic, if not foolproof, exemption.

Although it might have mattered less to the declining number of people—increasingly a few adult men—actually still put to death, the transformation of capital punishment from proudly public to carefully secluded was as dramatic and revealing as the reduction in capital crimes. Public executions were a traditional staple in many societies through the eighteenth century (including during the French Revolution), designed to allow criminals to confess their sins and ask for forgiveness—thus providing a presumably inspiring example—demonstrating to a wide audience the consequences of crime, and revealing the power and majesty of the state. In fact, although publics often enjoyed the scene, there had always been some drawbacks, particularly if the audience sympathized with victim rather than the state or used the occasion to foment disorder. These downsides loomed larger by the early nineteenth century, as cities grew and crowds became less reliable. At least as important, however, was the new view of death's horrors. Even if some capital punishment remained essential, authorities increasingly believed that public displays offended the sensitivities of the civilized and pandered to the worst instincts of those who might still enjoy the spectacle.

New York State was the first to ban public hangings, in 1835, and gradually all other states followed suit—Kentucky being the last. Parliament banned public executions in Britain in 1868. France maintained public executions in principle, but began to keep the crowds so far away that they could see very little.

American leadership in this move was fascinating, because, as we will see, the nation began to lag behind global trends 150 years later. The American Revolution prompted considerable rethinking of all sorts of traditional practices, particularly in the northern states, and opened the door to fuller implementation of Enlightenment ideas—including ideas about appropriate punishment. Along with the new thinking about death—where the United States also led, as in the development of garden cemeteries—this generated major innovations in the approach toward those executions still regarded as necessary. What had once seemed obviously desirable—exposing the public to the most awful punishments for crime—now seemed dangerous and demeaning. To be sure, there were some complexities. American authorities made quite a spectacle of the hanging of the conspirators in Lincoln's death, and even in the twentieth century, press accounts of certain executions could be quite vivid. In a few states also, the move to private executions was slightly qualified by a requirement that a few civilian volunteers be present to witness the event. Generally, however, official distaste for display of death marked an important change in U.S. practice.

With U.S. example leading the way, from states like New York and then Pennsylvania, European countries began to rethink their practices as well. German cities started to worry about public executions as contributions to moral decay and disorder. When old-style beheadings occasionally misfired—requiring a second or even third blow of the ax to sever the head, as happened in Hamburg several times in the early nineteenth century—the pressure to figure out some better approach mounted appreciably. Hamburg officials simply stopped executions for thirty years after 1822, and when they resumed them, they did them in private. All this seemed an essential part of modern progress—as one reformer put it, "old laws had to be enlightened with the torch of progress." Lower-class taste might still be debased, but it was up to progressive officials to establish new levels of decency around the phenomenon of death. In 1854, after much debate, Hamburg reestablished executions, but in private, with only a few wealthy and respectable male citizens allowed to attend. The guillotine was now used to avoid mishaps that had occurred earlier employing the ax, and "the machine was erected in a way that the witnesses could hardly see the body of the condemned, and the head, after being suspended from the torso, immediately fell into a bag under the scaffold." Death was now too dreadful to be viewed. Of course, popular newspapers actually increased their coverage of mayhem and violence, but this was an ambivalence about modern approaches to death that would continue to the present day.[2]

Britain obstinately refused to abandon hanging in favor of more modern types of execution, but it, too, ended the public spectacle. The last man to be publicly hanged was an Irish nationalist, Michael Barrett, in 1868—convicted of blowing up a prison wall in an effort to free other Irish prisoners. Two days later, after months of debate, the British Parliament passed the Act to Provide for the Carrying Out of Capital Punishment in Prisons. From this time until the last British executions, in 1964, hangings were concealed from public view. British leaders had decided—indeed, simply now took it for granted—that public executions were "a disgrace not only to civilization but to our common humanity." They were "barbarous and demoralizing" and "not in accordance with the spirit of the age." Indeed, many recognized that Britain had lagged a bit behind progressive international standards in failing to act even earlier. The terror of death was increasingly recognized: Criminals should at least be spared the need to deal with these terrors in public, and the public should be spared the need to contemplate the terrors through unnecessary stimulation. Novelists like Charles Dickens recounted their own revulsion at public executions, another sign that the rethinking of death involved a new level of squeamishness that inevitably affected policy. Some, of course, began to oppose the death penalty outright, although Dickens ultimately did not take this route. But surely, even if still necessary, it was believed that the act should be concealed.[3]

Critical historians have properly noted that the new movement to privatize executions was hardly a sign of humane sentiment, even though proponents at the time thought that it was. The executions still occurred, and concealment might in fact reduce pressure to rethink capital punishment more fully. And ordinary people were not consulted: Crowd appetite for witnessing death might not have changed and, as the popular press quickly realized, turned to other sources of lurid stories about death and violence. Still, the change, if complex, was substantial, a visible public statement that death needed to be rethought and, at least symbolically, reduced—at least in the eyes of elites and the "respectable" middle classes.

One final change emerged, although amid controversy over one specific matter: the progressive elimination of torture or defilement in addition to execution. Again traditionally, many societies had long inflicted punishments complementary to the death penalty as a means of responding to certain particularly awful kinds of crime—like leading a political protest. Bodies might be torn apart (sometimes, beginning before death and continuing afterward; sometimes simply to abuse the body, usually publicly, after death). By the eighteenth century, in the

Western world and somewhat beyond, these practices began to seem absolutely barbaric, and they largely ended. New controversy arose over a newer matter: the use of the bodies of executed criminals in anatomy laboratories. Concern about the growing hunger for cadavers—part of the early stages of developing more modern medical training, obviously overall intended to help combat death—surfaced in many societies, as we have seen. Many people worried about grave robbers, and some riots occurred in the late nineteenth/early twentieth centuries to insist on fuller protection. Several jurisdictions responded by designating certain criminals for dissection after execution—the idea was to provide a sufficient supply so that illegal depredations against corpses would stop. New York State passed such a law at the end of the nineteenth century. Punishment for particularly horrible crimes, the law suggested, could have dissection added as a part of the capital sentence. Fairly quickly, however, this also seemed too cruel, and the practice dropped away. Clearly, new ideas about the sanctity of the body in death, even for criminals, modified traditional practices and some well-meaning innovations alike.[4]

Changes in use of the death penalty tended to accumulate over time, well into the twentieth century. More nations or units like the American states created greater flexibility, and actual courts imposed death less and less frequently. Thus Switzerland extended full abolition of the death penalty from fifteen cantons in 1874, to nationwide elimination in 1942. Iceland abolished the penalty in 1930; Brazil essentially did the same in 1946. In the United States, Michigan was the first state fully to abolish capital punishment, in 1847; four other states banned it between 1907 and 1911, and seven more during World War I. Occasionally states restored the penalty after a few years, but even then they often administered it infrequently. Ohio, which resisted full abolition, sentenced 58 percent of those convicted of first degree murder to death in the years 1896–1900, but dropped this to 26 percent thirty years later. Nationally, 130 people were put to death in 1921, rising to 194 in 1936, but dropping to 82 in 1950—and this in a country experiencing considerable population growth.

A final revealing trend, even where the death penalty was not abolished outright, was the consistent effort to introduce methods of execution that would be as swift and painless as possible. Here again, the contrast with premodern impulses to inflict prolonged death on certain kinds of criminals was considerable. The guillotine, as noted, was an early entrant into the less-painful sweepstakes, although its use was tarnished by its frequent service during the Terror of the French Revolution. Efforts to simplify hanging dotted the midnineteenth century. The electric chair, developed around 1900, was touted as a modern instrument that would kill quickly and reliably, although it turned out to be not so reliable on occasion. Later in the twentieth century experiments with lethal injections were justified on the same grounds. Death, if essential for some crimes, should be merciful, although the debate over how best to live up to this standard continues even in the present day.

The varied attacks on death penalty traditions were linked to other innovations, as new attitudes about death were juxtaposed with traditional practice. The practice of dueling was increasingly the victim of more modern ideas during the nineteenth century, both in the United States and in Europe. Dueling had long been regarded as an expression of honor, a means of avoiding wider conflict. But codes of honor increasingly seemed old-fashioned, an aristocratic conceit in an increasingly middle-class Western society; and, like capital punishment, they generated needless risk of fatalities at a time when efforts increasingly focused on limiting the experience of death. So, despite centuries of custom, legislation and policing increasingly ended the practice, even on the U.S. Western frontier.

Change came rather late, however. Dueling actually increased in places like Italy into the 1880s (when an average of 269 affairs of honor occurred each year). Germany also had high rates, associated with dueling societies among aristocratic university students. Latin America just began to introduce dueling in the 1860s, imitating Europe. Affairs of honor increased particularly in association with modern politics and journalism. Argentina had more than a hundred duels a year, mostly with pistols, into the 1920s. But opposition rose as well: These fights seemed senseless—and when death was involved, truly tragic—and they detracted from the power of the state to control decisions about justice. U.S. and British opinion unseated dueling fairly early in the nineteenth century (except in the U.S. South, where it lasted longer). Christian churches, including the Catholic Church, opposed dueling with growing vigor. A Mexican critic called dueling a "perverse custom that human depravation inherited from times past" yet "sustained by so many modern barbarians in Civilization's midst." Although protection of the rights of the state loomed large, the fact that dueling's goal was to maim or kill the opponent produced much of the fervor behind the increasingly widespread opposition. Britain was frequently cited as a quintessentially civilized society that had outlawed dueling without any loss of honor or gentlemanly conduct. Despite vigorous defense of the practice from some members of the upper classes, state after state abolished dueling and began to institute police proceedings against any attempt to maintain the practice. Several countries in the 1900s, both in Europe and in Latin America, established honor committees, so that the offenses once solved by dueling could be resolved without violence. Mexican law in 1929 established these groups, with the provision that they could never authorize an outright duel—which by that time was considered a crime. Dueling persisted for a while in some places, partly because laws were not well enforced, but the practice faded dramatically after 1930. In many ways, the spontaneous end of dueling was a more revealing sign of changing attitudes about death risks than the formal shifts in law. Slowly, because the upper classes were involved, the growing belief that the administration of death should be minimized applied even in matters of honor.[5]

Darker Sides

There were setbacks amid the general trends. After World War I, European nations that turned fascist, from Italy to Germany and Romania, uniformly reestablished the death penalty and often used it widely, particularly of course on political dissidents. The fascist idea of the state's responsibility to generate order and the need to beat back political opposition combined to make the death penalty seem not only logical but essential, and fascist enjoyment of violence contributed as well.

Another set of issues arose in the United States after the Civil War and Reconstruction. Even as formal moves against the death penalty gained ground, a new thirst for lynchings developed in some places as a means of evading the niceties of the law and, even more, to intimidate racial minorities. Between 1882 and 1930, when the lynching mania was at its height, at least 3,386 African Americans died at the hands of lynch mobs, and over a slightly longer time period, at least 597 Mexican Americans were lynched as well.

Individual stories show the contradiction in the dominant policies toward death. In November 1928, a group of masked men abducted a man from a hospital in Farmington, New Mexico, where he was dying of gunshot wounds, and hanged him from a locust tree. He had been shot by a sheriff's posse, convinced that he had assaulted a farmer's wife; a local newspaper rejoiced that "the degenerate Mexican got exactly what was coming to him." Lynchings revealed how the passions aroused by certain real or imagined crimes, in a context of virulent racial hatreds, could override attitudes toward the administration of death that were winning ascendancy in other respects. The Holocaust would display the same brutal override on a larger scale in Germany. Modern trends were real, in the reconsideration of using death to retaliate for real or imagined crime or deviance, but they were vulnerable.

Abortion

Abortion was another aspect of death that came under new scrutiny—not so much because of concern about the deaths of fetuses, the twentieth-century focus that depended among other things on much better knowledge of fetal development than was widely available in the nineteenth century, but because of worries about deaths of mothers combined with other factors. Although some new abortion issues developed in western Europe, the United States headed this particular facet of innovation.

Abortion had never been accepted in Christianity, but it did not provoke wide comment until the 1830s. Abortions were only illegal after the fourth month of pregnancy—traditionally a distinction was drawn between before and after "quickening," and even then laws were not usually rigorously enforced. Many women attempted abortion in colonial America (and also western Europe and elsewhere), although mainly through the use of natural products that might induce abortion—such as derivatives from juniper bushes (until the decline of magic in the eighteenth century, magical incantations and rituals were also used). These procedures did not always work, which might have been one reason that the subject did not command great attention. They also did not depend on assistance from others, although midwives or local "wise women" might assist at least in providing advice. And of course it is impossible to know how much abortion there was, though in the absence of widely effective birth control devices we can assume some use as a means of countering unwanted pregnancies. Single women who found themselves pregnant were probably particularly eager, but families might also seek recourse, particularly given the fact that outright infanticide was more rigorously condemned. Abortion was certainly used in other societies. In eighteenth-century Japan, for example, fairly wide recourse to abortion helped limit population growth. Shintoism viewed abortion as a necessary evil, whereas Buddhism manifested mixed reactions, with tolerance and compassion both toward the "aborted spirit" and toward the woman involved. Abortion was seen not as ending a life but as returning a fetus to be reborn again later; particular rituals were available for aborted souls as well as for miscarriages.

Attitudes first showed signs of change in the nineteenth-century United States. A wave of state legislation began to outlaw the practice, and by 1880 it was criminalized almost everywhere. What caused this significant shift? In the first place, a new culture of middle-class respectability arose, adamantly opposed to sexuality before or outside of marriage and deeply concerned about the morals of the lower classes (and sometimes, of young people more generally). Abortion was seen as a means of escaping the responsibility of sexual license; attacking abortion (along with attacking birth control) was intended to help enforce sexual propriety. The nature of abortion also began to change, with more surgical procedures introduced. This had the potential for making abortion more common than before. Estimates by the 1850s suggested that as many as 20 percent of all pregnancies were being terminated by abortion, with upper-class women joining their less affluent sisters in seeing this as a necessary measure for birth control. (Indeed, realization that native-born women were more likely to use abortion than immigrants provided another argument: Abortion should be opposed as a means of ensuring the birthrates of the "best" Americans.) But rising numbers were not the only point. Growing reliance on surgery could also present new risks for the mother. Natural chemicals themselves could do damage, by poisoning the mother or harming reproductive capacity; hasty surgery could be even worse. Early laws against abortion, in states like New York, followed from publicized cases of maternal death resulting from botched procedures. Doctors took a lead in the widespread new campaign against abortion; the American Medical Association made this a major part of its platform virtually from its inception in 1847. Doctors were motivated by sexual prudery, by a sincere concern for women's health, and also by professional self-interest against midwives or other practitioners who often performed abortions. By attacking abortion, doctors were implicitly claiming a new role in regulating sexuality and childbirth. The U.S. emphasis on antiabortion had something to do with the fact that American doctors long had shakier professional credentials and public acceptance than their European counterparts and so were eager to develop new platforms to tout their indisputable professionalism. Thus in 1895 Dr. Joseph Taber Johnson, director of the Obstetrical and Gynecological Society, launched a campaign for the stricter enforcement of existing law, believing that it was up to medical professionals to take up the new fight. In the process, death of a fetus began gradually to be added to potential death of the mother as a reason to oppose abortion: Doctors urged the public to recognize that just because the fetus was not yet moving was no reason to believe it was not alive.

New attitudes toward death, in other words, played a role in a dramatic new stance toward an old practice, although only in combination with other factors. Initially the criminal focus was on the abortionists—who were the main targets of doctors—but increasingly blame spilled over to women seeking abortions.

European concern about abortion also developed—a British measure outlawed abortion in 1803—but the campaigns were less fierce and reasonably open practice still persisted—although far more in Protestant regions than in Catholic. In Berlin by 1900, for example, a quarter of all working-class women had had at least one abortion, in absence of adequately reliable birth control. Most European countries had laws against abortion by the later nineteenth century, but enforcement was constrained not only by substantial popular reliance on abortion as a means of controlling family size or escaping the shame of premarital pregnancy, but also by public opinion. Great sympathy might develop for young women who became pregnant because of sexual intimidation by employers, for example. French juries even acquitted many women who killed infants after birth, because of this concern. The disparity between official attitudes and actual practice, in other words, remained considerable, and although this applied to the United States, the European gap was greater.

Even greater tolerance for abortion developed elsewhere. Abortion persisted in Japan. A key move of the new Soviet government in Russia was to legalize abortion in the 1920s, and abortion remains a major source of birth control in Russia to the present day. (This policy predictably reinforced antiabortion in the United States, because abortion might now be linked to dangerous foreign radicalism.)

Even in the United States, however, abortion was a disputed topic. Many women resorted to illegal abortions, and not a few died. By the 1930s, 14 percent of all maternal deaths were attributed to botched illegal abortions, by shady practitioners who exploited young women and often ignored even basic measures of sterilization of instruments. A few tragic cases each year even found women attempting abortions on themselves, using such things as coat hangers. Widespread public sympathy continued to support abortions, and although this did not change the law, it did modify enforcement. (Even outright infanticide sometimes won exoneration in the courts, in the United States as well as in western Europe, in cases where a young woman had been abused by an irresponsible man.) Furthermore, legal provision for abortions where essential to preserve the life of the mother allowed doctors some leeway, and a number of abortions were performed in hospitals and clinics—particularly for women in the middle classes. Increasingly, however, abortions were seen as a resort of primarily lower-class women who refused to regulate their sexuality. And the pressure to enforce existing laws mounted, particularly after about 1940. By this point not only doctors, but also newspapers like the *New York Times* and key religious groups (first Protestants, then Catholics) joined in the effort. But greater rigor increased the need some women would feel to resort to illegal outlets, where the dangers were particularly great.

By the 1950s, even as antiabortion policing was at its height, the modern concern about death did not provide a clear-cut stance. New efforts to discourage death had helped motivate campaigns against abortion for the sake of mothers, but also with a growing realization—due in part to more precise anatomical research—that even early fetuses had life. But antiabortion measures could also provoke death, for laws regulated popular recourses only imperfectly and unquestionably made the (illegal) abortions that did occur more dangerous. Here was a topic that was becoming ripe for reconsideration in the second half of the twentieth century.[6]

War

New attitudes toward death were particularly applied to punishment and abortion, but they also touched other facets of policy to a more modest extent. War was a case in point. Many aspects of nineteenth-century war were shaped by factors independent of the new distaste for death and often ran contrary to the implications of the new attitudes. Technology made war more fearsome than ever before after 1850: Repeating rifles, more mobile cannon, and early versions of the machine gun allowed soldiers to kill each other at unprecedented rates, as the Crimean War and the U.S. Civil War would both reveal. To be sure, better measures of hygiene and medical care reduced deaths due to illness among troops, which used to kill more people than battles did, but the battles themselves became bloodier.

When new technology combined with racial disdain, the results could be fiercer still. Many attacks on indigenous peoples, during the U.S. westward movement and amid European imperialism, saw small numbers of Western troops mow down sometimes tens of thousands of native troops fighting with more traditional weapons and methods. A young Winston Churchill, later British prime minister during World War II, wrote the following after an 1898 battle in Sudan that pitted a small British force armed with twenty machine guns against 40,000 Muslim troops:

> The infantry fired steadily and stolidly, without hurry or excitement, for the enemy were far away and the officers careful. Besides, the soldiers were interested in the work and took great pains ... And all the time out on the plain on the other side bullets were shearing through flesh, smashing and splintering bone ... valiant men were struggling on through a hell of whistling metal, exploding shell, and spurting dust—suffering, despairing, dying.

The new technology of war prepared the world's most bloody conflict to that point, the world war that broke out in 1914. No new hesitations about death slowed the advance of more lethal weapons. New or newly enhanced hatreds born of racism or nationalism could add fuel to the fire, making it easier to justify the killing of others who did not share crucial identity.

It is also vital to note how modern military technology began to depersonalize the administration of death in war. In the Civil War, along with bombardments by cannon, soldiers still fought hand to hand, using bayonets. By the time of imperialist struggles in the later nineteenth century, and certainly by World War I, most killing was now from a distance, with the use of machine guns, more devastating artillery, and ultimately tanks and planes. The huge change in the military administration of death would create searing tensions between normal death standards and what happened in war.

But changing death attitudes did count around the margins, where war was concerned. The middle decades of the nineteenth century saw new efforts to provide medical care to wounded soldiers. Florence Nightingale's ministrations during the Crimean War were followed by expanded medical service during the Civil War. Results were still modest, but some lives were saved.

Along with medical care came new interest in caring for the bodies of those killed in battle. During the Mexican American War, before the heightened level of concern kicked in, more than 13,000 U.S. troops were left unidentified and often unburied, with no apparent sense that this was anything but normal. In the Civil War, however, efforts to ship bodies home intensified—this was one of the sources of the growing interest in embalming. Beyond this, Clara Barton, the founder of the American Red Cross, launched a campaign to identify bodies and inform families of the fates of their loved ones, an effort that extended for years after the war itself and began an investigative program in the United States that would expand greatly in the twentieth century. Even Lincoln's Gettysburg Address can be interpreted as a new sign of uneasiness over those killed in war, a belief that they deserve special attention and memory.

More direct efforts emerged to ease the clash between new attitudes toward death and the realities of war. In 1859 a Swiss banker, Henry Dumont, appalled at the lack of medical attention given to soldiers during the wars of Italian unification, began to urge the adoption of more international standards to improve care and minimize fatalities. His work caught the attention of the press, and celebrities like Nightingale and writer Victor Hugo chimed in as well. An international committee followed, that later became the International Red Cross. A variety of national governments agreed to follow certain standards during wars, and although these standards had no impact on deaths directly in battle they did work toward realizing lower levels of death among the wounded and also those that resulted from mistreatment of prisoners of war. The Red Cross, and later associated groups like the Red Crescent, also worked across international boundaries to minimize fatalities and suffering in natural disasters as well as wars—another sign of the new global humanitarianism related to the desire to constrain traditional sources of death. In 1864 the Geneva Convention was signed, initially among Western powers but gradually with the adherence of other states such as Japan.

The idea of the initial Geneva Convention was to protect prisoners of war, and although this went beyond issues of outright loss of life, the new concern for developing greater controls over death was certainly involved. It was no coincidence that just the next year a Confederate army officer was executed for murdering Union prisoners of war—another illustration of the new belief that even wartime behavior needed to be controlled where death was concerned. As a Brussels Protocol insisted in 1874, war should not "inflict unnecessary suffering" upon an enemy. In this spirit, later Geneva Conventions reached out more ambitiously, becoming the widest effort in human history to contain societies in conflict. A set of 1899 treaties, following an 1880 English "Manual of the Laws of War on Land," addressed asphyxiating gases and expanding bullets, leading to thirteen separate treaties among a number of nations in 1907. The movement continued with a new set of conventions in 1929, outlawing poison gas while also further regulating the treatment of wounded prisoners. In 1949, finally, four more conventions offered protection to people involved in shipwrecks and also to civilians generally in times of war. Insisting that military personnel be clearly designated by uniforms, the fourth convention explicitly stated that civilians should not be subject to attack—either directly or through indiscriminate action against areas in which civilians were present. All of this was backed up, in terms of international law, by increasing belief that individuals who violated the wartime standards could be treated as criminals—as occurred after World War II, with a number of Nazi officials at the Nuremberg trials.

The attempts to curtail death in war obviously swam against the tide of modern technology and modern passions. We will take up the tensions between the new standards that intended to limit death in war and the actual circumstances of twentieth-century war in a later chapter. The contrast with the more manageable issue of capital punishment was massive. But the discord was obvious as well, and the fact that military trends and modern death attitudes did not mesh set up issues for the future, issues with which global society continues to grapple today. At the least, facile acceptance of new levels of military slaughter was complicated by the growing aversion to death in other contexts.

Suicide and Murder

People killing themselves or others constitute a final aspect of the administration of death. The acts are often private and individual, but they, too, call for policies and public reactions in response; in both capacities they might have some relationship to changing attitudes toward death.

Tracing the actual history of suicide is a challenging task, although historians have launched some interesting efforts. Suicides in the past were often concealed, because of the shame involved to the victim and to his family. We know that, historically, suicide rates are higher in some regions than in others. Often this related to the length and darkness of winter, but other factors might be involved. It is difficult to determine whether new attitudes toward death affected suicide rates during the nineteenth century.

Suicide rates almost certainly rose, on a per capita basis, in Western society by the later nineteenth century. One study suggests that the increase had most to do with growing despair in later age, particularly when combined with unemployment, heavy drinking, and growing isolation and loneliness. Concern about suicide rates, as death itself became less fatalistically accepted, constituted an interesting feature of the nineteenth-century outlook, a blotch on any easy belief in progress.[7]

What is clear, and what provides another link between new attitudes and policy, is that suicide became a much more widely discussed and analyzed subject than ever before. The decline of religion encouraged more social science attention to a phenomenon once simply categorized as a sin. But the growing uneasiness with death also explains why more and more distinguished scholars felt that suicide was an issue to be probed, that factors should be identified that might allow societies to reduce the levels of an unacceptable human recourse. This discussion often led to anxiety that rates were increasing, although it was not always certain that this was the case; this, too, contributed to public attention to a type of death that was not easy to square with growing hopes for progress.

Europe led the way here. Statistical surveys of suicide began to appear from the 1840s onward. Medical professionals analyzed the brains of suicide victims, to determine whether recognizable forms of mental illness were involved. Social scientists worried that modern social conditions were generating higher rates of suicide. Émile Durkheim emerged as the leading scholar in the field. He argued that social stresses altered the brains of some people, predisposing them to suicide. Although probing marked regional variations, Durkheim argued that Europe overall was experiencing a disproportionate suicide rate owing to the decline of cohesive institutions such as guilds and religious communities, leaving more people isolated. His findings persuaded many people that modern conditions increased the propensity for suicide, a troubling conclusion amid growing hopes that death could be more constrained by modern progress. Durkheim believed that social reforms, generating new types of organizations, might counter modern isolation, but his pessimistic conclusions drew more attention. But some new policies were introduced, often under medical supervision. Doctors helped organize suicide watches in hospitals, asylums, and prisons, and treatments were developed for the suicide-prone, including traumatized veterans of World War I. The idea of suicide prevention was itself a fruit of modern thinking about death and its avoidance.[8] Changes in Western attitudes to suicide also affected Russia. Earlier religious judgments of suicide as a sin, a defiance of God, and a sign of demonic influence increasingly yielded to scientific inquiry. But in the Russian context of the nineteenth and early twentieth centuries, suicide began to be taken as a sign of social protest—possibly against noble landlords, possibly against the state; suicide was a diseased act, according to the scientists, but also possibly a sign of a diseased society. For this reason communist leaders, after 1917, would work hard to prevent or conceal suicide, viewing it as anti-Soviet, because in a society heading toward communism, the social causes of suicide should be declining.[9]

Suicide received new kinds of attention in one other respect. As policy procedures improved and court systems expanded, investigations into suicide increased, and in many countries courts of law, even juries, were required to decide on whether a suicide ruling was accurate, as opposed to foul play or natural causes. This helped expand the discussion of suicide. In general, juries preferred to think of suicide as an indication of mental imbalance or at least as stemming from uncertain causes, rather than as an outright crime; changes in law, in places like Britain, reduced the consequences of suicide rulings (which until 1882 could result in penalties on the families of the deceased), which made it easier for juries to register their discomfort with suicide without seeming punitive.

In Western society, murder rates fell, on a per capita basis, from the Middle Ages to the twentieth century, not every decade but in terms of overall trends, and the drop was probably considerable. Several factors were involved. Better government controls reduced private feuds and, later, imposed more police prevention as well. People seemed gradually to have learned greater restraint, so that even though weapons became more lethal, homicide became less common. Attitudes toward death might certainly be involved here: As death became less a part of accepted routine and more awesome, more people might have hesitated in administering it even in anger, and certainly governments urged police forces to work on reducing this crime, including bringing murderers to justice, more than any other.

Murders that did occur also became more widely noticed. Nineteenth-century newspapers, both in Europe and in the United States, highlighted juicy homicides, providing entertainment, but also serving to focus apprehension lest the crime get out of hand. As with suicide, discussion of murder and its prevention gained increased attention, another facet of the new levels of concern about death. Often, people in Western society believed that murder rates were rising when they were not in fact, a sign of uneasiness about modern society but also a symptom of the desire to reduce this traditional source of death along with others.

The United States shared an uneasy relationship with larger Western murder trends. From colonial days onward, the nation had a much higher per capita murder rate than western Europe did. More open frontiers, more abundant use of guns, less-effective governments, and more racial and ethnic tensions are usually combined in explaining this fact. The U.S. rate was even higher than that of Canada, despite the fact that both societies had frontier traditions and considerable ethnic mixing. Other societies had rates higher still: Most Latin American countries have higher rates than the United States, and Russia has also had higher rates at some points.

American rates did tend to decline in key periods, suggesting a rhythm similar to that of western Europe, despite higher levels overall. Thus rates dropped noticeably in the second half of the nineteenth century, compared with pre–Civil War violence (when ethnic mixing was particularly volatile, given new levels of immigration) and with colonial murder rates. Growing personal discipline and better policing were both involved, despite frequent public belief that modern conditions would drive murder rates up. Here, particularly, some link to broader reconsideration of death might have been involved. But the relationship was unstable: U.S. rates increased again in the first quarter of the twentieth century, but then dropped noticeably into the 1960s. A sharp rise occurred at that point, after which considerable stabilization developed, followed by a drop in the 1990s. Again, U.S. rates continued to exceed levels in other industrial societies, by as much as 400 percent (compared with Britain) or 800 percent (compared with Japan), although European rates themselves began to increase around 2000.

Overall, social concern about murder, and a hypersensitive awareness to real or imagined rates, did suggest some relationship to rising levels of discomfort with death. Whether this discomfort had much to do with the complexities and oscillations of actual murder rates, however, is difficult to determine. Other factors, including ethnic mixing and even gun policy, probably had far more to do with murder than did the evolution of attitudes about death. Some changes—for example, in the United States the noticeable decline of murder of strangers around 1900 but the increase of murders within families—are intriguing but probably irrelevant to the larger patterns of death and death policy.[10]

Conclusion

The impact of new ideas about death on public policies was both considerable and uneven. Some truly unprecedented initiatives developed in almost every category, most obviously concerning capital punishment, but also in aspects of abortion, approaches to war, and even new public efforts to prevent suicide. On the whole, more change occurred in the social administration of death than in the personal—that is, new attitudes toward death might have only limited impact on potential murderers or suicide victims, driven by their own demons, whereas legal frameworks were more widely affected; behaviors in war fell in between. But some change occurred in virtually all categories, and it was significant in several. Many developments, furthermore, set the stage for additional revisions later on. Continued anxiety over the death penalty, even after it had been cut back and privatized, would later lead to outright abolition in many regions, for example.

But unevenness was important as well. In the first place, the main developments occurred in the Western world, although they would have some impact on places like Russia and Latin America, which were in close contact with Western standards. There was more than a hint here of new global standards toward death policies, but global at this point essentially meant Western. Many societies retained quite different death cultures and death policies.

More important, even in the West itself, a variety of forces competed with the new ideas about death, often—particularly in the case of war—overriding them.

This complicated changes in the administration of death in the Western world and, perhaps even more, in the interactions between the West and other societies. The century in which death was seriously reconsidered was also the apogee of Western imperialism. Westerners could argue that they were bringing new standards of civilization to other parts of the world, and this could include new policies toward death. After the 1820s, for example, British colonial administrations in India worked hard to outlaw the sporadic traditional practice of *sati*, in which a widow would cast herself on the funeral pyre of her dead husband, effectively committing suicide, because life without the husband had no meaning. Indian reformers, taking a cue from the British, soon joined in this campaign. But for all these "progressive" impulses, the imperialists also brought military force and new levels of death in warfare, where new standards simply did not apply against the weaponry available and the rooted belief in Western superiority. Lessons about death on a global level in the nineteenth century, if lessons there were, were exceedingly complex.

Notes

1. Frank Hartun, "Trends in the Use of Capital Punishment," *Annals of the American Academy of Political and Social Science* 284 (1952): 8–19. Pieter Spierenberg, *The Spectacle of Suffering; Executions and the Evolution of Repression* (Cambridge, 1984).

2. Juergen Martshukat, "Nineteeth-Century Executions as Performances of Law, Death, and Civilization," in Austin Sarat and Christian Boulanger, *The Cultural Lives of Capital Punishment* (Stanford, CA, 2005), pp. 49–68.

3. V. A. C. Gatrell, *The Hanging Tree: Execution and the English People, 1770–1868* (Oxford, 1994).

4. Steven Wilf, "Anatomy and Punishment in Late Eighteenth-Century New York," *Journal of Social History* 22 (1988): 507–530.

5. David Parker, "Law, Honor, and Impunity in Spanish America: The Debate over Dueling, 1870–1920," *Law and History Review* 19 (2001): 311–341.

6. Leslie J. Reagan, *When Abortion Was a Crime: Women, Medicine and Law in the United States, 1867–1973* (Berkeley, 1997); James Mohr, *Abortion in America: The Origins and Evolution of National Policy, 1800–1900* (Oxford, 1978).

7. Victor Bailey, *"This Rash Act": Suicide Across the Life Cycle in the Victorian City* (Stanford, CA, 1998).

8. David Lester, *Thinking About Suicide: Perspectives on Suicide* (New York, 2004); Georges Minois, *History of Suicide: Voluntary Death in Western Culture* (Baltimore, 2005).

9. Susan Morrissey, *Suicide and the Body Politic in Imperial Russia* (Cambridge, 2007).

10. Roger Lane, *Murder in America: A History* (Columbus, OH, 1997).

CHAPTER 5

The Death Revolution
in Western Society
and Its Global Implications

The years 1880 to 1920 saw a transformation of the fundamental features of death, both in the United States and in western Europe. Trends that had been gradual since the later eighteenth century coalesced and accelerated, particularly in the area of infant death rates. Causes of death began to shift dramatically. So, finally, did the location of death, as the typical site of dying moved from home to hospital.

Changes in the physical aspects of death would continue to evolve after 1920. Infant death rates would fall still lower, the emphasis on degenerative diseases and accidents as opposed to contagious disease would become even more pronounced, hospitals would gain still further ground. It is also true that social divisions qualified the trends to some extent. African Americans in the United States continued to have much higher infant mortality rates than whites did—even in 2006. Rural people were less likely to make it to the hospital. But change affected all groups to some extent.

And the change was truly monumental. By 1920, the average Western family would not have to expect any children to die before adulthood. This was the first time in human history, certainly in the history of agricultural societies, in which this was the case. The results, not only for children who might traditionally have died but for parents and siblings, were immense—a tremendous reduction in the routine need to interact with death. Other changes were equally unprecedented: For example, by 1920 women had to give little thought to dying in childbirth, again a historic first.

Table 5.1 shows the dramatic reductions in death in key societies, along with some interesting variations. Throughout northwestern Europe, the United

79

Table 5.1 Historical Comparison of Infant Mortality Rates*
(Births per 1,000 Population per Annum)

	1880	1920
United States	246	82.1 (white); 131.7 (nonwhite)
Germany	214.3	104.57
Iceland	245	75
New Zealand	93.33	50.57

* Infant mortality rates are computed by taking the number of registered deaths of infants under one year of age per 1,000 registered births in the same year. Infant mortality statistics vary for a variety of reasons. Frequently, variations occur as a result of the definition of stillborn.

States, and New Zealand/Australia, rates dropped by at least 50 percent and often much more.[1]

Transformations this sweeping would later spread to other parts of the world. Japan experienced a similar death revolution between 1920 and 1960, punctuated of course by World War II. Other societies changed less completely, but moved in the common direction. The attention of communist regimes to public health and prenatal care, for example, moved Russia and then China away from traditional mortality patterns, although not quite to the achievement levels of the advanced industrial nations. There was something of a modern model of death, far different from traditional patterns, that was first established in the Western world around 1900.[2]

Changes of this magnitude, finally, inevitably affected cultural practices. It was impossible to maintain customary attitudes and rituals when the incidence of death was shrinking so massively for all but the oldest age categories. Here, however, greater complexity was involved. The death revolution touched cultures everywhere, but not necessarily with the same results. Even western Europe and the United States, joined at the hip in the death revolution, parted company to an interesting degree when it came to cultural outcomes.

A New Regime and Its Causes

The transformation itself can be stated simply enough, but we must not let the simplicity be deceiving. We're talking about one of the truly great changes in the human experience, assuming it persists, compressed into a surprisingly short period of time.

The reduction of infant mortality was the most important development. Levels had been dropping gradually in western Europe and in the United States since the later eighteenth century, a trend surely related to the cultural changes that generated greater grief and a growing sense of guilt when children passed away. Still, however, in 1880 20-25 percent of all children born in Western society would die in infancy, mainly from contagious respiratory diseases, diarrhea, and related diseases, including cholera; childhood ailments such as measles also took a toll. Life expectancy at birth, in the cities, hovered around thirty-five years. By 1900, in the industrial nations, the rate had fallen to 10 percent, and by 1920 it stood at 5 percent, and of course it continued to fall thereafter. Here of course was the major source of rising life expectancy at birth: Since the main constraint had been child-hood mortality, its substantial removal impelled longevity figures up dramatically. They had already reached fifty years by 1900, throughout the then-industrial world, and by 1950, when infant mortality pushed well below 4 percent, life expectancy surpassed seventy, and by 1999, again in the now-growing industrial world, which included Japan, South Korea, and the rest of the Pacific Rim, with infant death rates below 1 percent, a person could expect to live to nearly eighty.

Similar changes occurred for women concerning deaths in childbirth. In 1880, about 10 percent of all women could expect to die in childbirth (this did not of course mean that 10 percent of all childbirths killed the mother, it meant simply that over the span of active fertility one in ten women would die). Puerperal fever contracted during the birthing process was the most common cause of death. By 1920 deaths in childbirth had dropped dramatically, and the experience had become so uncommon that it began to pass from general expectancy.

Two developments accounted for these huge changes, although both were related to the shifts in culture that argued for a more active effort to hold death at bay. Public health measures helped reduce contagious diseases and diarrheal infections well before the advent of new drugs and inoculations (with the one exception being the expanding use of smallpox vaccines, spreading since the eighteenth century). Broader improvements in living standards, particularly in nutrition and to some extent in housing and general hygiene, provided the second major spur.

It was in 1855 that the English physician John Snow published his finding that cholera was caused not by "miasma" or "bad air," but by the presence of fecal waste in drinking water, a finding confirmed by the 1883 discovery of the offending bacterium, *Vibrio cholerae*, under the microscope. From the mid-nineteenth century onward, often even before absolutely precise science, Britain had been leading the way in public health measures that included underground piping for sewage and increasing efforts to provide clean drinking water. Regula-tion of food quality contributed as well by the 1880s, limiting the availability of contaminated meats and fish and requiring the pasteurization of milk. While British leadership was vital, western Europe and the United States, and by the 1870s, Japan, quickly followed suit. Cholera epidemics virtually disappeared in the industrial world after the 1880s, and other contagious diseases declined rapidly as well. The great influenza epidemic of 1919 brought a brief renewal of a classic problem, but it was the last massive contagion affecting industrial cities from that point onward.

Public health measures also included a growing provision of food supplies for infants even in the poorest urban classes. Here, reformers were motivated by a combination of humanitarian concern and nationalism. With birthrates dropping, many officials worried that population would begin to fall below the levels necessary to provide adequate military forces—France, after its loss to demographically more dynamic Germany in the war of 1870–1871, led the way here, but many other nations joined in. The solution was to attempt to ensure that children who were born would live to adulthood, and beyond general urban sanitation, provision of instruction in hygiene and, where necessary, government supplies of pure milk and other infant foods could work wonders. More traditional options, like finding wet nurses for children whose mothers could or would not breastfeed, began to decline rapidly, and although wet-nursing had not always been dangerous, it had on the whole contributed both to inadequate nutrition and to hygiene deficiencies.

Hygiene measures also began to reduce maternal mortality. A key source of infection for new mothers involved germs transmitted by caretakers, midwives, and even, more commonly, doctors who brought diseases from other patients literally on their hands. After brief confusion, including medical resistance to sterilization as an unnecessary nuisance, increasing requirements that doctors and other attendants wash their hands before assisting in deliveries began to cut into an age-old problem.

Supplementary public health measures included growing awareness of the desirability of draining swamps, in order to reduce infections from insects like mosquitoes, or the growing effort to remove horse droppings from city streets, a campaign soon facilitated by the decline in the use of horses outright.

General improvements in living standards meant that fewer mothers were underweight or debilitated when they gave birth, an advantage to their own life chances as well as those of their infants. Stillbirths declined: They had constituted 4 percent of all births in many European cities in the mid-nineteenth century, but by 1900 they had virtually disappeared, thanks to better food and housing. Housing improvements, along with related slum regulation, also reduced tuberculosis rates. Improvements in living standards included more provisions for opportunities to boil water, particularly important when dealing with infant foods, along with growing knowledge—actively pushed by the public health advocates and their government sponsors—of the importance of attacking germs and bacteria.[3]

Thanks to the dynamic duo, public health and greater prosperity, cities in the Western world for the first time began to display lower death rates than the countryside, where hygiene lagged and living standards were on average inferior. Here was another measure of the huge transformation in human exposure to death. More generally still, a growing number of ordinary people, as well as experts, had the means, knowledge, and desire to alter practices that had contributed to traditional levels of death. The combination was clearly and increasingly successful.

Further Impacts

Dramatic reductions in traditional mortality in the industrial world set a basis for additional developments, both in the most prosperous countries and in the world at large. Increasingly, new scientific and pharmacological developments added to the basic mortality revolution, while also helping to reduce death rates in other regions. The results could affect other human practices, while also challenging rituals and beliefs connected to death.

By the 1920s and 1930s, improvements in medicine began supplementing the results of public health and living standards in places like the United States and western Europe, and to an extent more widely. Discoveries of sulfa drugs and then penicillin provided new weapons against various communicable diseases; this could help drive down deaths rates even further among children, while also assisting older adults. Soon, new vaccinations also attacked traditional killers, like measles and, a bit later, polio. By the later twentieth century medicines that reduced blood pressure began to cut into mortality levels resulting from heart attacks and strokes. Through combinations of early detection, surgeries, and medication, there was even some progress concerning death rates in cases of cancer. All of these developments increased longevity. Not only life expectancy at birth, but also life expectancy at age fifty or sixty began to move up. Old age continued to be the death arena in the new pattern—the separation of childhood and death was still the big change—but old age itself was partially redefined, with death more likely to occur in one's eighties than the sixties or seventies, particularly in northwestern Europe and Japan but throughout the industrial world to some extent. A greater linkage between medicine and death-fighting developed as a result as well.

Gradually in the later nineteenth and early twentieth centuries, then more rapidly after 1950, echoes of the death revolution began to spread beyond the industrial societies. Some basic public health measures began to be introduced by 1900. European colonial administrations in Africa and Asia realized that, in order to protect the health of white settlements in the towns, some improvements in sanitation had to be developed for the more general urban population, because contagion did not rigorously respect racial boundaries. Humanitarian efforts added to the impulse, particularly in providing somewhat better care for expectant mothers and young children. Infant mortality levels remained much higher in Africa and Asia than in the industrial world, but they did drop in many places. By the 1950s, new technologies and the desire to win favor in the Cold War prompted more ambitious measures. In Sri Lanka (then Ceylon) for example, the annual death rate was abruptly cut in half in the 1950s, when the United States provided new pesticides against mosquitoes that could be sprayed from airplanes. These changes in death did not involve improvements in living standards in other respects; indeed, they sometimes amplified poverty. But the impacts on death rates were undeniable.

New communist regimes, beginning with the Soviet Union in 1919, fought traditional sources of death particularly vigorously. As early as 1918 the victorious Russian revolutionaries proclaimed that too many children had died "as a result of the ignorance and irresponsibility of the [czarist] state." The government rapidly expanded clinics and prenatal services, even amid great poverty. Officials sent out reminders and even insisted on personal visits if children were not brought in regularly for checkups. Hygiene was strongly emphasized in the schools, and children were urged to bring their parents into line. By 1960, despite huge intervening upheavals, infant mortality had dropped by 900 percent, to 3.8 percent of all children born, and by 1989 the figure had declined to 2.5 percent. Russia, clearly, had experienced a full death rate revolution of its own.

From the 1950s onward the new communist regime in China worked hard in the same direction. It set up neighborhood clinics in cities, with particular attention paid to prenatal guidance and children's health, and sent "barefoot doctors," who combined modern and traditional medicine; immunizations against the major childhood diseases spread rapidly. Child mortality, at 18 percent in 1955, had dropped to 3.7 percent by 2003, again a revolutionary result.

The death revolution had one further direct outcome, first in the West and then, gradually and unevenly, on a more global basis: It encouraged a reduction of the birthrate. Birthrates had been falling in the West even before the 1880–1920 transformations, but with still-fewer children dying, the impulse was extended. Outside the West, the inroads on infant mortality often occurred before much birthrate change, which of course pushed population levels up. But ultimately, families and even governments realized that with more children surviving it was important to have fewer born in the first place, lest they overwhelm resources. China, of course, explicitly adopted a severe limitation policy in the 1970s, but everywhere rates began to trend downward. This pattern, however, had some ironic potential where death was concerned. On the face of things, lower child mortality should have reduced parental anxieties, at least about physical security. But with fewer children born, parental investment in individual children went up; it became vitally important that all live, when there are only one or two in the first place, and the fact that overall statistics were now favorable might be inadequate assurance. Concern about the survival of one's own children, and therefore some complex emotions on the subject of children and death, could persist to a surprising extent, or even intensify.

The complexity might be compounded by new discoveries concerning young children and death. In the United States, for example, the phenomenon of unexplained deaths of infants in their cribs, from some kind of suffocation, began to gain public attention from 1948 onward. In the 1960s the idea of sudden infant death syndrome, or SIDS, won currency. The apparent existence of a new disease at least helped parents understand that they had done nothing wrong. But the concept could also increase parental anxiety. By the 1970s magazine articles were claiming that 35,000 children died annually from SIDS, which was at least five times the actual rate. Warnings multiplied for what was, statistically, a remote risk. Where children and potential death were concerned, massive improvements in fact might be seriously qualified by changes in cultural expectations and emotional attachments.

Causes of Death

The death revolution, where it applied in full force as in the West and East Asia, also involved fundamental transformations in what people died from. The traditional killers—respiratory diseases, infant diarrhea, and epidemics—receded dramatically, first through the public health measures and then through the medical combinations of inoculations and pharmaceutical treatments. In their place—since everyone could still expect to die—came a rising incidence of degenerative diseases, headed by heart attacks, strokes, and cancer, with growing rates of diabetes a factor as well. Accidents also claimed a growing number, particularly with the advent of automobiles.

These shifts, especially the new primacy of degenerative diseases, followed quite logically from the basic death revolution. They primarily affected older people, and with rare exceptions did not even require much worry or attention before later middle age. They were consistent, in other words, with the growing separation between death and most stages of life.

Here, too, however, there could be some nuances. The new killers struck from within. Their onset might not be perceived at all, until it was too late to do much. Certainly, precautionary attention focused on medical checkups and a growing array of tests: An individual, simply monitoring his or her own body, might not know what hit him or her until a heart attack or diagnosis of terminal cancer made the situation inescapably, and painfully, obvious. Some cultural observers speculated that the need to grapple with unseen agents of death could produce new levels of fear, compared with the more traditional battle with more visible problems such as the spread of an epidemic. Certainly, particularly for people prone to hypochondria, the possibility of worrying about one's own death did not disappear, and new anxieties might fester particularly in a climate in which, at least on the surface, the tolerance for discussion of death issues began to decline.

The Location of Death

The final component of the death revolution involved the replacement of the home by the hospital as the place where most people would expect to die. By the 1920s most people were dying, or at least pronounced dead, in hospitals in the United States. The same transition had occurred in France by the 1950s. Here was another change with huge potential implications for the experience of death and for attitudes toward it.

The change had several causes. Most obviously, improvements in sanitation, resulting especially from the implications of the germ theory, began to reduce the extent to which hospitals might actively cause disease or death. Most people who entered hospitals would now leave, alive and often improved. At the same time, hospitals began to offer positive attractions to people who were not simply impoverished and without alternative. A key development in the mid-nineteenth century was the advent of anesthesia. Childbirth could be easier, as well as, gradually, safer in a hospital setting than at home. Operations might now be contemplated as something other than a last resort.

Urban crowding and the location of work outside the home also made hospitals more attractive, again to people who were far from destitute. It became harder to care for the sick, not to mention the dying, in an urban apartment where most adults were out on the job during the day.

Gradually, of course, hospitals added further utility. New medicines and more refined surgery, and the advent of emergency care, increased the reasons to go to hospitals in case of serious illness or accident. The changes in the dominant causes of death also supported the movement to hospitals, where some hope might exist for cardiac or cancer patients or the victims of car crashes, either for cures or alleviation of pain or both.

For all the good reasons, the increasing use of hospitals did frame the final great change in the physical experience of death: the fact that it would occur amid medical personnel, in unfamiliar surroundings, away from family.

Conclusion

The death revolution dramatically altered a number of basic features of the death experience. It had global ramifications, although its patterns also created or enhanced some global inequalities in death rates and locations where death occurred. Inevitably, changes of this magnitude had major implications for the beliefs and rituals surrounding death—whether the issues involved individuals facing death or people or societies dealing with the deaths of others. Cultural adjustments, even upheavals, were inevitable. How successful they would be, in adjusting practices to the new realities but also to the ongoing burdens of death, would be a vital question.

Notes

1. "Neonatology on the Web: Infant Mortality," http://www.neonatology.org/classics/graham.html; Hallie J. Kintner, "Determinants of Temporal and Areal Variation in Infant Mortality in Germany, 1871–1933," *Demography*, Vol. 25, No. 4 (Nov. 1988): 587–609; Malcolm Fraser, "New Zealand—Infant Mortality Rates and Still-Births," *Journal of the Royal Statistical Society*, Vol. 92, No. 3 (1929): 428–444.

2. On mortality changes: E. A. Wrigley, *Population in History* (New York, 1969); Roger Schofield, David Reher, and Alain Bideau, eds., *The Decline of Mortality in Europe* (Oxford, 1991); John Gillis, David Levine, and Louise Tilly, eds., *The European Experience of Declining Fertility* (Cambridge, MA, 1992); Charles Tilly, ed., *Historical Studies of Changing Fertility* (Princeton, NJ, 1978); Ansley Coale and Susan Watkins, eds., *The Decline of Fertility in Europe* (Princeton, NJ, 1986) (an exceptionally important summary of massive studies in the Princeton Fertility Project). Richard Evans, *Death in Hamburg: Society and Politics in the Cholera Years, 1830–1910* (Oxford, 1987), is a significant case study.

3. Geoffrey Gilbert, *World Population: A Reference Handbook* (Santa Barbara, CA, 2002); John M. Last, "Public Health," in Robert Kastenbaum, ed., *MacMillan Encyclopedia of Death and Dying* (New York, 2003).

CHAPTER 6

Death as Taboo:
The American Case

The death revolution of the turn of the twentieth century—the progressive reduction of death rates for key age groups, and the transformation of the most common causes of death—soon produced a near-revolution in death culture. The United States took an early lead in this process, although it was not alone, and ultimately its innovations would be surpassed by changes in western Europe. Enough adjustment occurred, however, to ease some of the complexities that had built up during much of the nineteenth century, when rapidly rising discomfort with death was not matched by reductions in actual mortality rates. Indeed, the United States, along with western Europe, seemed at some points not just to downgrade death as a subject—this clearly occurred—but to make the phenomenon a virtual taboo. Although this judgment involves probable exaggeration, it is unquestionably true that aversion to death reached a level that created unhealthy side effects and new vulnerabilities.

It is not surprising that the unprecedented changes in human death of the early twentieth century would have massive cultural impact. It is, however, possible that some of the reactions generated more problems than they solved, and this issue remains alive even to the present day.

The death revolution seemed to resolve the cultural tensions that had been building up in the nineteenth century, by allowing a focus on the growing aversion to death. Now, with the death rate so dramatically reduced, it seemed possible to concentrate on the distaste alone. This impulse was enhanced by the growing role of doctors and other medical personnel, and hospitals, in framing death—for their task, assigned by their training and by public expectations, was death-fighting, their focus not the management of death, but its prevention, their failure not a poorly handled death, but death itself. New levels of aversion suited the professional realignment toward death perfectly, although their roots lay in broader cultural changes. The only problem was that aversion did not eliminate death, despite the huge changes in mortality rates: So the question was, how would the new practices and attitudes work when death, despite all the best efforts, became inescapable? Many critics contend that the new combination worked badly and that, despite a few more recent adjustments, it still works badly.[1]

Culture Clash

The most immediate cultural results of the death revolution, beginning to emerge in the United States right around 1900, although accelerated in the century's second and third decades, involved a fierce attack on Victorian beliefs and practices. We can see, with the benefits of historical analysis, that the contradictions between the new situations and nineteenth-century attitudes were not as sharp as the innovators contended: A strong discomfort with death pervaded both systems. But the actual death situation was so novel that the self-proclaimed trendsetters, writing for the most popular magazines of the teens and twenties of the new century, abandoned historical perspective in favor of stark modernity. Their recommendations did not win the U.S. public entirely, but they were widely influential in changing many of the assumptions and rituals associated with mortality.

Some popularizers proclaimed that modern society could now entirely abolish death before later age, and with it fear itself:

> Fear is the greatest source of human suffering. Until comparative recent times nature has been something unknown and the unknown has been a constant source of terror ... This burden of woe has now been lifted. Another view of nature now prevails. Man has cast off fear and finds himself master of nature and perhaps of all her forces, while in religion the gospel of love is casting out the dread monster of fear ... Few of us appreciate the profound security that we now enjoy: security of life, property, and reputation.[2]

This kind of sentiment, associated with a Progressive belief in the limitless possibilities of relying on science and reform-minded social organization, reflected a giddy optimism amid the rapid decline of infant and maternal death. It is difficult to say how widely the sentiment was shared. But, as we will see, many Americans began to act as if many conventional risks could or should be eliminated, such that death before a ripe old age had to represent a failure on someone's part. The cultural impact of the death revolution began to reach deep.

The most obvious focus of the innovators' enthusiasm involved an attack on Victorian grief and the rituals associated with grief. The features of grief that had most attracted nineteenth-century advocates—its capacity to take a person out of normal reality in reaction to loss—now became menacing. The editorial columns of magazines filled with opinion pieces about the outdated and dangerous qualities of Victorian emotion. Not only the changes in death itself, but growing delight in the here-and-now pleasures of growing consumerism, fed a distaste for emotional indulgence of death that—given death's retreat—seemed far less necessary and that contradicted the growing mentality of this-worldly pleasure seeking. To be sure, some articles, mainly by Christian apologists, maintained the older valuing of grief, as an appropriate response to death and a source of strengthened character; but the tone was now defensive, for the momentum was clearly moving away from grief.[3]

A number of arguments surfaced. If, as the Victorians themselves had contended, the dead would quickly ascend to Heaven and families would there reunite, why fuss about death at all? Why should it not be to all of us the Great Adventure? Why should we not look forward to it with anticipation, not with apprehension? Upbeat Christians could now readily argue that death need not disrupt the perpetual happiness that sensible believers should seek in all phases of their lives. In 1907 Jane Belfield wrote on death for *Lippincott's Magazine*, stressing the folly of great pain. After all, not only death but also reunion with family are certain, so death need not involve intense feelings at all but rather "emotions and aspirations hushed" as loved ones took it in stride. And after all, since death was now occurring mainly in old age, with its various aches and pains, death could be seen simply as a pleasant release from decrepitude. The elderly, it could be argued (perhaps particularly by those not yet old), would welcome death: "The stains of travel were gone, the signs of age had vanished; once more young, but with a wisdom beyond youth, she started with buoyant step and with a rising hope in her heart; for through the soft mist beautiful forms seemed to be moving, and faint and far she heard voices that seemed to come out of her childhood, fresh with the freshness of the morning, and her spirit grew faint for joy at the sound of them." Clearly, in this picture, neither fear for one's own death nor grief at the passing of an older relative made much sense.[4]

Popularized science attacked grief and fear of death from another interesting angle, during the same early twentieth-century decades. A steady series of popular articles countered the traditional belief that death involved pain. Many modernists argued that this belief was one of the sources of Christianity's hold on the masses, who used religion to counter anticipated suffering, but that it was empirically incorrect. This had another, huge set of implications regarding grief, for the new contention was that most deaths were actually rather pleasant. An article as early as 1891, while admitting that death did involve some natural dread of the unknown, contended that most actual deaths involved a "pleasurable sensation." Like going to sleep, death was a "slumberous condition, not unlike that at the end of a toilsome day."[5] Through the twentieth century, various scientists and religious authorities alike argued for evidence that people, even in sudden death, felt no pain. An extensive literature emerged about individuals who had gone through near-death experiences: They reported uplifting visions of light and peace—"delightful sensations" and "beatific visions." So why, the argument went, worry much about death at all? A few less-cheerful scientists chimed in that modern death usually resulted from a gradual deterioration of the organs, so there was no reason for particular emotion when the final stage of this process actually ended life. By 1914 *Living Age* magazine proclaimed that the whole idea of a "'death agony' is an unscientific conception," which in turn meant that the entire traditional atmosphere of death needed review. As another author put it, people should get used to the "hard facts of science" and stop emoting so much about what was not only inevitable but also rather tranquil.[6]

In this vein the *Fortnightly Review* contended that with medical improvements surrounding death, plus the new understanding that death need not be feared as painful, "death is disappearing from our thoughts.... Perhaps the most distinctive note of the modern spirit is the practical disappearance of the thought of death as an influence directly bearing on practical life." Death was losing its terrors—"regarded rather as a welcome friend than a grisly visitant"—so grief itself had no purpose. The death of others—presumably, mostly old and mostly enjoying the experience—"frequently causes more relief than grief to those who remain." At an extreme, arguments of these types began to be used in support of euthanasia—after all, since death was no big deal, why not put people who seemed to be suffering from untreatable illness out of their misery? There was also some praise for new, thrill-seeking behaviors like auto racing and airplane flying that showed a proper disdain for death. "The best psychology of life is equally the best psychology of death: be glad to live and gladly die." These extensions of the new attitudes were not uniformly shared, of course—Americans still in the main disapprove of euthanasia—but they suggested the sweep of a new cultural approach to death.[7]

American modernists also went through a phase of trumpeting a distinctive national approach to death that differed, not only from the past, but also from greater foreign, particularly European, traditionalism. Europeans were seen as tied to outdated mourning that was another sign that they were not keeping up with the benefits of modern life. For a few decades, at least, Americans took some pride that their nation was setting the contemporary pace for death as well as for other aspects of consumerism and economic progress.

But the main point was the need to revisit U.S. traditions themselves. Expensive funerals were attacked, a theme that would recur into the later twentieth century. It was ridiculous to spend much money or emotional energy on death. "We could never understand why old women should, as they unquestionably do, love to attend funerals, or how anybody could be induced, except as a matter of duty, to make a business or profession of the handling of corpses." It was positively immoral to encourage peoples' grief in order to get them to spend a lot on funerals.[8]

Grief itself was the key villain. As the *Independent* noted in 1908, "Probably nothing is sadder in life than the thought of all the hours that are spent in grieving over what is past and irretrievable." An emotion once praised was now condemned as useless, counterproductive psychological baggage. A healthy person would handle death without excessive emotion. And this meant, in the new wisdom, that people who did experience considerable or prolonged grief needed professional help. Modern "psychotherapeutics" must be invoked to help people escape the kind of grief that Victorians would have regarded as normal, along with medical attention to make sure that there were no physical causes of "melancholic feelings." This was a culture focused increasingly on the need for cheerfulness, certainly the ability to present a cheerful front to the outside world, and grief had no real place. A bit might be briefly tolerable, but weeks of tears suggested "something morbid, either mental or physical." Women were the worst offenders in this view: "When a woman cannot rouse herself ... from her grief there is need of the care of a physician." People must learn to handle death in a matter-of-fact way. "This may seem a very crude and heartless way to look at such a subject, but it is eminently practical and above all has the merit of being satisfactorily therapeutic. Nothing is more calculated to arouse people from the poignancy of their grief than the realization of a necessity to care for their health." Grief is, as another editorial put it rather pompously, a "contradiction in the universe, an attempt on the part of a drop in the sea to prevent the tidal progress of the ocean of life of which it is so small a part, yet every atom of which is meant to serve a wise purpose in all its events." Another magazine more simply called for a cultural "abolition of death."[9]

Some of this outpouring of modernism undoubtedly reached only a minority of Americans. Certainly the delight in a kind of science that would use the growing knowledge of the physical causes of death to urge people to take it in stride, as part of the natural course of things, probably won only a tenuous hold on a U.S. majority that remained conventionally religious. But two of the new claims clearly gained wide influence: first, the idea that grief was potentially dangerous and that a balanced person should be able to keep it under control, and that professional help should be called in where balance faltered; and second, the increasing tendency to believe that one's own enjoyment of life should take precedence over emotions at the deaths of others or, by extension, at the need to pay too much attention to other people's grief. Neither of these ideas was uniformly or consistently accepted, and we will see that there were certain occasions where the deaths of others continued to cause unexpected discomfort. But there was a tendency toward recalibration that would extend from this initial period of cultural innovation on through the twentieth century and into the twenty-first.

American (and some British) commentary urged that a "modern" approach to death was essential in dealing with the massive slaughter of World War I (the American attitude encouraged by the fact that American exposure was fairly brief, the loss of life far less great than that of the European combatants). Elaborate funerals, in this line of argument, were an insult to the courageous soldiers; the focus should be on the character of the brave men, not the sentimentality of the survivors. Tearful military funerals were "an old-fashioned chamber of horrors show"; they should be controlled in order to "let civilization have the right of way." The very increase of mortality that the war caused, according to the modernists, should help produce "greater wisdom and good sense in our mourning usages," so that people could get on with life rather than wallow in useless emotional distraction.[10] There was obvious irony here, which would become much clearer later on (see Chapter 11): The modern capacity to administer death in war clashed directly with growing distaste for death in other arenas. Efforts to control grief and extensive killing represented an initial experiment in dealing with the tension.

Certainly the modernist themes continued in the United States after the war, although a few religious leaders countered with articles in favor of the healing qualities of more traditional grief. A number of authors continued to emphasize that death did not involve pain, in one essay arguing that "even in cases of death from being torn to pieces by wild beasts, physical pain is surprisingly absent"–although the evidentiary base of the claim was not entirely clear. A number of women writers commented on their own evolution from Victorian excess, in which as children they had been encouraged to grieve, to a more healthy modern approach where positive self-control gained ascendancy over "fruitless recollection."[11]

By the end of the 1920s, the popularized discussion of death largely faded from the major magazines, replaced by other subjects. Although the modernist discourse had not persuaded everyone–again, religious traditionalists most clearly held out–it had been successful enough that the debate, as a frequent journalistic staple, could be closed. A new set of emotional guidelines had replaced Victorian culture.

The New American Way of Death

These emotional guidelines that resulted from the concerted attack on Victorianism had several consequences, during the debate period itself but even more when it ended. The first was a growing sense that, aside from attacking remnants of traditionalism, death should not be widely discussed at all. If it was no big deal, an unremarkable feature of the universe of nature, and beyond that largely an occasion for self-control, people would be best served by having the topic low on the public agenda. The subject might be indirectly addressed, of course, by recurrent articles on new medical advances that made this or that cause of death increasingly unlikely, but this merely confirmed the sense that the subject itself deserved little explicit comment. This was the context in which European and U.S. culture critics, by the 1960s, began to comment on death as the new cultural taboo.[12] Clearly, media officials had decided that the basic debate on death had been concluded successfully or that the new upbeat standards were too shaky to risk extensive review; in either case, the result was extensive silence, on grief as an emotion as well as on death itself. An occasional essay revived the debate themes about painlessness and lack of terror; thus a 1950 comment resurfaced the idea of nonchalance: "Look death in the face. His countenance isn't so terrifying as we are led to believe." A larger number of articles urged therapy for extensive grief, while blasting people who encouraged needless emotional pain. "Why is it that we are able to cast off conventions pertaining to every event in modern existence except the burial of the dead?" Even Christian popularizers, while giving a bit more credit to grief, talked about more "natural and happy" funeral occasions. A scattered number of commentators, finally, wrote to confirm that death had receded as a modern topic. As one triumphantly noted, while blasting a few religious traditionalists, "Modern knowledge ... offers to the intelligent person to-day [sic] a conception of living which is a positive answer to the old death fears." And an *American Mercury* article noted quite simply, "America Conquers Death." This sort of triumphalism, however, did not require death to be discussed very frequently; an occasional confirmation of the new wisdom should suffice for people who ought to be paying attention to other subjects.[13]

Relative silence also pervaded medical manuals, when it came to death. Nursing handbooks, particularly between the 1920s and 1950s, provided short, matter-of-fact paragraphs on how to recognize impending death and how to lay out a corpse. Both doctors and nurses long emphasized concealment of probable death from a person, lest unacceptable emotions develop and in order to protect medical personnel from emotions of their own. The focus, of course, was on prolonging life. Even advice on how to inform relatives once death occurred was terse—this was simply not the purpose of medical activity.[14]

The major exception to the general impulse toward silence involved the desirability of touting the wonders of psychological therapy for people who could not get with the new program. From the 1920s onward most therapists had accepted the modernist approach, defining their "grief work" as an attempt to get the emotion under control, to treat it as a problem. Freudians acknowledged that some grief was essential to free people from ties to the deceased, but they also contended that psychological damage would occur if the emotion were not transcended fairly quickly. Other schools gave even less credit to grief, viewing it as an immature form of separation anxiety. Most people, of course, would handle the emotion sensibly, but counseling was available for anyone else, for retention of grief symptoms was a clear form of maladjustment. "Chronic grief syndrome" was applied to any clinging dependency, most common among women, when a spouse died. By the 1960s, popular terms for excessive grief included *mummification* and *despair*. By the 1970s counselors were advising even older widows to find new interests in life, new identities, in order to break unhealthy ties with the past. Some therapists explicitly attacked the idea that grief was a result of love, arguing that grief when a spouse died showed a previous love-hate tension with the guilt portion, not loving nostalgia, causing the undesirable emotion. Mental health meant breaking bonds and avoiding dependency, and grief, contradicting both goals, became the target for ongoing attack.[15]

One final topic warranted recurrent comment even after the debate period had crested, and it suggested some of the complexities of the new approach. The subject was children and advice to parents on how to deal with death as part of their responsibilities in socialization. And the context involved not only the growing aversion to death but the special achievement of rapidly declining child mortality rates that made it particularly painful to think of death and childhood in the same embrace. Logically, of course, if death was uncommon before later age and entirely natural, the idea of acquainting children with death might have raised no particular problems. But this was not the case, which means that something beyond logic was in play. The need to protect children physically from death extended to a felt need to protect them emotionally as well. Children, increasingly precious now that the birthrate was low and precisely because babies were unlikely to die and so were open to more extensive parental emotional investment, were increasingly seen as emotionally vulnerable, too feeble to handle something potentially so overwhelming as death. Good parents must be very careful lest they arouse childish fears. Obviously the old Christian habit of scaring children with death continued to be seen as dreadfully wrong—this had been part of Victorian advice literature as well. But now, so too was the Victorian habit of trying to train children in grief. Since the emotion was now undesirable, and since children needed to be shielded from intense emotion of any sort, it now seemed best to keep any references to death away from the young. As one expert noted, explicit discussion of death might make children even afraid to go sleep. Of course it was easier than ever before to keep children from much awareness of death: Death no longer occurred at home, most children would not experience the death of a sibling or a young parent, and grandparents increasingly lived separately from the nuclear family unit. And proper adults were not supposed to mourn extensively, another basis for keeping mum.[16]

The new expertise thus called upon parents to keep children away from death or thoughts of death, even with Victorian sugarcoating about family reunions in Heaven. *Parents' Magazine* cautioned against "conjuring up a heaven of angels and harp playing," for "inevitably the small girl or boy will discover that mother and father are not certain about the after life. Such a discovery augments the fear of death." Many experts urged carefully evasive phrasing so that children would get no images of death of any sort. Referring to a grandparent's death as "all through" might be a good idea, in this context. "Fear of death arises when the child imagines not mother or grandmother, or the bird, but himself being covered up with dirt. That much the child can imagine; that much is within the child's observable experience. But if the child gets the idea that a dead person is 'all through,' the identification of himself with the dead person or animal is more difficult." Parents' letters to advice magazines suggested that they worked increasingly hard to obscure any idea of death. Most obviously, as the experts increasingly suggested, they kept kids away from critical care units of hospitals (where children were usually banned, partly for practical but also for emotional reasons) and above all from funerals.[17]

Children might be told that most death resulted from old age. "If such an explanation is grossly inappropriate," one expert wrote, "reference may be made to a most unusual illness which none of us is likely to get." Avoidance was the key: Children must not be encouraged to contemplate their own death at all, because their psyches might be overwhelmed. Parents must keep their own grief in check, of course. A key reason for the attack on traditional forms of mourning, like wearing black clothing, involved the need to spare children any thought of death. Where information had to be provided, "let us give the fact to the child with as little emotion as possible." Death should be acknowledged quickly, lest children suspect dark secrets, but ceremonies as well as emotion would best be removed. One school, by the 1980s, even banned reference to the *dyeing* of Easter eggs—they were merely to be colored—lest children confuse the term and start thinking about death. Even events of World War II, the experts urged, should be presented to children in the most matter-of-fact way, without signs of fear or distress. With this kind of tone, experts hoped, "the child ... will meet many minor death references as just one more interesting phenomenon."[18]

True to the advice, popularizers began removing death emotionality from the media available to children. Killing occurred, in boys' stories and cowboy movies, probably more often than before, but without emotional context. Victorian staples such as prolonged illness or a life plucked too soon dropped away. Death was matter of fact, no emotion involved; heroes did not stop to ponder consequences. In the 1930s Disney began to sanitize traditional folktales, removing death references and emphasizing happy endings. Even deaths of animals were minimized in fiction and in the real life of family pets—dead bodies were disposed of secretly, and replacement pets were often quickly provided to distract the children from sadness.[19]

The dramatic new approach to death and children was both consistent and inconsistent in terms of the larger cultural change. It certainly translated the growing desire not to discuss death very often in any direction. It certainly provided a cultural mirror to the actual changes in physical death: Both in fact and in culture, death and childhood were increasingly separated. But there was glaring contradiction as well: If death was not a major issue, why spend so much effort concealing it from children? And what about the later consequences: If children gained little experience with death themselves, would they grow to be adults capable of handling the phenomenon as casually as the experts advised? The new U.S. culture toward children's experience with death was understandable in historical context, but it reflected a response that was not entirely thought through and that harbored vulnerable inconsistencies.

There was no question about the larger intent, and by the mid-twentieth century it was showing up even in popular etiquette manuals. Manners writers had maintained Victorian standards into the 1930s, recommending extensive symbols of mourning and real care in dealing with the emotions of others. Mourners needed active sympathy, although Emily Post, the leading guru, did begin to write that elaborate funerals might be a bad idea because they would stir up even more emotion. Ultimately, however, innovation caught up even with the etiquette writers. By 1952 Amy Vanderbilt suggested that the main subjects that should be focused on when death occurred were the practical issues like wills, bank accounts, and any medical formalities. Funerals and mourning should be kept short—Vanderbilt praised the decline in wearing any distinctive mourning attire—stressing that the emotional mood after a death should be as light as possible. Friends of the bereaved should express sympathy, of course, but they should be careful not to encourage grief. Avoidance of grief gained new praise: "It is better to avoid the words 'died,' 'death,' and 'killed' in such [condolence] letters. It is quite possible to write the kind of letter that will give a moment of courage and a strong feeling of sympathy without mentioning death or sadness at all." Most revealing was the advice to the bereaved themselves, who now had an obligation to control themselves in a positive manner. Grief simply must not be intense, because it was impolite to others. "We are developing a more positive social attitude toward others, who might find it difficult to function well in the constant company of an outwardly mourning person." Whatever went on inside should be kept carefully under wraps. Vanderbilt explicitly noted that World War II had helped encourage this modern approach to death, where too much grief would have damaged morale and given comfort to the enemy. Manners commentary more generally addressed the same theme of aversion to intense grief. Stories might discuss the problem of peer reactions—"her friends were again feeling a little critical of her, saying to one another that it would be a pity if poor Marian should allow grief to make her 'queer.'" The message was widespread. Etiquette, probably the most conventional and change-resistant sector of popular culture, had given over to the modernists: Death, handled conventionally, could turn out to be rude, a source of alienation among friends.[20]

The Impact of Culture

The new U.S. attitude toward dealing with death was a striking historical innovation. It also generated a wide variety of criticisms, not only from traditionalists but from other angles as well. Most basically, although it reflected the death revolution, it risked foundering on the fact that death still happens. If the dominant approach to death involves ignoring the subject, downplaying emotion whether one's own or others', and keeping children particularly ignorant, what happens when death happens anyway, as it always will—death of others or, perhaps even more ominously, contemplation of death of oneself? Is the emphasis on emotional control even consistent with widespread ignorance and inexperience? Is death not likely to provoke even wilder emotions from people who have been encouraged not to think about it and who, as children, are kept away from the death that does occur?

In fact, the U.S. majority never fully bought into the new culture. They accepted large elements, but they maintained several older emphases as well, which proved quite functional in several key death settings; they also registered on some of the criticisms of the new culture as these circulated from the 1960s onward, introducing some additional modifications. The result continued to be strongly shaped by the new culture, which meant that it did have some ongoing vulnerabilities; but the amalgam was more complex than the new culture suggested. Additionally, of course, a host of subcultures in the United States added their own variants.

The new culture did shine through, for the majority of Americans, in three crucial respects. First, most Americans absolutely agreed that, when death threatened, the first call should be to modern medicine; death should be fought as long and as hard as possible. Second, most Americans increasingly agreed that a proper society should be able to prevent death before later age, by eliminating risks, and that when death did occur prematurely, someone ought to be blamed. And third, most Americans progressively dropped most of the traditional rituals associated with death, agreeing that the death of others should not significantly interfere with normal life.

Combating and Preventing Death: New Crusades

Medicalization became the key response when most Americans faced the prospect of death, for themselves or for loved ones. Even in a society that, by comparative standards, remained quite religious, spiritual authorities took second place to doctors and medical settings when it came to a final illness. Public expectations and advancing technology supported a steady, sometimes dramatic series of improvements in the capacity to prolong life. Particularly impressive, in the second half of the twentieth century, was the growing ability to respond to accident victims, restoring life and, often, serviceability, where the same injuries once would have produced fatalities. But life-support systems for people suffering from diseases also developed extensively, at an extreme, producing new debates about when death actually occurred. A highly politicized court case in 2006 involved Terri Schiavo, a Florida woman in a coma, diagnosed as being in a permanent vegetative state in terms of brain wave activity. Most doctors (as well as her husband) said she could never recover, but she could be kept alive indefinitely by means of a feeding tube attached to her abdominal wall. Grieving parents and a Republican governor pressed for legislation that would prevent the tube from being removed, although ultimately she was allowed to die. More generally, by the later twentieth century it was estimated that up to 40 percent of the nation's unusually large and rapidly growing medical expenses went to treating people suffering from terminal illnesses. Some of this expense, to be sure, involved the palliation of pain or other treatment efforts undertaken before the terminal situation could be fully determined. But it was clear that many Americans, for themselves and even more for members of their families, believed that they could face death with a clear conscience only after heroic, and very costly, medical procedures had been attempted.

Fighting death also increasingly applied to issues of prevention, although there were a few interesting blind spots. From the 1920s onward, U.S. society became increasingly safety conscious. In part this responded to new threats, most notably automobiles, which caused a significant increase in accidental deaths, including deaths of children, during the first third of the century; new household appliances also posed dangers. But more than objectivity was involved; many Americans, and their public officials, became reluctant to tolerate even remote chances for death that once had been taken for granted. Safety training began to be introduced in the schools by the early 1930s, particularly to help children deal with automobile traffic. Driver's tests and highway regulations, including speed limits, also began to be widely introduced. Safety obsessions increased by the 1960s, with new measures to protect the unwary in the home: safety caps on medicine bottles, "childproof" devices for electrical outlets, and mandatory car seats were among the steady crescendo of measures intended to limit risk of accidental death or injury. Measures like bicycle helmets, usually required by law for children, were particularly interesting. No other society, including many in which bicycle riding was far more common than in the United States, imposed such strictures; Dutch riders experimented briefly with helmets and decided that they were too much nuisance and too unattractive and almost uniformly jettisoned the devices, even as they poured into the streets on daily commutes.[21]

Not just safety was involved. Again from the 1920s and 1930s onward, Americans, prodded by soap companies that helped pay for school programs, were encouraged toward ever-greater hygiene precautions. Regular bathing became a national habit, urged, among other things, on immigrant families sometimes suspected of being less clean than was desirable. Germs must be combated, lest they bring unnecessary disease and (at an extreme) death. Americans began to bathe more frequently than any other people in the world, and they soon vaunted more bathrooms per family than any other society as well, and although hygiene was not the only factor in this formula, it played a large role. By the early twenty-first century, germ concerns, heightened by wider fears, prompted a growing mania for the use of plastic gloves, intended to prevent receipt or dissemination of contagion. During the 1970s, after long hesitation, the U.S. majority was also finally persuaded that smoking was a dangerous risk, threatening premature death from a variety of causes, including, most obviously, cancer. Public safety campaigns helped bring about an impressively speedy reduction of smoking rates, with Americans changing more rapidly in this regard than any other society. Again, regulatory measures soon joined in as well, with increasingly widespread and severe limitations on smoking in public places. Attitudes to remaining smokers hardened: They were confined to out of the way places, often outdoors, and shunned as pariahs. Growing fears of the health effects of secondhand smoke helped explain this fierce rejection, but so did widespread beliefs that smokers were somehow symbols of death and of an ominous lack of personal self-control. Moralism in the United States became a big part of the crusades against potential sources of death.

A few important inconsistencies emerged. Although Americans regulated driving speed more closely than most societies, they did not accept the low speed limits that would most demonstrably serve to limit highway fatalities. Reducing speed to 50 to 55 miles per hour was too great a price to pay to achieve maximum safety.

Despite massive injunctions to keep weight down, and widespread dieting, Americans continuted to put on the pounds, particularly from the 1980s onward, when obesity rates increased dramatically. Disputes about the true dangers of being overweight helped explain this inconsistency, but the simple fact was that many Americans knew their eating habits posed greater risk of early death down the line, but kept on munching anyway. It was obvious that other needs could override the undoubted desire to minimize risks of death.

At the other extreme, death concerns, particularly associated with children, could also prompt anxieties and regulatory responses that went well beyond what the actual facts of the situation called for. The taming of Halloween was an intriguing case in point. U.S. children had long played a variety of pranks on this holiday, and trick-or-treating was a central feature. The whole sequence of activities began to seem too disorderly to many adults, and there were some safety risks in children roaming about the streets. But the clearest spur to change involved reports in 1982 that children were being given poisoned candy and razor-blade-filled apples. None of the poisoning reports was ever verified: The only objective problem involved three cases in which pins had been stuck into candy bars in the Long Island area. But belief, when risk was involved, easily outpaced reality. Cities began limiting the hours for trick-or-treating, and parents began accompanying their offspring and pouring over the goodies received before authorizing consumption. With more objective backing from accident statistics, but still with the risk of excessive interference, regulation of fireworks on July 4 constituted another case in which traditions were jettisoned in favor of maximum protection from death or accident.

U.S. society, proudly resistant to undue government interference in many aspects of life, willingly accepted an impressive sequence of safety constraints by the later twentieth century, and the progression of measures showed no sign of slowing. Safety signs and fences were far more prominent in U.S. parks and other public settings than in similar areas in most other parts of the world. Where risks of death were present, even if statistically modest, Americans could not entirely trust themselves to be properly prudent.

The same fundamental dislike of mortality risk showed, finally, in the increasing national tendency to seek and punish causes for premature (or even not particularly premature) deaths that did occur. Distaste for death was too great to allow easy acceptance of accident or chance—someone or something had to be available to blame. The change showed up in law. From 1910 onward, when a court ruled that car companies should anticipate wear and tear on tires that might result in accidents, even years after a car was purchased, in tort law cases, U.S. courts frequently ruled in favor of people who had been injured or killed in such accidents. A jury thus orders a lawn mower company to pay the family of a man who died from a heart attack $1.75 million, because the attack occurred when he was trying to start a mower. A man is robbed and killed on a street near his hotel, and the family sues the hotel and successfully wins the case. From the 1980s onward, asbestos companies were successfully sued for not warning victims, who had died from product-related lung cancer, about risks that were simply not known when the damage occurred. A 2005 Texas case further extended the responsibility of companies to warn about risks of death associated with the use of their product: The manufacturer of a pain medication was held liable for not listing the risk of the possible slight increase in heart attacks, in a case where the individual had actually not taken the medication very long and had died of a different kind of heart ailment altogether. The rapid increase in medical malpractice suits most directly linked the new ideas about blame with the unusual U.S. propensity to litigate. To be sure, only one fatal accident in about two hundred actually resulted in a lawsuit by the latter twentieth century, and many companies managed to protect themselves from blame. It remains true that large numbers of Americans found significant risk of death unacceptable. They might have abandoned the optimism of the early twentieth century, as they found the modern world more dangerous than they wished, but they sought the same goals: a life in which the intrusion of death, or thinking about its risks, were largely absent.[22]

Impact on Ritual

The most obvious link between the new culture of death and widespread practice involved the significant and fairly steady changes that began to occur in death ritual from the 1920s onward, some of them picking up trends already visible in the later nineteenth century. Formal mourning declined in virtually every respect. Special clothing was abandoned, except for wear at funerals themselves, and by the late twentieth century, even for wear at funerals. Markings on homes progressively disappeared, as did black-edged cards that had been used to announce deaths. Employers became increasingly reluctant to allow time off for mourning, beyond a day or half-day for the funeral itself—this was a change the effects of which were further compounded when women began to work widely outside the home, in the 1950s and 1960s; by this point no one in the family might be available to organize extensive displays of grief. Sympathy hardly disappeared, but most people were expected to resume normal functioning fairly quickly. And all this occurred, of course, in a situation where death now occurred outside the home, surrounded by the apparatus of death-fighting in hospital intensive-care units, which filtered contact even with the anticipation of death.

At an extreme, critics contended, modern U.S. death began to look like this: a subject that no one thought about, for self or others, save on rare occasions; that was regarded as an alien and blamable intrusion when attention was forced on it; that was approached in terms of medical death fighting until this failed and then disposed of with a minimum of emotional or ritual fuss. Although this was an editorial view, not a carefully balanced assessment, it surely contained elements of truth, both for groups like doctors dealing with death and for individuals facing death of themselves or others.[23]

Modifying the Culture

Although real changes occurred in association with cultural hostility toward death, three kinds of complexities developed as well, through the twentieth century and into the twenty-first. Several subcultures resisted the full application of modernism. Mainstream Americans continued to use the funeral home as a significant adjustment to the starkest kind of modernity, as a place where grief could be acted out. And the criticisms of U.S. modernism, gaining ground in the 1960s, produced some additional modifications as well. Modernist death still prevailed in many ways, and as we will see, it did bring some demonstrable drawbacks, even when all the adjustments are taken into account. But the picture was more complex than some critics allowed, and the United States might have generated a distinctive contemporary death amalgam in the process.

Many U.S. groups continued to enjoy distinctive death practices. Many Jews argued that their religion's approach to death, with traditional rituals, family-community interaction, and set periods of prayer and recollection for the dead, provided real comfort even in modern society, even for people whose temple attendance was usually nominal. Funeral services in African American churches were frequently more emotional, with more open expressions of grief than were common in many other U.S. communities. Another interesting feature, developing as an innovation around the year 2000 but with antecedents in older African practice, involved the "personalized theme" funeral. African Americans had long buried some daily items, like tools or clothing, with the dead body itself, retaining the idea that this would speed the passage to the next life and avoid adverse engagement between the spirits of the dead and those still alive. In a modern incarnation of this idea, adjusted to the practices of funeral homes and embalming, African Americans began to construct funeral settings based on objects identified with the individual: sports gear could form a theme, or mechanics' tools. A cooking scenario, complete with chickens and other favorite foods and utensils, was another popular theme. Several companies, like Perpetua, Inc., emerged to orchestrate this kind of personalization. The idea was to turn the funeral into a celebration of an individual's life. Obviously, the goal was to downplay grief as well. As one funeral home director put it, with personalization "It's not like you're at a funeral home; it's like you're at home. It makes it just a happy place to be." But whereas the attack on grief might seem modernist, the extent of attention paid to the dead harked back to older impulses. Many African Americans also began to place emblems of a dead relative on cars as a sign of mourning; and the practice of taking out commemorative advertisements in newspapers, complete with portraits, to note not only a death but also its anniversaries, spread widely as well. Many African Americans contended that however menial their life, in a community suffering from ongoing inequalities, at least people could look forward to a big sendoff in death. Clearly, this cultural tradition was capable of interesting innovations while resisting the more general tendency to limit attention to the fact of death.[24]

Other Americans, by the early twenty-first century, also moved toward the use of pictures and celebrating life stories in funeral or commemorative ceremonies. This suggested a further attack on grief, but it also encouraged more elaborate attention to the deceased.

Funeral home practice, although often still fairly restrained and subdued, constituted an even wider qualification to the general movement to distance death. Here was an institution founded in the Victorian era, that both separated death from the home and institutionalized grief—somewhat modern but not fully so, by the strictest new cultural standards. The funeral home continued to flourish despite—or indeed because of—its somewhat old-fashioned trappings, including a muted, religious-like atmosphere and somber, sympathetic attendants. The premium on careful embalming remained, of course; part of the farewell ceremony involved looking at the body and deciding how well it represented what had once been a life. Funeral home viewings, extending often several evenings after death occurred, did allow most Americans to feel that proper rituals had been observed and grief had been duly and publicly expressed. People attending a visitation quickly established community, sharing their sorrow and commiseration, often evincing or witnessing quite raw emotion, but emerging with a sense that some closure had been reached.[25]

The strictest modernists, to be sure, derided the funeral home and the attendant gravesite ceremony and marker. Jessica Mitford's landmark 1963 study, a muckraking effort, took the funeral industry to task for exploiting emotion and making big money in the process.[26] And burial costs were substantial in the United States, precisely because of the ceremonies involved. People still wanted high-quality caskets, and although cemetery markers were more modest than those of the nineteenth century, they could still cost a fair sum. But spending money, surely, was part of the process of feeling that the dead had been properly honored. Only when a body was not available for viewing did most Americans seem to feel really uncomfortable with the combination of new and old procedures they employed to handle the deaths of others.

Indeed, it seems clear that a new version of the good death emerged in the contemporary United States, a death that would allow most loved ones to believe that they had done the right thing, including expressing some real sorrow without being overwhelmed by it. Start, first, with a death in later age, when not surprisingly people could come to terms with the inevitable most readily. Add a significant effort to fight the disease that would bring death, often including extensive, and expensive, hospitalization, urged on by loving relatives eager to make sure everything possible was done in the medical setting so that grief could be delayed and guilt minimized. Follow with a tasteful, again not inexpensive, funeral home setting in which family and community could share a real, though professionally organized and relatively brief, experience of mourning, around a body carefully dressed up to avoid any impression of decay. Add perhaps a bit of celebration of the past life. End with burial in a coffin impervious to dirt, with at least a modest marker that some relatives might periodically revisit as a sign of remembrance. All of this was neither traditional nor Victorian nor modernist, but a clear mixture of elements that, in combination, noted death more than modernists might like but did not allow it to creep too extensively into normal life.

Finally, modernism itself was directly challenged by a new breed of death experts in the 1960s and 1970s, particularly in the United States, but in western Europe as well. Spearheaded by widely read gurus like Elisabeth Kübler-Ross and by elements of the antibourgeois counterculture that emerged in these decades, a variety of arguments attacked the modern effort to downplay death as superficial, for society as a whole, and psychologically damaging, for those who faced death of self or others. Death and dying courses proliferated for a time on college campuses, to help people learn how to discuss the phenomenon more elaborately and to understand what it involved so the process could be invested with less pain and more dignity. Much of the criticism focused on overreliance on medical personnel to deal with death—death fighting rather than death acceptance—and by their lack of relevant training. Grief, in this new argument, should be welcomed, not constrained—it was part of a healthy reaction and was preferable to the silent misery, even depression, that so often resulted from efforts to cope in private silence. Kübler-Ross detailed her famous stages of reaction to the inevitability of death, from denial to anger to acceptance, and argued that modern society must create spaces where the individual could find outlets for open emotion and in which family members could participate in the process of painful adjustment and ultimate acceptance.[27]

This counterattack, along with common sense adjustments by many ordinary Americans, modified the modernist, anti-death culture in some measurable respects. Children began to be shielded from death less systematically: Many families now took them to funeral homes and to funerals, so that they could vent their own emotions and learn more clearly what death was about. A growing number of U.S. states began to authorize living wills, in which people could stipulate their desire to die with dignity and to avoid expensive, heroic medical measures that might prolong life but without quality. Living wills most commonly requested that no efforts at revival or life support be attempted when real recovery or full brain activity were unlikely. A number of therapists began to reduce their sense that deep grief was unnatural, in favor of more sympathetic and individualized treatments—although the notion that "grief work" might be essential against excess persisted. Doctors reconsidered their own approaches in many cases, encouraged by the new thinking; they became more candid with patients and families about terminal situations, reducing their sense of personal failure in favor of encouraging better adjustment to death. Individual Americans, according to many polls, began to think about death more often, or at least to admit they had such thoughts. The 1970s indeed saw a revival of a kind of guidance that had been available prior to the twentieth century: the advice book on mourning. Bookstores by the 1980s and 1990s usually had ten to fifteen titles in hand, by authors such as Harold Kushner and Stephen Levine; and the books usually argued that death caused serious grief, which in turn resisted a great deal of effort over a prolonged period of time. In contrast to pure tradition, the new advice emphasized individual approaches, not set community norms; but whatever the course, death required concerted attention.

The modification process, however, should not be overdone. Reactions in the early twenty-first century often directly recalled the purest modernist responses of seventy years before. Thus children might be shielded in new ways: The nursery song about the old lady who swallowed a fly, which traditionally ended with her swallowing a horse, after which "she died, of course," was now modified in children's publications to "she's full, of course"—imaginative, but lacking the punch that the sudden evocation of death could offer. On another front, the American Cancer Society revealingly seeks to distance itself from a dreaded topic: "In no way do we want to be associated with a book on death. We want to emphasize the positive aspects of cancer only." Or finally, on a more meaningful front, a hospital patient has DNR—do not resuscitate—clearly marked on his chart, but the attending physician uses the defibrillator five times to bring him back to life, meaning that his last days were spent in intensive care, on tubes, during which time relatives came in to say their last good-byes, which he could not hear. Impressions of an unrealistically, even harshly anti-death society persist.[28]

Change showed in the U.S. reception to the hospice movement, one of the most important innovations in U.S. response to death, which was imported from western Europe. But, here, too, there would be limits to change. The U.S. hospice movement, most immediately brought over from Britain, began in the 1970s. It was designed to provide a realistic alternative to medical death fighting, in cases where a disease was terminal in all probability. Hospices offered advice and facilities for individuals to adjust to their fate, often with assistance in easing pain toward the greatest possible dignity in death. Families gained attention as well; they were encouraged to attend the ailing individual, as once occurred within the home, so that they, too, could recapture the benefits of a more traditional good death, beginning a grief process before death actually occurred and having a chance to settle any outstanding disputes or tensions. All parties involved in hospice care might feel that death was being confronted in a setting designed to provide comfort and group support and amid personnel for whom these purposes, and not death fighting, were the objects of training and reward. Often, indeed, with hospice assistance, the actual death could occur in the home, which is what most hospice patients said they wanted.

Group adjustments, the ongoing effectiveness of fairly elaborate funerals, and the countermeasures introduced in the final decades of the twentieth century added up to a rich and complex environment for death in the contemporary United States. Individuals could find diverse approaches, and probably individual personalities could carve appropriate responses more freely than ever before. Collectively, a mixture of tradition, strong doses of Victorianism, and modernism clearly prevailed, and there was no reason to argue that it could not be effective. Certainly, the culture-critic argument, that death had become a fearful taboo, was overblown, at least after the modifications of the 1960s and 1970s.

Leading Problems

At the same time, elements of the mainstream approaches clearly did not work as might be desired. This means, first, that death can always be difficult; no system is ideal. But second, it means also that more of the modernist limitations persisted than might be imagined, given the reasoned objections and alternatives. Contemporary American death practice, like the actual death patterns themselves, was substantially new, and it had huge downsides that had at best been slightly ameliorated. If there was a contemporary good death—in later age, medically delayed but perhaps with a hospice ending, cushioned for survivors by the tempered grief of the funeral home—there were lots of bad deaths still.

The most obvious contemporary vulnerability where death is concerned—a classic human problem to be sure, but definitely in new form—involves deaths of children and young adults. These deaths are now rare, which is the good news; but they are not nonexistent, and the modernist culture makes them very hard to handle—the bad news. Standard rituals, including the funeral home routines, do not easily suffice when the vigorous sense that these deaths should not have occurred and, often, guilt are added to normal grief. Brief adjustment periods, with little visible mourning, do not provide adequate help. Many people faced with these deaths find little community sympathy, beyond an initial brief response—for most people have no relevant experience. Many people carve out individual approaches that do work. But signs of difficulty remain. Many marriages collapse in divorce after the death of a child—because accepted forms of grief no longer tie family members together, as in the nineteenth-century ideal, and parents frequently blame each other for a death that should not have occurred. Many people seek out strangers for help: From the 1950s onward, in many U.S. cities, grief groups formed, which were composed of people who had experienced the death of a child or young spouse, and who simply could not find the necessary response except from people who shared the experience. *Thanatos* groups (from the Greek word for death) and an organization known as Compassionate Friends spread widely in the United States. The fact that members of these groups were otherwise strangers was trivial in light of the bond they had that differentiated them from the social mainstream. And of course, many people now facing unacceptable death did continue to turn to therapy in hopes of managing emotions that surpassed the bonds of available ritual or of the support from family and friends.

A more extensive issue involved people facing their own death, frequently amid loneliness and alienation. A few, to be sure, might be comforted by the knowledge that medical care would provide everything possible and that afterward there would be appropriate funeral home gatherings, but for many these contemporary trappings might not suffice. The good contemporary death was good more for family members, convinced that everything possible had been done, than for the dying themselves. A recent Institute of Medicine report puts the problem starkly: "a significant number of people experience needless suffering and distress at the end of life."

A revealing change: Most contemporary Americans now hoped to die a sudden death, presumably from accident or heart attack. This was not the traditional choice, where spending some time dying allowed for appropriate farewells amid family and community support. It was not the choice of loving relatives, for whom a sudden, unexpected departure created sharper grief and guilt amid lack of preparation. But it was the choice of individuals themselves. The change partly reflected the fact that the most common lingering form of death now became cancer, rather than respiratory disease, and cancer brought pain and difficult medical treatments in its wake. But it partly reflected the extent to which dying in any form was now unpleasant to contemplate; it was better just to go without warning.

And this in turn reflects larger limitations of the contemporary U.S. death process. The subject is still not widely discussed. Although children are less rigorously excluded than before, they certainly learn that death is an uncommon, unpleasant topic. With little normal discussion, the whole prospect of death looms as an unknown and terrifying inevitability. Few people, because of the remoteness of the subject and the lack of much experience with death even into middle age, make significant preparations for their own deaths. And when death actually approaches, unless it is indeed sudden, it is faced in hospitals or nursing homes, cut off from most familiar contacts and surrounded by intimidating technologies.

Although hospital authorities have become more aware of the need to help handle the dying process, the steady improvements in medical technologies and the growing concern about lawsuits for malpractice have pushed them in the opposite direction. Death frequently occurs amid scary machines and batteries of precautionary tests. The dying continue to lack control over their own dying process. Attempts to keep them alive still take place, often against their own repeatedly expressed wishes to experience dignity over prolongation. The hospice movement, designed to redress this problem, has accomplished much, but its impact has been limited. Only 19 to 25 percent of dying Americans have any contact with a hospice, and even this minority figure is misleading, because contacts often occur too late for the hospice volunteers to do much good, delayed until the final days because of insistence by doctors and well-meaning relatives that death fighting and heroic medical acts should continue well beyond any probability of success. Minority groups, in particular, have little awareness of the hospice alternative. Concern about Medicare fraud further limits access to hospices, because insurance coverage becomes uncertain. And the story does not end there: Seventy-five percent of all Americans do not know that hospices facilitate home care. Eighty percent say they know that predeath stipulations, such as living wills, are desirable, but almost no one follows through, because thinking about death in advance is so painful. And hospitals not infrequently overrule living wills anyway, concerned that they might be sued if every medical alternative is not attempted despite the expressed wishes of the patients that heroic measures be avoided. The individuals involved, now very sick and often quite old as well, are often not in a position to protest, and relatives often hesitate to take the responsibility themselves.[29]

The goals of Americans who are dying are clear and not particularly new—"relationships and belonging"; "having control"; and "being human." They are often not fulfilled or are incompletely fulfilled. It is as if the contemporary United States purchased some key gains, notably less premature death and usually less pain in death, at the cost of a culture that would sustain the dying themselves. Contemporary modernism, although slightly modified, seems to limit putting into practice available knowledge about what most people want as they die. Loving relatives, eager to limit grief and guilt, and medical personnel both contribute to the tendency. So does lack of preparation on the part of individuals themselves, who fail to explore what is known about how best to organize an inevitable part of life. There is insufficient opportunity to explore death in advance, and a host of cultural features contribute to this dilemma.

One final issue deserves attention. Distaste for death helps generate some novel public reactions when a particularly inappropriate symbolic death occurs. Widespread public mourning at the death of Princess Diana—still young and beautiful at the time of her death—was a powerful international display in which many Americans joined, laying flowers and wreaths in numerous places. But Americans might have been particularly eager for healing rituals and monuments when death's presence might otherwise seem overwhelming, and we will explore the wider manifestations of public emotion in Chapter 11.

Conclusion: How Large Does Death Loom?

Several points are clear about the contemporary history of American death—beyond the encouraging facts of the death rates themselves. Culture and associated rituals and symbolism changed a lot, which was both inevitable and (at least in some ways) desirable, given the dramatically new death patterns. Many older ideas were vigorously attacked, although some of them changed in fact slightly less than the attacks suggested. Some initial transformations were partially revisited. It is fair to note that contemporary death is still quite a new phenomenon, in historical terms, which makes it unsurprising that some responses are still being refined.

Some of the changes that did occur had complex consequences. Children now usually did not die. This encouraged a sense that childhood and any experience of death should be newly separated. It promoted a belief that death fighting was the only appropriate response to threats of death among children, for it was hard to admit that any death in this category must be acknowledged or accepted. Adult anxieties about risks to children measurably increased, even though most risks declined, because it was so hard to contemplate even an unlikely possibility that a child might die; Americans, for whatever reason, carried the worries about security and safety unusually far. Finally, when a death did occur to a child, guilt and outrage might know no bounds. The process, once painful but common, now became rare but truly agonizing. It was difficult to know how to adjust reactions for the unfortunate few who had to experience the unlikely tragedy.

The other disparity that was revealed was between what people around the act of dying preferred—to see themselves as caring relatives or effective doctors or nurses—and what dying people said they wanted to happen. The dying "won" when they died fast and unexpectedly, against the best efforts of emergency medical teams and amid the lack of preparation of their families. But the wishes of others seemed normally to prevail when death stretched out over any period of time. The two most striking innovations in the actual settings for death—the modern high-tech hospital and the funeral home—did not directly address some of the key wishes of the dying themselves and might even contradict these wishes. Culture critics identified the problems, but had only limited success in compensating for them.

Several key questions remain, which are far easier to raise than to answer. We have argued that contemporary U.S. culture largely seeks to downplay death. At the same time, however, aspects of the nation's entertainment portray death as a routine staple, suitable for thrills or even laughter. The average U.S. child, growing up with television and the movies, sees many thousands of people die before his (slightly less commonly her) eyes. Earlier efforts to limit the sense of death in the media—an old Hollywood rule that a gun shooter and a gun victim should not be shown in the same frame, so that children would not have to directly confront the cause of a death—quickly faded amid growing media violence and gore from the 1970s onward. Gruesome death scenes became more common than ever before. What messages did this send to a culture that was, for the most part, unattuned to death? Why, in fact, were the images even popular if death had become such an unpleasant topic? Many critics argued that children, even older children, were incapable of understanding the meaning of death given the larger contours of contemporary culture, so that the violence in their media had no real meaning except perhaps to encourage a few to experiment with violence on their own, not understanding from real experience what death was all about. But the overall package was odd, to say the least. Perhaps it was troubling as well.

Accusations of superficiality flowed glibly from many of the 1960s culture crit-ics. Is a society encouraged to think little about death capable of understanding the deeper meanings of life? Is an individual who thinks about death rarely if at all not just vulnerable to lack of preparation for his or her own actual pass-ing, but missing something about the real nature of humanity? The distaste for death can easily be associated with other aspects of consumer culture, eager for quick thrills and surface pleasure but incapable of deeper appreciations. The resultant criticisms deserve some attention, but they are hard to evaluate, and they are not, in a context in which so many aspects of death have changed in fact, necessarily accurate.

The biggest issue involves the extent to which Americans were in fact successful in downplaying the importance of death—or whether they really wanted to. The modernists wanted to remove death as a normal concern. And without question, a healthy adult in middle age, with a normal brood of kids, could pass many years without thinking seriously about death as a personal concern, beyond watching some people kill other people on the television screen (knowing of course that they did not really die, unless the news was on) and maybe wondering occasionally about the well-being of surviving parents. Children, seeing no real death around them, might have a particularly difficult time defining the experience at all. Even for adults, relative innovations such as the funeral home seemed to many to allow a social visit to a departed friend or relative, but not much serious engagement. The injunction of modern manners, to keep grief away from others, certainly could contribute to a sense that death could be largely ignored.

Granting personality variations, however, there was another side to this coin. Lack of familiarity with death and lack of any easy ability to discuss the subject with others might make it loom larger when the thought became inescapable.

Fears might easily go up—fears about the uncertainty of one's own death, and even fears about imagined threats to family members. Death might become a bigger deal than it had been before, if less often contemplated. Was melancholy about death, as an unconsidered and underexperienced topic, related to rising rates of emotional depression and (in some groups) suicide in the United States?

Whatever the views about this complex scorecard, one point was very clear: There were certain kinds of death that Americans cared about very deeply, even more than in the past. In no sense was the subject minimized down the line. Expectations about death were partly new, but they could be vigorous even so, and they could generate intense responses when they were violated. The subject could also engender profound divisions within U.S. society, another result of a rapidly changing experience. Death in these senses remained a very big deal, even in the course of U.S. history itself.

Notes

1. Phillipe Ariès, *The Hour of Our Death* (New York, 1981); Ralph Houlbrooke, ed., *Death, Ritual, and Bereavement* (London, 1989); Elisabeth Kübler-Ross, ed., *Death: The Final Stage of Growth* (New York, 1975); Ivan Illich, *Medical Nemesis: The Expropriation of Health* (London, 1976).

2. G. T. W. Patrick, "The New Optimism," *Popular Science Monthly* 82 (May 1914): 492–503. See also Basil King, *The Conquest of Fear* (New York, 1921).

3. Lymon Abbott, "Christ, Secret of Happiness: The Joys of Sorrow," *Outlook* 83 (11 August 1908): 837–838; "Heart of Sorrow," *Outlook* 72 (6 December 1902): 775; see also "The Reality of Sorrow," *Outlook* 73 (24 January 1903): 197; Charles F. Dole, "Of Sorrow and Pain," *Current Literature* 29 (December 1900): 694.

4. Rev. W. R. Inge, "The Vesper Hour," *Chautauqua* 62 (April 1911): 260; "The Great Adventure," *Outlook* 103 (22 March 1913): 605; Jane Belfield, "The Passing: An Emotional Monotone," *Lippincott's Magazine* 80 (September 1907): 374; "At the End of the Journey," *Outlook* 70 (25 January 1902): 216.

5. "Euthanasia: The Pleasures of Dying," *New Englander and Yale Review* 55 (September 1891): 231, 232–241.

6. H. B. Marriott-Watson, "Some Thoughts on Pain and Death," *North American Review* 173 (October 1901): 540–553; "The Dying of Death," *Fortnightly Review* 72 (August 1899): 246–269; "A New Medical Conception of Death," *Current Literature* 47 (October 1909): 453; see also Elie Metchnikoff and Dr. Henry Smith, "Why Not Live Forever?" *Cosmopolitan* 44 (September 1910): 436–446; "Pain, Life, and Death," *Living Age* 281 (May 1914): 368–370; "The Conquest of Love and Death," *Current Literature* 53 (August 1912): 1968.

7. "The Psychology of Sudden Death," *Literary Digest* 47 (December 1912): 1120; "Grieving," *Independent* 64 (1908): 476–477.

8. Richard Fisguill, "Death and La Mort," *North American Review* 199 (January 1914): 95–107; "The German Idea of Death," *Living Age* 286 (August 1915): 523–529; "Editor's Diary," *North American Review* 186 (October 1907): 307–308; Arthur Taylor, "Pioneer Inquiries into Burial Lots," *Survey* 28 (September 1911): 815–824.

9. "Grieving," pp. 476–477.

10. "The New Mien of Grief," *Literary Digest* 52 (February 1916): 292; see also "The Presence of Death," *New Republic II* (May 1917): 45–47; "Poor Death," *Living Age* 290 (September 1918): 360; "The Abolition of Death," *Current Opinion* 62 (April 1917): 270–271; "The Unseemliness of Funerals," *Literary Digest* 54 (April 1917): 1170; "And the Mourners Go about the Streets," *Unpartizan Review* 12 (July 1919): 176; Corra Harris, "Politics and Prayers in the Valley," *Independent* 71 (1916): 195. On World War I, Paul Fussell, *The Great War and Modern Memory* (New York, 2000).

11. "Agreeable Physical Aspects of Death," *Current Opinion* 72 (June 1922): 797; Sidney Lovett, "The Vocalism of Grief," *Atlantic Monthly* 130 (December 1922): 758–766; Sarah N. Cleghorn, "Changing Thoughts of Death," *Atlantic Monthly* (December 1923): 812.

12. Geoffrey Gorer, *Grief and Mourning in Contemporary Britain* (New York, 1965). See also Ernest Becker, *Denial of Death* (New York, 1997).

13. H. A. Dallas, "What Is Death?" *Living Age* 332 (Febrary 1927): 354–359; "The Tranquility of Death," *Reader's Digest* 56 (February 1927): 354–359; Marian Castle, "Decent Christian Burial," *Forum* 91 (April 1934): 253–255; M. Beatrice Blankenship, "Death Is a Stranger," *Atlantic Monthly* 154 (December 1934): 649–657; Mabel S. Ulrich, "What of Death in 1931," *Scribner's Magazine* 89 (June 1931): 559–560; Milton Weldman, "America Conquers Death," *American Mercury* 10 (February 1927): 216–227; "Problems of Living," *Scholastic* 36 (April 1940): 31.

14. Cas Wouters, "Changing Regimes of Power and Emotion at the End of Life," *Netherlands Journal of Sociology* 26 (1990): 151–155.

15. James Averill and E. P. Nunley, "Grief as an Emotion and as a Disease; A Social-Constructionist Perspective," *Journal of Social Issues* 44 (1988): 79–95; J. Bowlby, *Attachment and Loss*, 3 vols. (Harmondsworth, 1971–1980).

16. D. A. Thom, *Child Management* (Washington, D.C., 1925), p. 14; Daniel Anthony Fiore, *"Grandma's Through": Children and the Death Experience from the Eighteenth Century to the Present*, unpublished honors paper, Pittsburgh, 1992; Peter Stearns and Timothy Haggerty, "The Role of Fear: Transitions in American Emotional Standards for Children, 1850–1950," *American Historical Review* (February 1991); S. M. Gruenberg, ed., *The Encyclopedia of Child Care and Guidance* (New York, 1954), p. 170.

17. Ruth Sapin, "Helping Children to Overcome Fear," *Parents' Magazine* 8 (August 1933): 16; see also Donald A. Laird and Eleanor C. Laird, *The Strategy of Handling Children* (New York, 1949), p. 77; C. W. Hunicutt, *Answering Children's Questions* (New York, 1949), p. 22; Harold H. Anderson, *Children in the Family* (New York, 1941), pp. 104–105; Letter to Mrs. Frances Tuttle, Lucile, and Stephen, 9 August 1943, Tuttle Family Papers, Arthur and Elizabeth Schlesinger Library on the History of Women in America, Radcliffe College.

18. Allan Fromme, *The Parents' Handbook* (New York, 1956), p. 66; Mrs. Theodore (Alice McLellan) Birney, *Childhood* (New York, 1905), pp. 28, 239; Dorry Metcalf, *Bring-*

ing up Children (New York, 1947), pp. 62–63; see also Sapin, "Helping Children," p. 16; "In the Midst of Life," *Parents' Magazine* 20 (September 1945): 142; see also Lynn Chaloner, "When Children Ask about Death," *Parents' Magazine* 7 (April 1932); Sophie Fahs, "When Children Confront Death," *Parents' Magazine* 18 (April 1942): 34; Mary M. Green, "When Death Came to School," *Parents' Magazine* 22 (April 1947): 20.

19. Jack London, *The Call of the Wild* (New York, 1903), pp. 180–181; see also Evelyn J. Swenson, "The Treatment of Death in Children's Literature," *Elementary English* 49 (1972): 402.

20. Emily Post, *Etiquette: The Blue Book of Social Usage* (New York, 1934) 1st ed., (New York, 1922), pp. 413–417, 496; Amy Vanderbilt, *New Complete Book of Etiquette* (New York, 1952), pp. 121, 126.

21. Peter N. Stearns, *Anxious Parents: A History of Modern Childrearing* (New York, 2003), pp. 36–38.

22. G. Edward White, *Tort Law in America: An Intellectual History* (expanded edition, Oxford, 2003); Robert Rabin, "The Historical Development of the Fault Principle: A Reinterpretation," *Georgia Law Review* 15 (1980–1981): 925–961.

23. Elisabeth Kübler-Ross, *Death: The Final Stage of Growth* (New York, 1986).

24. Suzanne Smith, "Laid Out in Big Mama's Kitchen: African Americans and the Personalized Theme Funeral," in Peter N. Stearns, ed., *American Behavioral History* (New York, 2005), pp. 159–180.

25. Gary Laderman, *Rest in Peace: Cultural History of Death and the Funeral Home in Twentieth-Century America* (New York, 2003).

26. Jessica Mitford, *American Way of Death* (New York, 1963).

27. Kübler-Ross, *Death: The Final Stage of Growth* (New York, 1972).

28. Sharon Kaufman, … *And a Time to Die: How American Hospitals Shape the End of Life* (New York, 2005); Sandra Gilbert, *Death's Door: Modern Dying and the Ways We Grieve* (New York, 2005), p. 106.

29. Christie Davis, "Dirt, Death, Decay and Dissolution: American Denial and British Avoidance," in Glennys Howarths and Peter Jupp, eds., *Contemporary Issues in the Sociology of Death, Dying and Disposal* (New York, 1996); Kübler-Ross, *Death: The Final Stage of Growth* (New York: 1972); Illich, *Medical Nemesis*. Darwin Sawyer, "Public Attitudes toward Life and Death," *Public Opinion Quarterly* 46 (1982): 521–533; Donna Dickenson and Malcolm Johnson, eds., *Death, Dying and Bereavement* (London, 1993); see also an excellent review of post-1960s developments, John W. Riley Jr., "Dying and the Meanings of Death," *Annual Review of Sociology* 9 (1983): 191–216; Margaret Stroebe et al., "Broken Hearts in Broken Bonds," *American Psychologist* 47 (1992): 1205–1212; Wouters, "Changing Regimes of Power and Emotion at the End of Life": 151–155.

CHAPTER 7

The Comparative Context: Global Patterns of Change

During the nineteenth and early twentieth centuries, the United States had been on the cutting edge of change concerning the rituals and assumptions surrounding death, with the new emphasis on grief, the redefinition of cemeteries, and the rapid gains of funeral homes and the practice of embalming. U.S. changes in the latter twentieth century, extending but also significantly modifying Victorian patterns in light of the death revolution, were significant in their own right. However, several other parts of the world innovated more extensively than the United States did in this new period. U.S. patterns, as a result, remained distinctive, but in more complicated ways.

Global trends involved a host of variables. Huge differences in living standards generated great variations in mortality rates. Japan and parts of western Europe raced ahead of the United States in mortality rate decline by the end of the twentieth century. Less internal inequality, better public health, and wider medical coverage accounted for the differences—which meant that several societies went farther in the death revolution than the United States did, although the basic directions were similar. Other parts of the world cut mortality more slowly, thanks to greater poverty, less widespread health measures, and, in some cases, worse environmental degradation. But change occurred almost everywhere by the latter twentieth century, pushing infant mortality rates below previous levels, if not yet to the levels of the advanced industrial societies. Death rates rivaled traditional levels only in a few parts of Africa, in the 1990s (where in some cases they were deteriorating thanks to famine, civil strife, and the impact of AIDS), and in special cases such as Iraq. Change was widespread, but the massive differences in timing and extent mattered as well.

Culture was the second key variable. Some cultures proved much more open to a reassessment of death than others. Here, too, the United States was in

some ways more a middling case—of change within tradition—than a continuing pioneer. Some societies, at another extreme, even discussed restoring earlier
customs after an intervening period of change. By the early twenty-first century,
for example, some Mongolians reverted to a traditional pattern of taking dead
bodies out into the wild. It had once been believed that allowing animals to feed
on the dead was a contribution to nature, reducing the need to prey on other
animals.[1] Now, with the ending of the communist regime in Mongolia, some pur-
ists found meaning in a return to earlier practices (along with a fierce resistance
to alternatives like cremation). Again, cultural variation could be both extreme
and intriguing, and there was no clear, global pattern of change.

Modernization or Random Change: A World in Flux

Changes in death, and most notably the trends toward reduction of infant mortality and the introduction of new medical procedures, although very unequally
distributed, had some general implications for existing rituals and beliefs. The
example of Western cultural change might push in a similar direction. Not
surprisingly, by the mid-twentieth century some widespread signs developed
that previously elaborate death practices were being rethought, toward greater
simplicity and reduced family involvement. Not only changes in death itself,
but growing urbanism and increased attention to consumer pleasures prompted
reconsiderations. Hospitals also expanded in cities everywhere. The tendency in
Africa, for example, to minimize the time devoted to grief and family arrangements, discussed earlier and highlighted by Nigerian novelist Chinua Achebe,
is one among many symptoms of the tendency to reduce elaborate traditional
responses. At the same time, there were other forces at work, including new religious influences or for a time the advent of communism. And previous practices
had been so varied and changes in death rates were so uneven that it would be
misleading to talk about some general global modernization of death cultures.
The better model involves a few widespread impulses along with considerable
ongoing commitment to diversity—both within and among major societies.

Signs of simplification, suggesting lowered concern about death at least on the
surface, multiplied in many different places. Middle-class Mexicans dropped the
traditional celebration of the day of the dead. Traditionally, All-Saints' Day had
been an occasion for visits to dead relatives, the decoration of graves, even parades
of death figures; it was widely believed that spirits came from beyond to pay a visit
at this time. Increasingly (partly because the day of the dead became a growing
tourist attraction, which already diluted its spiritual content) people stopped
observing many of the customs, substituting U.S. Halloween icons instead, from
pumpkins to trick-or-treat candy, far removed from any overt connection with

the dead. All this in a country in which death once seemed central to national culture, with a leading intellectual describing how the Mexican once "chased after death, mocked it, courted it, hugged it, slept with it; it was his favorite plaything and his most lasting love."[2] Koreans increasingly shifted death ceremonies to hospitals or funeral parlors rather than using their homes. A traditional three-day mourning period was shortened or remained unobserved entirely.

Communist regimes inevitably attacked traditions, partly through their general campaigns against religions or customary beliefs such as Confucianism. In China, for example, old people might still pay annual visits to cemeteries, believing that they were communing directly with ancestors, but the young and the middle-aged, although they might accompany their elders out of love, simply didn't believe in ancestor contact and thought the whole process was confusing and boring. Russian communists worked hard to provide new funeral practices—called "red funerals"—to replace religious rituals. They also often seized funeral stones in cemeteries to use as building materials. Cremation increased, partly as a means of disposing of political dissidents. New rituals abounded, including placing workers' tools at grave sites to substitute for crosses and singing songs instead of religious chants. Religious practices returned after 1989 in some cases, along with fancier burial sites and markers for the newly wealthy. Death ritual was hardly displaced in the Russian case, but it was greatly altered, and ultimately the main result was increasing individual variety in the way people celebrated funerals and decorated graves.[3]

The Russian example already suggests how simplification and redefinition could lead in diverse directions, for here the emphasis was more on new creativity than on downplaying cemeteries and ritual. A fashionable Moscow cemetery, the Novodevichye, used for artists and officials from the 1920s onward (after Stalin had destroyed some more traditional sites), indeed became a haven for original displays and witty sayings. One general bedecked his tomb with a miniature tank; an airplane designer stipulated a plane; a performer had a life-size statue with a cigarette that periodically glowed as if being puffed. All in all, it is perhaps the liveliest graveyard in the world, suggesting a new mood, to be sure, but not a rejection of attention to death and the dead.

Japan, in its treatment of death, as in so many issues, provided a particularly interesting case of significant modern change combined with some continued traditions, which resulted in diversity. Not surprisingly, Japan had maintained elaborate rituals in dealing with death, designed particularly to protect against the dead person harming the living through impurities and to incorporate the dead in the panoply of family ancestors. (Significant specific variations did depend on the religion involved, most notably Shintoism versus Buddhism.) Two basic purposes were reflected in the common practices of establishing two graves: one to house the actual corpse, the other to serve as an ancestor memorial.

Many superstitions accompanied death, such as the idea that a pregnant woman must not attend a funeral. Rituals involved washing and otherwise purifying the body, often with incense, having family members dig the grave, and forming an elaborate procession as part of the funeral process.

Western influence, growing secularism, and expanding urbanization began to cut into tradition from the late nineteenth century onward, but with particular force after World War II. Japan participated vigorously in fighting death through public health measures and formal medicine, and the nation achieved the world's lowest infant mortality levels by the 1990s. Rituals shifted as well, partly because of medicalization. The Japanese quickly adopted Western black as opposed to East Asian white as the color for mourning clothing. The first funeral parlor opened in Tokyo in 1887, as urban people lacked time and space to conduct rituals themselves. Gradually, rituals themselves became less elaborate and processions declined. The first hearse was imported from the United States in 1917, although hearses were elaborately decorated with Japanese symbols such as dragons and phoenixes. Cremation gained popularity with growing knowledge about infectious disease. Use of funeral halls expanded rapidly in the 1970s and 1980s, as family members became unwilling to tend to dead bodies themselves and as beliefs about impurity declined. A positive memory of the dead person increasingly predominated over ancestor preparation and combating death pollution. The growing role of hospitals as sites where death should occur also reduced opportunities for family involvement. At the same time, with expanding prosperity, funeral costs tended to rise, and individual variants expanded, although there were accusations of "mass production" and standardization by the commercial funeral companies. The double grave site virtually disappeared, as did the elaborate community procession; but funeral altars, particularly within Buddhism but even among more secular families, became more ornate and elaborate, symbolizing a new desire to believe that paradise had already been achieved in death, rather than requiring earthly assistance—another sign of an attempt to take a more positive attitude toward death. Parting rites, rather than traditional goals, increasingly predominated; a 1995 poll showed 60 percent of all Tokyo residents believing that the funeral was a time to say good-bye, not a preparation for peaceful rest or spiritual advancement. Another innovation involved "pre-funerals," or *seizenso*, designed to celebrate an older person before death, which took some of the emotional and economic pressure off families when death actually occurred and when memorial services might be quite brief. Older Japanese often vigorously disapproved of the currents of change: As one eighty-four-year-old put it, "Look at young people today in the presence of death ... the first thing they do is call a funeral company. They act like helpless children. Such an embarrassing situation never arose in the past"—when presumably people were more certain of how to behave.

Another intriguing change, culminating quite recently, involved the transmutation of death from community/family responsibility to a more individual event. This was part of the movement away from elaborate rituals like the processions, but it was also involved in a historic shift in defining death itself. When death was seen as a family event, Japanese policy resisted the idea of brain death in favor of cessation of the heartbeat as the means of determining when death occurred. This reduced the need for family members to decide when death occurred. Family decisions also almost always argued against organ transplantation (which were technically illegal under a 1968 statute), believing the body should not be interfered with. But the possibility of saving lives through transplants began to gain ground in the 1980s, with individuals making the decision to accept transplants or to offer them on their own. In 1997 a measure that established brain death as legal death was passed into law, opening up wider transplant opportunities.

Japanese patterns followed Western precedent in key respects, copying some elements directly, as in the recent shifts concerning brain death, and adopting some others as part of the wider process of urbanization and the growing role of medicine. Timing varied, with Japanese changes cresting somewhat later, but directions were quite similar. In general, Japanese attention to death declined, and their desire to emphasize a positive outlook increased. But these important similarities should not obscure key distinctions. For example, the Japanese acceptance of suicide as a means of defending personal honor was a persistent difference. More broadly, the new emphasis on altars in the funeral process, to aid remembrance, differed from U.S. and European practices, both in terms of specific ritual and at least in part in terms of goals. Although ancestor worship declined, a lingering element informed the process of innovation in Japan. The pre-funeral was a unique Japanese contribution, again emphasizing the desire to celebrate the older individual and to stress remembrance. Along with some elements in the communist societies, Japan provides the best example of a potential "modernization" pattern in dealing with death, which was pioneered in the West. But the variants are vital as well; it would be dangerous to press a single modern pattern too vigorously, even amid significant change.[4]

Furthermore, beyond modern diversity, other forces were at work besides simplification and a new distaste for death and tradition. Religious change was important in many areas. Korean practices reflected modern medicine and some decline of ritual. But the spread of Christianity among a growing minority was at least as significant. Where Christian influence prevailed, traditional beliefs that people lived in the world of the dead until birth and then returned there after death, with shaman-led funerals helping to return the dead to their original homes, simply dropped away. Now funerals were led by priests and often preceded by a wake for viewing the dead body, along of course with distinctive prayers and more Western-style mourning clothes (dark suits for men instead of the customary sleeveless hemp coats). This was an important set of changes, but not entirely in a modernist direction.

In Cameroon, in Africa, the spread of Christianity had an even more dominant impact during the twentieth century, combined of course with the fact that death rates did not drop dramatically. Traditional burial rituals had suggested the social hierarchy, with the privileged being given marked graves and interred with many material objects and the poor being dumped in the forests. With Christianity, ceremonies still might reflect economic differences, but everyone (including women) received a grave. More time was spent on death rituals, in contrast to earlier rushed efforts, hurried because the dead were considered polluted. Children were encouraged to attend funerals, in contrast to the past when the association of death with fear encouraged their exclusion. The dead were now to be remembered, rather than forgotten (in principle), because of the association of death with evil. To be sure, concessions to tradition occurred, as would be expected: Christian rituals applied right after death, but then later activities were conducted to please ancestors, who were still seen as having certain powers. And cemeteries did not spread widely, because it was better to keep ancestors near their family. But the larger point is that significant change moved in directions far different from Western modernism or communist innovation.[5]

The same general pattern accompanied the spread of Christianity among indigenous peoples in Peru. Here, too, the Christian religion encouraged formal burial, a departure from tradition, where the dominant emphasis had been on getting rid of the body quickly because of the danger of its return as a demonic creature. Prayer to God vied with prayers for ancestors, although some combinations involved praising God for the existence of the ancestors.[6]

Obviously, great variety prevailed, as had always been the case. Perhaps over time a more systematic modernism will win out, particularly when and if the death revolution spreads more widely and uniformly. To date, rich combinations of tradition, modernism, and new religious forces literally defy generalization.

And this means that U.S. patterns, with their own interesting blend of nineteenth-century innovations, some traditional beliefs, and a fair chunk of modernism, particularly on the medical side, in one sense fit right in. They are distinctive, just as most other societies carve out distinctive approaches. They do not, in any systematic way, seem to ignore death more than several other modern societies do (indeed, as is obvious, some traditions distanced the dead far more than most contemporary Americans do). By the same token, there is no particular sign that contemporary American practices are having any sweeping global influence. Bows to Westernization, as in Japanese and Korean funeral colors, include American example. American missionaries display influence of another sort. But there is certainly no clear "Americanization" of the global approaches to death—far less, for example, than in the case of eating habits or sports interests. Death can be held apart from a considerable amount of global contagion, even when its rituals change considerably.

Western Europe

If global patterns help set a framework for understanding U.S. changes and continuities, they offer at most general guidance toward assessing how U.S. approaches to death stand up to scrutiny. But there is a more precise comparative context that requires more rigorous analysis.

The most revealing comparative patterns, in terms of interpreting U.S. developments from the mid-twentieth century onward, involved western Europe. Here was a society culturally very close to the United States that participated in a similar basic death revolution—similar in nature and in timing—and with active, ongoing contacts that made mutual imitation easy. Not surprisingly, many continuing changes did proceed in similar directions, as Europeans like Americans partially reassessed what death meant and how it should be handled. But vital distinctions opened up as well, difficult to explain but with fascinating implications. Whereas the United States had developed clearer innovations than western Europe in death rituals in the nineteenth century, in the twentieth century, the equation reversed, with Europe outstripping its younger transatlantic cousin.

Common trends included a new concern about grief. European authorities did not attack grief as loudly as their U.S. counterparts did, or with as much emphasis on therapy. But the impulse was widely shared: Elaborate grief did not fit a modern society where death was so extensively held at bay before later age. Elaborate mourning was limited in World War I, despite, or perhaps because of, massive slaughter, lest widows' public grief undermine wartime morale and give comfort to the enemy. Hostility to emotional display continued thereafter. Immigrants into western Europe, like South Asians in Britain after World War II, accustomed to more open expressions of grief, found themselves criticized and constrained, for example, by hospital authorities.[7] On a related front, by the latter twentieth century, few people changed their regular routines, beyond a day or so, in response to the death of a family member. Europeans greatly reduced mourning symbols and ceremonies, and as in the United States, this raised new questions about whether death and grief were being adequately handled. Change came earliest to the wealthier classes, with urban poor and rural people clinging longer to older customs, but it steadily extended.

Death moved out of homes and into hospitals, again in a familiar pattern, with a new profession of funeral directors taking a growing role in handling arrangements after death. This profession began to gain greater recognition in Britain early in the century, and then organized further in the 1930s—here, too, broadly paralleling U.S. patterns although with a slight time lag.[8] Again, workers moved more slowly in using new facilities than the middling and upper ranks, because of cost factors and more traditional attitudes alike. But the trends were clear. As in the United States, concerns mounted that doctors, as death fighters, did not handle death well, often ignoring the needs of grief and failing to deal honestly with terminally ill patients due to their tendency to equate death with failure.

But amid these vital similarities, two major differences emerged. Europeans increasingly shattered traditions by widely adopting cremation instead of conventional burial. And they modified medical death fighting with growing efforts to preserve greater dignity in death, while seeking to limit physical pain.

The cremation movement was striking.[9] Cremation was not authorized in Britain at all until a law in favor of it was passed in 1902, which followed from the initial modernist current. In 1919 only 1 percent of all British dead were cremated. But by 1998 the percentage had soared to 72. The practice was accepted by the Church of England in 1944, and by the Catholic Church in 1965, bowing to overwhelming popular support. In contrast, by 2000, only 25 percent of all U.S. corpses were cremated, as modernism continued to encounter deep traditional resistance to destroying the body. In Europe, cremation seemed a sensible response to growing urban crowding, high costs (cremations were much cheaper than traditional funerals and burial sites), and the general movement to reduce the ceremonialism associated with death. The greater hygiene involved in cremation was also widely appealing. Once death occurred, the new European goal seemed to be remembering the departed amid a minimum of fuss.

Before death occurred, however, there was growing interest in reducing some of the problems associated with excessive medicalization and the loneliness and isolation felt by many older people as they faced death.[10] Innovation was again more dramatic than in the United States, although in a sense it sought to use new means to regain some of the features of a traditional good death. The hospice movement thus sprang from a less-fierce insistence that every medical means be taken to hold death at bay, for even a few additional weeks or months. People were encouraged to accept a terminal illness—one's own, or that of a family member—and to move to a setting in which the emphasis was on family and community contacts, counseling to minimize fear and promote dignity, and appropriate treatments for pain.

An even more dramatic departure—approved in the United States only in the state of Oregon amid widespread national disapproval—was a growing European interest in legalizing medically assisted death, where death seemed inevitable along with increased pain and loss of quality of life. Here the Dutch led the way, legalizing medically assisted death. It could be administered, however, only after careful screening was done to ensure that a clearly terminal condition existed and that the choice had been made voluntarily. The Dutch, after considerable discussion, provided partial legalization in 1985, and full authorization in 2001, arguing that loss of dignity and excessive dependence were sufficient reasons, assuming official approval, to allow a person to seek assistance in death. Requests for this outlet went up steadily, primarily in cases of cancer, and although most were not approved, by 1995 2.3 percent of all deaths in the Netherlands involved approved medical assistance.[11]

Overall, taking various innovations into account in the final decades of the twentieth century, Europeans seemed bent on producing a somewhat different modern equation from that in the United States. Authorities talked of an "active orientation to death," with the people involved insisting on greater control over their own process.

What caused the unexpected differences? The most obvious factor, particularly around the widespread selection of cremation, involves the greater secularism that gained ground in Europe over the previous century or more; the decline of religion opened doors to greater innovation than occurred in the United States, whether for better or for worse.[12] To be sure, death still called forth religious sentiments among many Europeans—about half, in Britain—even among many who ignored religion otherwise in a society where active religious practice normally engaged only about 11 percent of the population. It was possible, also, that the experience of more massive death rates in the world wars opened Europeans to a greater willingness to reconsider what death meant and how it should be treated. Were contemporary Europeans somewhat less awed by death than their U.S. counterparts, less impelled to spend heavily both on fighting death and on memorializing it through somewhat more traditional funerals? It is also important, of course, that Americans had made some modern adjustments to death earlier than their European counterparts, during the nineteenth century, which might have reduced the need for further reconsideration. Funeral home burials were after all not traditional, and they worked well enough to preclude an active interest in further innovation; Europeans, who had not engaged in these changes so extensively, were open to looking at more radical alternatives such as cremation and even medically assisted suicide.

Developments in western Europe, and to a lesser extent in the United States, have occasioned impassioned debate between those who believe that death has become a taboo in contemporary society, with great damage done to people facing their own death or that of a loved one, and those who grant major change but argue that the result is a more rational approach to the real issues death involves. British sociologist Geoffrey Gorer mounted a particularly vigorous attack on contemporary European patterns in 1965, saying that death was surrounded by such secrecy and concealment that it had become equal to pornography in the nineteenth century, and just as dangerous to personal and societal health. Neither side of this dispute, which also raged in France and elsewhere, takes adequate account of the extent to which death has changed, which demands some major change in response—the nostalgia team is most guilty here—or of the variety of personal needs and reactions that exist. The debate is important, nevertheless, and not easily resolved.[13]

Within this debate rest also key aspects of the comparative issues between western Europe and the United States. To one of the leaders of the contemporary deterioration thesis, Philippe Ariès, U.S. patterns are preferable to European because the United States changed less: It surrounded death with more religious apparatus, it encouraged more ritual and expenditure, and it has not in the main succumbed to innovations like cremation. And, therefore (Ariès paid less attention to U.S. levels of medical involvement), U.S. reactions are less distorted than those European impulses that seem, in his argument, to trivialize an experience that must not be downplayed.

This comparative approach merits consideration. Pro-Europeans might reply that the U.S. approach does less for the dying than do European innovations such as the more extensive use of the hospices; Americans may have more ritual—although European pro-modernists properly argue that their rituals, although much reduced, remain serious and meaningful and that individuals can choose levels of elaboration (including, of course, traditional burial, which a minority still opt for) according to their personal needs.[14] A pro-modernist might go on to contend that U.S. rituals actually distract from attention to the dying, with their primary focus on protecting loving relatives from feeling guilt through extensive medicalization and the comforts of the funeral home. To be sure, key accusations about the vulnerabilities of modernity apply to trends in both societies: the heavy reliance on doctors, the embarrassment about death in front of children, the reduction of mourning. And some counterarguments apply to both cases as well, as traditional practices are subject to reexamination in light of modern medicine and a desire to limit physical and psychological pain. But the differences across the Atlantic do fit into the modernist-traditionalist debate as well.

The debate, though, insofar as it focuses on specifics like mourning or cremation, might obscure a more important point. U.S. distaste for death is in one sense at least greater than that in Europe: The greater insistence on fighting death to the utmost, regardless of costs and often regardless of the wishes of the dying, shows a degree of discomfort that no amount of traditionalist overtones can conceal. In this key respect, the U.S. taboo may weigh more heavily than the European.

Again, the issues in the basic debate and in its comparative extension are not easily resolved. What is clear is that the U.S. and the European patterns of innovation are intriguingly different and that they present somewhat different sets of strengths and weaknesses. And as death becomes more common again in both societies, thanks to an aging population, we can be sure that the debate will continue.

Notes

1. Michel Heike, "The Open-Air Sacrificial Burial of the Mongols," http://www.userpage.fu-berlin.de/%Ecorff/im/Texte/burial.html. August 15, 2006.

2. Na Kyung-so, "Today's Funeral Culture," *Koreana* 16 (2002): 32–37.

3. C. Merrivale, "Revolution among the Dead: Cemeteries in 20th Century Russia," *Mortality* 8 (2003): 176–188.

4. Dennis Klass and Robert Goss, "Spiritual Bonds to the Dead in Cross-Cultural and Historical Perspective: Comparative Religion and Modern Grief," *Death Studies* 23 (1999): 547–568; Satsuki Kawano, "Pre-Funerals in Contemporary Japan," *Ethnology* 43 (2004): 155–165; Jiro Nudeshima, "Obstacles to Brain Death and Organ Transplantation in Japan," *Lancet* 338 (1991): 1063–1064; Yamada Shinya, "Funeral Rites and Changing Perceptions of Death in Contemporary Japan," *Mortality* 9 (2004): 27–40; Hikaru Suzuki, *The Price of Death: The Funeral Industry in Contemporary Japan* (Stanford, CA, 2000); Andrew Bernstein, *Death Rites, Politics and Social Change in Imperial Japan* (Honolulu, 2006).

5. Michael Jindra, "Christianity and the Proliferation of Ancestors: Changes in Hierarchy and the Mortuary Ritual in the Cameroon Grassfields," *Africa* 77 (2005): 356–377.

6. Glenn Shepad, "Three Days for Weeping: Dreams, Emotions, and Death in the Peruvian Amazon," *Medical Anthropology Quarterly* 16 (2002): 200–229.

7. Shirley Firth, "Approaches to Death in Hindu and Sikh Communities in Britain," in Donna Dickinson, Malcolm Johnson, and Jeanne Samson, eds., *Death, Dying and Bereavement* (2nd ed., London, 2000).

8. Peter C. Jupp and Tony Walter, "The Healthy Society: 1918–1998," in Peter C. Jupp and Clare Gittings, eds., *Death in England: An Illustrated History* (New Brunswick, NJ, 1999).

9. Jupp and Walter, "Healthy Society"; Pat Jalland, "Victorian Death and Its Decline: 1850–1918," in Jupp and Gittings, eds., *Death in England*.

10. Clive Seale, "Demographic Change and the Experience of Dying," in Dickinson, Johnson, and Katz, eds., *Death, Dying and Bereavement*.

11. Phillip Kleepsier, *Life and Death Decisions* (Washington, DC, 2003).

12. Tony Walters, "Secularization," in Colin Parkes, Pitts Laungani, and Bill Young, eds., *Death and Bereavement across Cultures* (London, 1997).

13. The Philippe Ariès argument is summed up in "Death Denied," in Dickinson, Johnson, and Samson, eds., *Death, Dying and Bereavement*; for a contrary view, Tony Walter, Jane Littewood, and Michael Pickering, "Death in the News: The Public Invigilation of Private Emotion," in the same collection; Geoffrey Gorer, *Death, Grief and Mourning in*

Contemporary Britain (London, 1965); the French debate is summarized in Patrick Hutton, "Of Death and Destiny: The Ariès-Vovelle Debate about the History of Mourning," in Peter Homans, ed., *Symbolic Loss: The Ambiguity of Mourning and Memory at Century's End* (Charlottesville, VA, 2000).

    14. Peter Homans, "Introduction," in Homans, ed., *Symbolic Loss.*

CHAPTER 8

From Personal Death
to Social Policies

The reconfiguration of death in modern culture, its physical and ritual transformation in terms of personal experience, inevitably affected the various forms of administration of death by society. The changes triggered new debates about death as a punishment or death in war. The modernist approach to death did not, however, dictate uniform approaches to death as an element of social policy, which is why fierce disagreements often arose. Other factors besides attitudes about death affected areas like abortion or military strategy. Furthermore, different regions continued to vary in death experience, both because of different material circumstances—death rates still varied widely, as did levels of population growth and population pressure—and different cultural traditions. As a result, specific groups but also specific regions reached divergent conclusions about death policies, quite obviously on issues such as the use of suicide killers as part of war or terrorism. Divergences often powerfully shaped the U.S. position in world opinion and also the global impact of U.S. policies, particularly in the military arena but also in international debates over issues like population policy. Impulses in the United States often departed from new norms in others areas, most obviously from those in western Europe. No smooth globalization of death described policies in the later twentieth and early twenty-first centuries, any more than it described the variety of contemporary rituals. What was pervasive, however, was a series of new questions about death policies, as against earlier traditions and nineteenth-century innovations alike.

The following chapters take up the important arenas of policy debate and outright policy change. Each chapter shows how the growing discomfort with death combined with, or conflicted with, other key factors. Distaste for death sometimes predominated—as in European attacks on the death penalty or in fervent opposition to abortion in U.S. international policy. In other cases, different goals won through, although even here the goals often had to be adjusted to death concerns, as in the pro-abortion arguments, or in elements of U.S. military policy. Comparison remains essential, both to highlight different decisions about how to incorporate new attitudes to death and to explain why the differences generated explicit disagreements over international standards.

Modern technology and changing standards prompted several redefinitions on the borderline between the personal and the policy arena, which is what the remainder of this chapter takes up. When, for example, was a person dead? Traditionally, most societies registered death when the heart stopped beating. Modern medical technology, however, both facilitated and encouraged a different standard. During the 1940s the electroencephalogram (EEG) was introduced, charting brain activity. New research on comas revealed that some people, although technically alive in the sense of heartbeat, had little or no brain activity. At the same time, new devices began to allow preservation of life in new ways. Respirators, initially used for polio victims, sustained patients whose lungs were not functioning and who otherwise would have died. In 1967, Christiaan Barnard, the South African physician who performed the first successful heart transplant, declared a young woman "brain dead," ended ventilator support, which terminated her breathing, and then immediately removed her heart for use in his patient. During the 1970s, many U.S. states and various European countries began defining brain death diagnosis as the means of determining the cessation of life (and therefore the possibility of removing organs for transplants). The United States codified practices in 1981, in the Uniform Death Act, and every hospital developed a detailed procedure for declaring brain death. Most European, Australian, Latin American, and Asian countries followed suit, although as we have seen, Japan delayed for two decades.

More than formal legalities were involved in this change. The power of doctors to arbitrate death increased: They were the ones who interpreted the brain scans and on the basis of those interpretations could turn off life support machinery. Surgeons involved in the growing organ transplant business—itself of course designed to provide yet another means of prolonging life—took the lead in attacking "obsolete criteria for the definition of death [which] can lead to controversy in obtaining organs for transplantation." But while the new criteria advanced, providing legal protection for surgeons, actual specialists continued to vary considerably in their definitions of brain death. Some critics argued that brain death was pronounced far more frequently in transplant centers, where the need for organs was intense, than in other settings. Physicians also had to be instructed that some patients could show signs of life, particularly right before a ventilator was turned off, even when they were clinically brain dead—clasping their hands, for example, or shivering.[1]

The situation was ripe for debates about whether a person was really dead or not. True to expectation, a major case in Florida in 2005 emerged over a patient whom most doctors had pronounced brain dead, and whose husband wanted life support removed, but whose breathing and heartbeat were sustained by machines and whose parents insisted that she might ultimately recover. Massive court proceedings and national controversy erupted, with prominent conservatives arguing for extension at all costs, before a final ruling that the support mechanisms could be withdrawn and the patient allowed, by any definition, finally to die.

For most people, of course, heroic prolongation of life, even against a patient's wishes, was the most common modern problem when death neared—not the niceties of extreme definitions. But the novelty of definitions, and the unprecedented arguments that could ensue, provided vivid reminders of how new many aspects of contemporary death have become—and how difficult it might become for an individual to control the criteria involved with death.

Medical definitions and technologies were also involved in some of the new debates about the effective beginning of life, after conception; here was a significant component of the new controversies over abortion and its relationship to death, which we take up in the following chapter.

Medicine played yet another role, although a complex one, in one of the other striking new aspects of death in the contemporary period: the possibility of discussing individuals' wishes to die and the relationship of doctors to these wishes. Unprecedented concerns about what some people began to call the "right to die" developed for several reasons. The modern pattern in which people when very ill were frequently in hospitals and even more commonly under medical care created a sense that the only way to escape the pervasive interest in prolonging life at all costs was to establish a new countervailing right to end life when a patient wished—and that the medical establishment should in fact cooperate by providing the kinds of painless methods that modern drugs could supply. The "right to die" surfaced, then, as a deliberate countermeasure to the standard medical commitment to keep people alive even when any quality of life seemed impossible to recover—a new method of achieving the kind of release that, before the advent of modern medicine, nature itself often offered. But the rise of certain kinds of diseases, particularly cancer, that involved great pain, mounting incapacity, and loss of dignity provided its own spur to the new interest in access to assisted deaths. The advent of AIDS, and the aging of populations in industrial societies, with the greater incidence of diseases like Alzheimer's that accompanied this, provided added motivation. Why should modern medicine not simply fight death, but contribute to better deaths, when the alternative was months or years of hopeless struggle against wasting illness? At the least, right-to-die advocates urged greater legal clarity for people who wished to guard against being kept alive beyond any hope of real recovery, at a point in which a disease might deprive them of the ability to speak out directly.

The idea of a right to die first surfaced publicly in the 1930s, in proposals in Britain to allow voluntary euthanasia for seriously ill adults. The British Parliament vigorously rejected a proposal in this vein in 1935. In 1938 the Euthanasia Society of America was founded, the precursor of modern right-to-die movements in the United States. In 1950 a U.S. doctor was acquitted of killing a terminally ill cancer patient with an injection of air, although he admitted to committing the act: Elements of the public clearly were beginning to think that there were circumstances when death should be assisted, even though the law had not yet shifted. In 1968, another doctor proposed a bill in Florida to allow people to put in writing their wishes concerning end-of-life medical treatment, should they become unable to communicate later on. The American Medical Association at this point opposed living wills, urging discussion between patients and doctors instead; but the American Hospital Association backed a bill of rights that would include the right to refuse treatment.

Discussion and legal action heated up in the mid-1970s, both in the United States and in Europe. In 1976 the New Jersey Supreme Court ordered doctors to remove a respirator from a young woman in a coma, Karen Ann Quinlan, even though she was not brain dead; sustained by a feeding tube, she lived for another decade. In the same year California passed the first living will law. But the Catholic Church came out against these laws, although a papal decree in 1980, while opposing mercy killing, did permit the increased use of painkillers and a patient's refusal of extraordinary measures to prolong life. By 1982 the American Medical Association endorsed the withdrawal of treatment in hopeless cases, and growing numbers of doctors reported massive pressure from many terminal patients, and sometimes their families, to assist in death. By 1986 the association even supported the end of feeding and hydration for dying patients who requested this, and for those in permanent coma. A growing number of court rulings confirmed the right of patients to refuse medical treatment, sometimes ordering hospitals to conform to requests stated earlier; a 1991 federal mandate insisted on provision of information about advance arrangements, but here, too, many health care professionals ignored explicit directives.

Debate certainly continued, and continues to this day. Various courts also ruled against ending support for patients in vegetative states, and many hospitals, fearing lawsuits, insisted on keeping people alive at all costs. Whereas Catholic positions softened, increasingly countenancing living wills, many fundamentalist Protestants took a harder line, making religion a continued variable in the discussions as well. Debate among doctors was lively as well, not only on living wills but on the more radical idea of assisted deaths. Some physicians by the 1990s were obviously collaborating with patients' requests—4 percent of all doctors in one survey in the state of Washington, for example; a far larger percentage of physicians dealing with AIDS patients in the San Francisco area in the 1990s—but others ignored them in favor of insistence on heroic medical measures.[2]

American discussion of going beyond not maintaining life at all costs, to actually assisting in death, took a new turn in the 1990s with the efforts of Dr. Jack Kevorkian, in Michigan, to use a "suicide machine" to help patients end their own lives—often people in the early stages of Alzheimer's disease, as well as victims of terminal cancer. Charges of murder against Kevorkian long led to no convictions, and other doctors publicly admitted their assistance with prescriptions that they knew patients would use to kill themselves, again without court action. By 1991 a book instructing people on how to commit suicide reached the top of the best-seller lists. Legislative proposals to legalize suicide, however, mainly failed, for example, in both California and Rhode Island (although Rhode Island later ruled that assisted suicides were felonies, rather than capital crimes). Many states explicitly outlawed euthanasia in any form. And Dr. Kevorkian was ultimately imprisoned for murder, after taking part in a large number of assisted suicides. Only Oregon, with its referendum authorizing doctors to prescribe lethal drugs to terminally ill patients who requested them, fully defied the general trend, persisting in its commitment despite massive federal efforts to overrule the law. (The referendum first passed in 1994, was then struck down by a federal court, and was reinstated only in 1997 in the "death with dignity" act, with many safeguards against frivolous or ill-informed decisions; between twenty and thirty people a year availed themselves of the opportunity during the early 2000s.) Referenda in four other states failed, because even people who favored innovation in principle hesitated when it came time to vote.

Similar variety prevailed in other parts of the world, although as we have seen, some areas seemed ready to move further than the United States. In 1995 the Northern Territory of Australia became the first jurisdiction to allow doctors to take the lives of terminally ill patients who requested their help in dying; a sixty-six-year-old man suffering from prostate cancer, using a computer-activated syringe to inject himself with a lethal dose of barbiturates, became the first person to take advantage of the law, in 1996. The Netherlands and Belgium allowed assisted suicides—where doctors were involved—and also voluntary euthanasia. Switzerland joined Oregon in allowing physician-assisted efforts, preferred because the involvement of doctors allowed more systematic standards to prevent the mentally ill, for example, from abusing an opportunity intended only for the terminally ill. Canada's Liberal Party endorsed a reform effort in the late 1990s, and public opinion polls in many Western countries suggested that between 50 and 80 percent of the public backed the idea of new opportunities to obtain death with dignity. World conferences sought to support further explicit change, as in a 2004 meeting in Tokyo. But this remained, globally as well as in the United States, an area where the range of potential innovation was hard to calculate, where there was far more talk than formal action.[3]

Suicide constituted a final category in which new death concerns involved both policy and personal issues. Innovations were less striking here in one sense, because concern about explaining and preventing suicides had already emerged in Western society in the latter nineteenth century.

Global variations became more visible, however. Several societies maintained somewhat greater tolerance for suicide than was true in the West, on grounds of the greater importance of honor than of life—a theme among some Japanese, including a few traditionalists who committed dramatic suicides to protest undue Western influence in modern Japanese culture after World War II. Religious confidence might also provoke suicides, when the individuals believed that they would gain heavenly reward for suicidal acts of violence. Thus, although Islam strictly prohibited suicide, suicide in the professed interest of defending faith or nationality might win considerable approval. Japanese suicide bombers in World War II, and suicide bombings as part of terrorism in the early twenty-first century, challenged Western notions of appropriate respect for life. There was an occasional revival of *sati* suicides for Hindu widows, despite the fact this was against Indian law.

Within the West itself, and increasingly in places like Japan, efforts at suicide prevention mounted, building on earlier initiatives. Many cities established suicide "hotlines," providing sympathetic counseling designed to dissuade attempts at taking one's own life. During the latter twentieth century, growing concern responded to clearly rising rates of suicide among teenagers, in several industrial countries, including the United States. Rates might have tripled in the United States between 1965 and 1987, making suicide one of the top causes of death among adolescents and young adults. Parents and school officials were urged to keep careful watch for symptoms of suicidal impulses, because the idea of choosing death at a young age proved particularly repugnant. Research was active as well, seeking biological causes as well as more obvious prompts such as disappointments at school or in romance. A variety of organizations provided help lines and active counseling. In part because of new interventions, youth suicide rates seemed to stabilize in the United States by the latter 1990s; but they began to increase in Japan after 2000, rising 22 percent in 2003 alone.

Concern about suicide, particularly given periodic surges, added a new and unwelcome contact with death for many worried parents. And although primary explanations involved family instability, loneliness, and the pressures of modern schooling, some authorities wondered whether the dissociation of ordinary life and the experience of death—save in fictionalized media contexts—might have played a role in new youth behavior, with troubled adolescents less aware of the finality of death than their counterparts had been in more traditional settings.

In various ways, then, suicide could disturb some of the wider modernist assumptions about death in societies otherwise proud of their advanced economies and progressive achievements.[4]

Policies involved in defining the end of life and dealing with individual desires to seek death mixed old issues with very new concerns, all in a context of rapidly changing medical practice and technology. Shifts in death expectations, some of them encouraged by aspects of modern medicine, presented new issues for individuals eager to have control over their own passing and for lawmakers trying to set standards amid obviously varied constituencies. Division and debate, including controversies over the possible causes of suicide and potential remedies, constituted one inevitable result in the United States and in other societies where the newest kinds of issues penetrated at all. Everywhere, additionally, debate and policy were complicated by considerable unwillingness to talk about death too frequently, particularly in areas where the personal and the political intertwined in novel ways. These hesitancies proved less relevant on topics where discussion had already been established by shifts in the nineteenth century, most notably abortion and the death penalty.

Notes

1. Margaret Brindle and Gerald Salancik, "The Social Construction of an Institution: The Case of Brain Death and Organ Transplant Industry," in John Wagner, ed., *Advances in Qualitative Organization Research* (Stamford, CT, 1999), pp. 1-36.

2. P. Schmitz, "The Process of Dying with and without Feeding and Fluids by Tube," *Journal of Law, Medicine and Health Care* 19 (1991): 23-26; James Hoefler, "Diffusion and Diversity: Federalism and the Right to Die in the Fifty States," *Publius* 24 (1994): 153-170.

3. Marjorie Zucker, ed., *The Right to Die Debate* (Westport, CT, 1999); Margaret Battin, Rosamond Rhodes, and Anita Silvers, *Physician Assisted Suicide: Expanding the Debate* (New York, 1998).

4. Adina Wrobleski, *Suicide: Why?* (New York, 1995); A. F. Garland and E. Zigler, "Adolescent Suicide Prevention: Current Research and Social Policy Implications," *American Psychologist* 48 (1993): 169-182; J. A. Grunbaum and others, *Youth Risk Behavior Surveillance–United States* (Washington, DC, 2003).

CHAPTER 9

Abortion Disputes and
Contemporary Death Culture

New policies toward abortion began to be introduced in many countries by the 1950s and 1960s, particularly in the Western world. The changes generated bitter arguments, particularly in the United States, that called upon very different assumptions concerning death. These assumptions, combined with other factors, affected national political alignments in the United States, helped determine international policies concerning family planning, and more briefly colored the political process in several west European states.

As before, some regions were largely exempt from the dispute. Abortion continued to be widely practiced in Japan, and as the Japanese government began to encourage a lower birthrate in the 1950s, to limit population pressure, abortion rates might even have climbed. New efforts did develop to encourage other methods of family planning, including fairly ready access to birth control devices for teenagers, but abortion remained an option. Reliance on abortion remained considerable in Russia and Eastern Europe as well, again as a basic means of family planning. In the early 1990s, for example, Russian women had almost twice as many abortions as there were live births, and in Hungary the abortion rate actually rose after the fall of communism. Only in Poland, where the collapse of communism after 1991 gave greater political influence to the powerful Catholic Church, did significant new opposition to abortion access surface; a 1993 law banned abortion, except where the mother's health was at risk. Overall, in this region and some other parts of the world, abortion was cheaper than contraception, which explained its obvious currency.

New interest in abortion also surfaced in countries like China and India where interest in limiting the birthrate—in China, legal requirements for limitation—combined with traditional gender preferences. New methods of determining the sex of the fetus led many Asian families to abort females, hoping for an opportunity to try again to conceive a male without risking excessive family size.

In the 1950s, most west European countries, along with the United States, continued to outlaw abortion unless some threat to maternal health was involved. In Catholic Spain, even mother's health took a backseat to saving the life of a fetus. As we have seen, various criteria had combined to produce at least an official antiabortion stance: concern about possible death to mothers from botched abortion attempts, religious commitment to saving the unborn as human beings with souls, and a growing belief that human life began with conception. These attitudes reflected some traditional thinking along with the new hostility toward death—particularly the deaths of children, where concern might easily spread from the born to the unborn; complicating the picture, however, was a simultaneous belief that abortion might somehow encourage sexual immorality. Although enforcement of abortion laws varied, their existence undoubtedly affected abortion rates and practices, and in the United States policing rigidified from the 1940s onward. In contrast to the 1920s and 1930s, when many practitioners, including even some chiropractors, openly offered abortions—a Portland, Oregon, practitioner, Ruth Barnette, performed more than 40,000 operations—authorities now tightened up, raiding clinics, interrogating women, requiring hospitals to toughen their codes of conduct. Presumably, this shift reflected more general cultural pressure to urge women to devote themselves to family life, to encourage population growth in a climate of war and Cold War, and to counter the signs of growing permissiveness in sexual behavior. In the minds of some, abortion became associated not only with sexual license but also with communism, and in the climate of the early Cold War, repression was the order of the day.

Several factors reopened discussion, however, with some new efforts forming in the later 1950s, followed by then a more massive surge in the following decade. Tighter enforcement itself, which pushed some young women toward clandestine abortions that could endanger their health, even their lives, and which put many doctors in a difficult conflict between patients' demands and the letter of the law, was one element. Concern about maternal deaths clearly shifted from attempts to outlaw abortion—the nineteenth-century approach, backed by many doctors—to a realization that some abortion would occur regardless of the law and that women's health might be much better protected if abortion was legalized and available in regular medical settings. Medical advances also made it increasingly difficult to claim that a woman's life was at stake, such that terminating a pregnancy could be justified under most Western law. This put new pressure on advocates, and on many doctors themselves, to reconsider abortion more broadly. These developments help explain why many doctors now took a lead in abortion advocacy, because of what they experienced in terms of female suffering with botched abortions and the anguish of unwanted pregnancies—a huge reversal of the nineteen-century equation.

Discussion also reopened through a combination of new sexual practices and new ideas about women's rights, and this new context almost certainly outweighed death concerns among most of the new supporters of abortion rights. Between the 1940s and the 1960s—historians debate precisely when the change occurred—sexual activity increased in a number of ways, much of it outside of marriage and most of it aimed at recreation and pleasure rather than procreation. Women's age at first intercourse went down in most social groups, but particularly the middle classes. This "sexual revolution," clearly identified by the 1960s, swept through the United States and western Europe alike. Much of it depended on new access to birth control devices and changes in birth control measures such as the pill. But recreational sex, particularly among young people, might certainly still occasion unwanted pregnancies, which is where a new look at abortion could come in. At the same time, and more important still in terms of legal considerations, women's rights advocacy began to regain momentum by the 1960s, in the United States in a context in which arguments about civil rights were already intensifying for other reasons. Defending women's right to choose whether or not to have a baby, or as abortion rights advocates often put it more generally, defending women's rights over their own bodies, became a crucial plank in the platform of latter-twentieth-century feminism, in the United States and elsewhere. These rights were often seen as overriding detailed discussion about what constituted death for a fetus—particularly a fetus in the early stages of development. Abortion advocates, particularly in the United States, pressed to have the issue discussed as a matter of equity to women, not primarily as a question of death.

Equity arguments could be enhanced, again particularly in the United States, by data that suggested that poor women and those of minority races were particularly blocked by laws against abortion. Wealthier women could find ways around restrictions and also had more abundant access to birth control information and devices. Social as well as gender equity could bolster arguments for change.

The reopening of abortion law also occurred in a climate of growing concern about global population levels. World population would triple in the twentieth century, from two billion people to more than six billion, and many analysts worried about resultant pressures on resources and the environment. Here, too, modern concerns about death could enter in to some extent: Children born into great poverty, in societies where population levels were outstripping food supply, risked higher death rates in the future—even if, as the population boom itself demonstrated, these rates had not yet widely kicked in. And if population growth was getting out of hand, it was easy to argue that any reasonable form of

birth control, including abortion, might be vastly preferable to endless intensification of the current trends.

In the United States, in the 1960s, the decade of civil rights, active discussion
of abortion policy surged, there were more open changes in sexual behavior, and
there was a renewed focus on feminism. Prior to this point, abortion had been
regarded as a political taboo, but now—and for the next half century—it became
inescapable in the public arena. Major moves to legalize abortion occurred in
New York, California, and elsewhere, and it became obvious that—even in states
with large Catholic minorities—a majority of opinion supported legalization, at
least on the Pacific coast and in the Northeast. In 1969 the California Supreme
Court ruled that banning abortions was unconstitutional (*People v. Belous*). In
that same year, the National Association for Repeal of Abortion Laws formed,
and the National Organization of Women, a powerful, newly established feminist group, supported repeal of abortion bans. Many men, including numerous
doctors, formed part of the advocacy groups, but individual feminists provided
a vigorous spur, some citing their own experiences with illegal abortion or with
barriers to abortion, even in cases of rape or incest. Catholic groups mobilized
strongly against this surge and managed to delay legislative action in many states,
but in 1970, the New York Legislature repealed the abortion ban, in a law that
was cited as precedent three years later in the U.S. Supreme Court's *Roe v. Wade*
decision. Hawaii and Alaska also legalized abortion. Women began to travel
to these states when they sought abortion, which created additional pressure
for wider change. Then, in 1973, capping this long movement, the Supreme
Court's decision made it unconstitutional to ban abortion. Many doctors and
other practitioners quickly responded by setting up abortion clinics. Supporters
of abortion trumpeted their commitment to women's freedom of choice. Rates
of actual abortion increased notably, although they later stabilized and even
dropped a bit.[1]

A significant minority of Americans dissented passionately from these changes.
The hierarchy and official organizations of the Catholic Church, in the United
States and worldwide, vehemently opposed abortion. In the Catholic view, a
soul and therefore effective human life began with conception, and abortion
constituted murder, purely and simply; the attitudes that had once gone into
opposition to infanticide were now applied to efforts to protect the embryo and
the fetus. As Mother Theresa put it, "I feel that the greatest destroyer of peace
today is abortion, because it is a war against the child, a direct killing of the innocent child, murder by the mother herself." Many individual Catholics actually
dissented, often out of concern for the lives of mothers that could be jeopardized
if safe abortion procedures were not available, but the position of the Church
remained adamant. Catholics were joined, and often surpassed in vigor, by the
growing fundamentalist Protestant minority, equally persuaded that life began

at conception and that abortion was therefore a form of murder. By the 1980s, as religious commitments expanded in the United States and with the related expansion of conservative Republicanism, antiabortion forces—or as they termed themselves, right-to-life forces—were on the upswing. Many states passed measures restricting abortion, some of which were thrown out by the courts on grounds of the *Roe v. Wade* precedent. Efforts to limit abortion in the later stages of pregnancy and attempts to restrict access of minors without parental permission were common targets, and they gained some success particularly in the Midwest and the Great Plains states. A number of states also imposed waiting periods, often designed to give the mother a chance to change her mind. Finally, campaigns of intimidation constrained abortion clinics, prompting some to close outright.

There was no question that many opponents of abortion deeply believed that it was murder, no matter what the phase of the pregnancy. A doctor and former director of an abortion clinic was quoted as saying, "There is no difference between a first trimester, a second trimester, a third trimester abortion or infanticide. It's all the same human being in different stages of development." New medical procedures, like ultrasound, that allowed views of embryonic movement, confirmed many in the conviction that life was at stake. Opponents claimed that abortion counselors deliberately lied to pregnant girls about the development process, claiming that fully formed babies were "just tissue, like a clot." Counterarguments developed, of course, with other doctors arguing that early embryos should not be regarded as children and insisting on the issue of women's deaths where legal abortions were not available. Disputes about death were not the only factors involved in the controversy, but they loomed large.[2]

Abortion, and with it attitudes toward death and definitions of the effective beginning of life, became a massive issue in American politics, within many states and certainly at the national level. Improvements in medicine added to the debate: It became possible to save fetuses as young as twenty-seven weeks (five weeks younger than the age previously regarded as potentially viable), and this provided additional ammunition for the pro-life camp. Claims of life expanded still further: Many conservatives even opposed the use of embryonic stem cell tissue, taken from embryos for use in fertility clinics that would otherwise be discarded, on grounds that this, too, was an abuse. Widespread opposition also applied to "day after" birth control pills, which some right-to-lifers claimed constituted murder of a potential human being as fully as did outright abortion.

As before, the debate was not just about life and death, although there was sincere commitment on both sides of the political divide about these issues in themselves. Many antiabortion advocates remained deeply concerned about sexual behavior and not just protection of life. They often opposed birth control measures, particularly combating efforts to make birth control information available to teenagers, despite obvious U.S. problems with sexually transmitted diseases and relatively high U.S. rates of teenage pregnancy. Campaigns to convince young people that they simply should not engage in sex and that birth control might detract from this moral purity drew almost as much passion as did the right-to-life campaign. And this broader canvass meant that "pro-choice" forces, although increasingly on the defensive, were not just defending abortion but sexual freedom more generally.

Emotions ran high, and not just in election campaigns when candidates' views on abortion were carefully probed and hotly debated. Some antiabortion extremists not only attacked abortion clinics but in a few cases even killed doctors or other personnel.

Clearly, in this vital extension of discussions of death, Americans simply could not agree, creating an open political wound that showed no signs of healing. Debates arose in other societies, with results pointing in various directions. By the early twenty-first century, strong Catholic influences in some Central American states generated stronger antiabortion policies. In 2006 Nicaragua passed legislation outlawing abortion, even when the mother's health was at risk.

Abortion policy controversy also surfaced in western Europe, but with results rather different from those in the United States. Debate arose a bit later than in the United States, and it focused more on legislation than court action—a pattern suggested in the initial, state-by-state discussions in the United States but then superseded by the Supreme Court decision and efforts to attack or defend it in the courts. Deep religious objections to abortion played a role in European politics, particularly in the Catholic countries, but this factor was far more muted than across the Atlantic because of Europe's greater secularism and the related absence of any significant Protestant fundamentalism. Above all, Europeans on the whole managed a greater balance between protection of women and protection of the fetus, avoiding the either-or rights debate that so polarized Americans. This meant in turn that all the concerns about death were served to some degree, although in a framework that, by U.S. standards at least, involved some obvious compromises. There was also less concern about using abortion policy as part of a larger strategy to control sexuality.

New discussions in Europe were definitely framed by the same factors that operated in the United States, including dramatic changes in sexual behavior and world population growth. European feminism also surged, although on average slightly less vigorously than in the United States during the 1970s. There was also, however, less pronounced or systematic conservative backlash than occurred in the United States in the 1980s.

Change occurred quickly. Great Britain passed a landmark abortion rights bill—the Abortion Act—in 1967; only Northern Ireland was exempt from this reform, and there abortion was possible only to protect a woman's "mental health."

British liberalization triggered discussion elsewhere, partly because some women began to travel to Britain for operations illegal in their own countries—a form of "abortion tourism" that for a few years included Americans as well. Awareness of rates of illegal abortion and the dangers involved increased at the same time.

Legalizations occurred throughout Europe and Canada during the ensuing fifteen years. Only Belgium and Ireland, the latter because of particularly great Catholic influence, held out. Ireland even attempted to limit the rights of women to travel to Britain for abortion, occasioning some bitter discussion reminiscent of U.S. levels. The Netherlands legalized abortion in 1981, until the twenty-second week of pregnancy, after which a woman had to be in a "crisis situation" to qualify. Slovenia legalized abortion in 1977, Turkey (a Muslim country eager to gain admission to the European Union and usually under secular leadership) did so in 1983. Spain was one of the last European countries to ease restrictions, but even there Catholic opposition was finally overcome, in 1985.

French patterns were instructive, particularly in comparison with the United States but also in contrast to its own past, for the country had long been known for tough restrictions (although often lax enforcement), particularly given long-standing concerns about inadequate population growth as well as the influence of the Catholic Church. A striking French law in 1975 legalized abortion up to the tenth week of pregnancy if the woman was in a "situation of distress"—a phrase that received no definition and was largely ignored in practice. The law stipulated that abortion was not to be used as birth control, although, again, this was not easy to enforce. A patient must be informed of other options, such as adoption, through a private interview and some educational pamphlets, and had to wait at least a week between application and the actual operation. In other words, French law placed more complications around abortion than did many American clinics, without actually restricting access in the early stages of pregnancy. (Switzerland introduced other hurdles, including the requirement that two doctors had to agree to an abortion before it could be performed.) After the tenth week, however, only therapeutic abortions, for the health of the mother, were permitted. The law occasioned vigorous discussion, along lines familiar in the United States, but after it was passed most dissent vanished. The Constitutional Council maintained that the statute adequately respected life, and its success was also due to its obvious compromise between conflicting interests, indeed conflicting views of death. As one commentator put it, "the legislation as a whole is pervaded by compassion for pregnant women, by concern for fetal life, and by expression of the commitment of society as a whole to help minimize occasions for tragic choices between them." The law was accompanied by vigorous efforts to disseminate birth control devices, to avoid unwanted pregnancies, and therefore violation of the fetus in the first place. Financial support for unwed mothers was also increased.

In France and in Europe generally, legalized abortion usually occurred in a hospital setting, rather than in specialized abortion clinics, which also reduced occasions for attack. In Germany and elsewhere, as in France, abortion law focused on issues of human life, not women's rights or a fetus's right to life, and this, too, facilitated compromise and acceptance even amid considerable division of opinion.[3]

To be sure, debate did not end, even in Europe. Catholic concern and the presence of growing Muslim populations provided ongoing religious objections to abortion. The U.S. antiabortion campaign also fueled some European spill-over. But the issue did not create political battlegrounds on the eastern side of the Atlantic, except to an extent in Ireland. Indeed, new drugs like RU 486, which provided contraception after sexual intercourse, were quickly accepted in Europe, precisely because they further limited the need for formal abortion; in contrast, these drugs were long mired in controversy in the United States. Some countries also reduced the age at which a woman could consent to an abortion, from eighteen to sixteen, partly because of concern that Muslim girls would encounter serious family problems if they had to inform their parents that they were pregnant without being married. The trends obviously ran counter to the more conservative measures being considered in the United States, which among other things tried to require more rather than less active parental involvement.

Abortion in the contemporary context raised problems throughout the Western world, because of a commitment to protecting the life of a fetus if not throughout pregnancy, at least in its later stages. Many people agreed that life began before birth and that therefore attitudes toward death—whether traditional, in the sense of protecting a soul, or more modern in the sense of avoiding death wherever possible—did apply. The situation was complicated by concerns about maternal health and mortality and certainly by wider debates about contemporary sexuality. Policy problems and political divisions could be limited, the European example suggested, by making protection of the fetus clear although not absolute, and by separating the abortion issue from any more general concerns about sexuality or the marital status of pregnant women. Here is where the lesser involvement of religion in the European context played a particular role, more than around definitions of life and death. Active promotion of birth control, including promotion among teenagers, did dramatically limit abortion rates in Europe, which, in turn, tended to confirm the more modest reverberations of debates by the 1990s and beyond.

The abortion issue, and particularly intense U.S. concerns, had one final impact on the international front. Frustrated by court rulings in the United States, many U.S. antiabortion activists pressed for efforts to use U.S. policy to discourage abortions in other countries. In 1984 President Ronald Reagan enunciated what became known as the Mexico City Policy, requiring that any nongovernmental organization receiving U.S. funds, for example, in the area of health or family planning in developing nations, would neither perform nor actively promote abortion as a method of birth control. This policy was rescinded by Bill Clinton in 1993, in one of his first acts in office, but restored by George W. Bush in January 2001—again, almost immediately after inauguration. Clearly, international abortion had become a bit of an American political football. The most recent ruling applied to State Department grants as well as Agency for International Development operations. The Bush ruling further extended even to organizations participating in discussions about legalizing abortion—a move opponents quickly described as a Global Gag Rule.

Many international observers widely condemned the American stance, because of the importance of abortion in protecting women's health in many developing countries. The centrality of abortion in family planning in many poor societies, plus the need at least to be able to discuss abortion options when the mother's life was endangered, made the U.S. ruling particularly delicate. Many organizations, in Africa for example, found themselves caught between funding needs and what they saw as best policies. In Kenya, withdrawal of U.S. funds forced the closing of five clinics offering prenatal care; other researchers claimed 50 percent reductions in family health operations in rural areas. The further claim was that a growing number of African women were obtaining unsafe abortions, at great risk to their own lives, because of the narrowing of options.

Abortion concerns surfaced also at the level of global policy discussions concerning population control. United Nations conferences on population policy frequently ended in bitter dispute, with arguments over abortion contributing to the outcome. There was considerable agreement on the issue: World population levels threatened the well-being of many societies, strained the environment, and could contribute directly to conflict. What to do about these levels was far less clear, given dramatic differences on policies relating to life and death.

A 1994 conference in Cairo, although ultimately producing a more harmonious if somewhat bland result, highlighted the divisions. The Norwegian prime minister (a doctor by training) presented a characteristic west European view, which admitted a concern about abortion but believed that it could be managed as part of more general commitment to popular well-being:

> I am pleased by the emerging consensus that everyone should have access to the whole range of family-planning services at an affordable price. Sometimes religion is a major obstacle. This happens when family planning is made a moral issue. But morality cannot only be a question of controlling sexuality and protecting unborn life. Morality is also a question of giving individuals the opportunity of choice, of suppressing coercion of all kinds and abolishing the criminalization

of individual tragedy. Morality becomes hypocrisy if it means accepting mothers' suffering or dying in connection with unwanted pregnancies and illegal abortions, and unwanted children living in misery.

None of us can disregard that abortions occur, and that where they are illegal, or heavily restricted, the life and health of the woman is often at risk. Decriminalizing abortions should therefore be a minimal response to this reality, and a necessary means of protecting the life and health of women.

The prime minister went on to claim that the legalization of abortions in Norway ended illegal operations while not increasing the overall number of abortions—which were among the lowest in the world.

Other delegates vigorously opposed this stance. An Iranian representative, referring to Muslim views, argued against any tolerance for abortion, except when the life of the mother was at stake. The United Arab Emirates spoke out against any implication that abortion might be used as part of family planning. The Vatican specifically noted its belief that "human life begins at the moment of conception. That life must be defended and protected. The Holy See can therefore never condone abortion or policies that favor abortion."[4]

Efforts to reach a compromise that might refer to abortion while renouncing any endorsement for its use as birth control failed. The conference did manage to generate a statement broadly endorsing some effort at birth control, with particular reference to promoting the education of women so that they could make informed choices. But a detailed population control agenda did not emerge, because it simply could not. There was, quite simply, no international consensus about how to both limit population growth and provide adequate protection for human life.

New issues surrounding abortion could be handled within individual societies, as in much of western Europe, where compromises were carefully struck. They did not loom large in some societies where abortion was simply accepted or in other societies, such as most of the Middle East, where there was little dissent from the idea that abortion was evil. But the issue could polarize certain societies as well, because of rooted internal disagreements over what constituted death and what constituted the priorities most deserving legal sanction. And it could certainly inhibit any effort at international consensus. The kind of implicit international agreement that had emerged over the centuries on infanticide—in principle if not always in practice—was nowhere in sight concerning the unborn.

Notes

1. Leslie Regan, *When Abortion Was a Crime: Women, Medicine and Law in the United States, 1867–1973* (Berkeley, 1997); Katha Pollitt, "Abortion History 101," *The Nation*

270 (2000): 10; Rosemary Nossiff, "Discourse, Party and Policy: The Case of Abortion, 1965–1972," *Policy Studies Journal* 26 (1998): 244–256; Johanna Schoen, "Reconceiving Abortion: Medical Practice, Women's Access, and Feminist Politics before and after Roe vs. Wade," *Feminist Studies* 26 (2000): 349–376.

2. http://www.gargaro.com/abortionquotes.html, accessed Feb. 26, 2007; Warren Hern, M.D., *Abortion Practice* (New York, 1984); Beverly McMillan, "How One Doctor Changed Her Mind about Abortion," Focus on the Family pamphlet (Colorado Springs, CO, 1992); http://www.iol.ie/~hlii/theresa.html, pro-life quotes from Mother Teresa, accessed September 21, 2006.

3. Mary Ann Glendon, *Abortion and Divorce in Western Law: American Failures, European Challenges* (Cambridge, MA, 1987), pp. 18–19 and passim; Genevieve Parkes, "Redefining the Legitimacy of Anti-Abortion Pressure Groups in Europe," *Journal of Social Welfare and Family Law* 21 (1999): 285–294.

4. United Nations, *Report of the International Conference on Population and Development*, Cairo, September 5–13, 1994.

CHAPTER 10

The Death Penalty
and Its Enemies:
New Global Divisions

Increased revulsion against death, new efforts to fight or conceal it, might logically lead to further attacks on the death penalty, picking up the reform efforts of the nineteenth century and the quieter, though not uniform, trends of the early twentieth century at least in the Western world. This is exactly what happened in some places. More systematic attempts to ban the death penalty entirely led not only to domestic reforms but also to unprecedented efforts to use world opinion to attack this use of death everywhere. Both new and old organizations joined the parade: Various human rights groups—nongovernmental organizations like Amnesty International—took up the cause, and they were joined by a newly activist papacy and Catholic hierarchy. The death penalty, these reformers argued, was wrong no matter what the crime involved.

Countercurrents existed as well, however. A number of societies simply persisted in believing that the death penalty was essential. No society tried to go back to the rampant use of death that had prevailed before the nineteenth century, but certain kinds of crimes still, in many areas, seemed to require the supreme sacrifice. Equally interesting, a few societies, headed by many U.S. states, actually reversed the modern trend and began to insist not just on restoring the death penalty but on employing it actively. Here was another crucial rift over death in the contemporary world.

There were several reasons to build on earlier trends and fight the death penalty more vigorously and systematically after World War II. The horrors of the war itself, and the revelations of massive imposition of death during the Holocaust, encouraged many countries to take a second look at their own practices. Increased awareness of the misapplication of the death penalty added fuel to the fire. New technologies—from fingerprinting to, later, genetic identifications—made it increasingly possible to discover after the fact when the wrong person had been executed. No decade passed, after 1960, without some revelations of this sort in areas where the death penalty persisted.

In the United States, and to some extent elsewhere, evidence of biased use of the death penalty created new concerns as well. By the 1950s a variety of studies showed that the death penalty was far more likely to be imposed on poor people than on rich for the same crimes, simply because the rich could afford better defense lawyers and would make a better impression on juries. The warden of Sing Sing prison even earlier, in the 1930s, had blasted the death penalty for the inequality of its use. "Not only does capital punishment fail in its justification, but no punishment could be invented with so many inherent defects ... The defendant of wealth and position never goes to the electric chair or the gallows."[1] And there was more: The imposition of the penalty was also racist. African Americans, Mexican Americans, and immigrants were disproportionate victims. Twice as many African Americans as whites were put to death in North Carolina in the middle decades of the twentieth century, for example; nationwide, between 1930 and 1950, African Americans were overrepresented among the executed by 550 percent, in relation to their share of the population as a whole. Famous cases, including the execution of seven black youths in Martinsville, Virginia, in 1951 for rape, drew increasing attention to the racial inequities of death penalty imposition, particularly in the southern states. As a backer of a bill to abolish capital punishment in the District of Columbia argued, "As it is now applied the death penalty is nothing but an arbitrary discrimination against an occasional victim."

Even the modern secrecy in administering the death penalty was used to argue against it. If death was so essential, a new breed of reformers argued, why did the district attorneys and others who sought its imposition not go to see it? Warden Lawes again: "Is it necessary as an example to others to kill the murderer? If it is, why surround the act with so much secrecy? It is surely not a deterrent example to perform an action furtively. If the state really believes that execution is necessary to deter others, it should execute open and unashamed. Does not this furtiveness carry the suggestive thought that the spectacle of legalized killing by the state breeds on the part of the unthinking masses a hardened outlook toward murder which is harmful rather than effective as a deterrent?"[2]

Changing attitudes produced one definite result in the United States by the early 1950s: the definitive end to lynchings. For several decades a growing segment of the public in the West and South had been turning against lynching, on grounds that even if the death penalty was still justified it had to be applied through careful legal proceedings, not mob action. International opinion weighed in as well, with growing protests from the 1890s onward at these contradictions of American ideals of civil rights and human dignity. Mexico increasingly intervened against lynchings of its citizens. Japan as well as Europe blasted the violence directed toward African Americans. Japanese headlines, for example, featured stories like "White Brutality: Lynching against a Black" or "An Atrocious Lynching," noting that "we can hardly imagine such brutality has occurred ... in a civilized country." Protests from Britain, Germany, and elsewhere added to the chorus, prompted by visiting African American rights advocates. "Even the most intelligent foreigner," noted one at a Berlin confer- ence, "finds it difficult to believe that colored men, women and children are still being lynched in the United States." Hundreds of letters and petitions . reached American embassies after publicized lynchings, and European papers often sent correspondents to the South to cover the most vicious attacks. In this climate, with both domestic and foreign outrage against unwarranted death, U.S. governments began to act. Gradually, the federal government recognized a responsibility to move against lynchings. Shock at Nazi racial policies in the 1930s and 1940s helped solidify American opinion against these extremes of racial violence. Changing attitudes and better policing ultimately ended the long history of lynching. The last lynching of a Mexican American occurred in 1928, the last attack of this sort on an African American occurred in 1951. Federal legislation specifically directed against racist violence stiffened, particu- larly from the 1960s onward.[3]

Change in Europe and Latin America

In terms of the death penalty itself, European initiative proved crucial. The British case was instructive—although in fact the British did not in the end provide the leadership they had on other death issues. A major new move occurred in 1948 as the British government introduced an experiment suspending capital punishment while a special Royal Commission looked into alternatives to imposing death in cases of conviction for murder. British politicians had recurrently debated the death penalty since the middle of the nineteenth century, although after the number of crimes punishable by death had been reduced primarily to murder and executions had been moved from public to prison venues, no actual change occurred. During the 1920s and 1930s, several reform groups worked vigorously to reintroduce the idea of full abolition. As a Church of England leader argued in 1935, these groups believed that "few public actions would at the present time so much demonstrate and secure an advance in the ethics of civilization as the abolition of the Death Penalty." The modern aversion to death could not have been more clearly applied to the question of punishment. Public senti- ment continued to suggest questions about capital punishment as well. About half of all death sentences passed during the 1920s and 1930s were commuted, particularly of course where women were involved. A 1938 public opinion poll found 45 percent in favor of abolition outright, a minority still but suggesting movement toward change (as was true in northwestern Europe generally).

New opportunities for reform emerged when the Labour government took power in 1945, for British Labourites were far more sympathetic to abolition than were conservatives. Reform advocates, including many police and prison officials, urged that the death penalty did not really deter serious crime and constituted in itself an offense against humanity. "The knowledge that society is deliberately hunting a man to his death, and when it has caught him taking away his life with the hideous trappings of legal execution, cannot fail to lessen the respect for the sanctity of human life ... It is absolutely no answer to say that the convicted man has himself taken human life, since by carrying out the act of execution society is rendering itself culpable of precisely the same act as that for which the condemned man has been convicted." A host of opinion leaders, including all the major newspapers, moved against capital punishment.

In the actual parliamentary debate in 1948–1949, however, the reformers lost. Conservative opposition hardened; the belief that the death penalty was an essential instrument against crime remained widespread. Attention to the reduction of whipping in prison—where abolition was enacted—actually hurt the capital punishment reform: Conservatives, and much of the public, contended that with one deterrent now removed, it was unsafe to take away the other. Increasing crime rates and a sense that the war had unleashed new forces of disorder also prompted public hesitation. Death penalties enacted against some Nazi war criminals, in the Nuremburg trials, also contributed to a sense that certain acts were so dreadful that only death could compensate. Up to 75 percent of the British public now favored retention of capital punishment as the only suitable response to deliberate murder—the old idea of a life for a life was very much alive, as one newspaper put it. Proponents argued that the death penalty was essential to show that some crimes are more awful than others, and that "wickedness" had to be judged and treated as wickedness as part of maintaining an active community conscience. Inept leadership on the part of the Labour Party, now in some disarray more generally, also entered in. Opponents continued to hammer home that capital punishment did not in fact deter crime, that it was really only an act of social retribution that was morally indefensible—but they failed.[4]

The issue reemerged almost immediately, however, and by the 1950s it was back on the British legislative agenda. The sense of moral uncertainty about the death penalty had become widespread, even if public opinion was still fickle on specifics. Furthermore, a number of key trials in which there was considerable suspicion that innocent people had been condemned to death helped revive reformist agitation. Even conservative opposition began to moderate. The result, however, still fell short of full transformation. A new Homicide Bill, passed in 1957, provided the first legislative breakthrough on capital punishment for a century, by dividing homicides into greater and lesser categories, with only the first, or capital, type now subject to the death penalty. This was a compromise that satisfied few groups fully, but it did show that opinion on this classic issue was once more on the move.[5]

More forceful action occurred in other countries, with Great Britain joining in a bit later. Sweden and Denmark had abolished the death penalty after World War I. More states took action after World War II: Italy, Finland, and Austria. Germany moved against capital punishment, for any crime, in the early 1950s. Spain and at last Great Britain enacted abolition of capital punishment for crimes other than war crimes in the 1960s and then extended this to crimes under military law or in wartime as well. By the end of the 1960s, all the member states of the European Common Market had agreed on action. Public opinion varied, and in some cases abolition occurred against majority sentiment; but nowhere was there great outcry, and by the 1960s debates were usually minimal.

By this point, in fact, the whole European Union—which was beginning to expand rapidly—made abolition of the death penalty a requirement for membership. Official memoranda also pledged the organization to oppose the death penalty in other places, including particularly the United States. The moral fervor involved, at least among the European leadership, was undeniable: "Although Member States' experiences in abolition varied in time, they shared common ground—that of the inhumane, unnecessary and irreversible character of capital punishment, no matter how cruel the crime committed by the offender." The penalty was "a denial of human dignity." European arguments went on to contest any factual basis for believing that capital punishment deterred crime, and in any event, civilized punishment should emphasize rehabilitation, not retribution. They further stated that in the long run maintaining human dignity would have the most positive impact on the crime rate. The chance of miscarriage of justice, even when the greatest care was taken, provided the final argument. "As a result, criminal policy programmes were intentionally humanized in order to pursue the view under which the State's actions should not have human beings as victims, but also that of the promotion of the human person as one of the major purposes of criminology."[6]

In 2003, Protocol 13 of the European Convention on Human Rights went into effect, the first legally binding international treaty to abolish the death penalty in all circumstances with no exceptions—going beyond the required action by individual member states. A long, arduous, and frequently seesawing debate seemed to have come to an end throughout much of the European continent.

The United States: A Different Drummer

For several decades in the mid-twentieth century, U.S. trends seemed to echo those in Europe—recalling the fact that a similar basis for opposition to capital punishment had been emerging since the late eighteenth century, with U.S. leadership on some points in the nineteenth century. Executions in the United States declined fairly steadily from the 1930s to the 1960s, with 166 a year in the Depression decade and 72 in the 1950s. Public opinion moved steadily toward opposition. In the 1930s, about 62 percent of all Americans still favored the penalty. Men were more supportive than women, East Coasters less supportive than people in other regions, the more educated slightly less supportive than the less. By 1966, only 42 percent favored capital punishment, with only 11 percent having no opinion; by this point, although most of the earlier divisions still prevailed, some Catholics were beginning to move into the opposition camp, whereas previously they had been slightly more favorable than Protestants. Republicans regularly favored the penalty more than Democrats did, although here, too, there was a decline over time. African Americans were consistently more opposed than other Americans.[7]

Several factors encouraged changes in the public view during the 1950s. Many people were revolted by the execution of Ethel and Julius Rosenberg for espionage in 1953. The Caryl Chessman case in California, involving execution of a convicted criminal who had written several popular books, and the fact that his crime was kidnapping for purpose of robbery—which many people thought should not be regarded as a capital crime—also drew fire. A murder conviction of a prominent Ohio doctor in 1954 (a case that became the basis for the movie *The Fugitive*), where later evidence proved that someone else had done the crime, also contributed to changes in public view, although the death penalty in this instance had not been imposed. Growing public awareness of the continued racial bias in administration of capital punishment, with the wildly disproportionate number of African American victims, added another element to the rising chorus of concern.

Many individual states began to ban capital punishment entirely. Delaware did so in 1958, Alaska and Hawaii did so upon becoming states in 1959; Oregon rejected the penalty in the public referendum in 1964. Political leaders in many regions voiced opposition, and several liberal Supreme Court justices began to invite challenges to the constitutionality of the death penalty. A host of groups arose to carry the cause further.

During the late 1960s and early 1970s the Supreme Court sent mixed signals about capital punishment in several rulings, but its deliberations helped call the death penalty into question nationwide, and executions were actually ended for several years pending a more definitive ruling. The ultimate issue was whether the death penalty represented "cruel and unusual" punishment, thereby violating constitutional rights. The California Supreme Court made this ruling in 1972, and then in June 1972, a 5-4 majority of the federal Supreme Court, in *Furman v. Georgia*, delivered the same finding, holding the death penalty in violation of the Eighth and Fourteenth Amendments. A leading opponent of capital punishment hailed the ruling: "There will no longer be any more capital punishment in the United States." More than 600 death row prisoners had their sentences commuted to prison terms.

But optimism was premature, for within four short years the nation pulled away from the European-Latin American pattern, restoring capital punishment in many states with a vengeance. Backlash to the *Furman* ruling developed quickly, particularly in southern states like Florida. By 1976, thirty-five states had passed new death penalty laws that sought to skirt the Supreme Court's objections. Even more revealing was the fact that public support for the death penalty began to climb rapidly, reversing the earlier trend. By 1976, 66 percent of all Americans favored capital punishment.

What was going on? Clearly, confrontation with a death penalty-free society galvanized resistance. Anxieties about a rising crime rate—not always accurate, in that crime rose less rapidly than people believed, and even at points declined when public opinion insisted that doom was at hand—contributed greatly. Many Americans reacted against the apparent license of the 1960s, coming to believe that a larger dose of tradition was essential against forces of disorder. Conservative politicians, particularly, although not exclusively, Republicans, played on law and order themes and often boasted that they would not hesitate to impose death to keep criminals in line. Surges in conservative sentiment and in fundamentalist Protestantism—both involving currents aligned with the death penalty—changed the national context. Cold War tensions might also have contributed, making Americans more anxious to shore up defenses against threat than were western Europeans or Latin Americans. Was there a racist element as well, in reaction to civil rights gains and in belief that African Americans were disproportionately likely to commit foul crimes? Certainly the reintroduction of the death penalty resumed the pattern of racial distinctions, and many Americans seemed to accept this without question. One study suggested a strong correlation between states with large percentages of African Americans and commitment to the death penalty—although an even stronger correlation with levels of income inequality, indicating also an anxiety about threats to wealth such that the death penalty seemed a vital defense.[8]

In 1976 the Supreme Court, in *Gregg v. Georgia* and some related cases, reversed field and ruled that the death penalty did not automatically violate constitutional protections, when judges and jurors were given guidelines to decide between prison and a death sentence for people convicted of capital murder. The ruling argued that capital punishment did not violate "the evolving standards of decency which mark the progress of a maturing society"—in direct opposition to definitions of progress in death in many other societies by this point. The United States had decided once again that the death penalty might be essential to deter crime and constituted a legitimate form of retribution.

The result was, by pre-*Furman* standards, a torrent of U.S. executions, propelling the nation to the top rank of death-wielding societies at least in terms of state policy. Although many individual states continued to ban capital punishment or, like New York, hedged it with virtually impenetrable constraints, others, headed by Texas and Virginia, jumped in with every appearance of enthusiasm. During the thirty years after *Gregg*, 1,050 people had been executed by thirty-six states or the federal government. For a time, until a new ruling in 2005, several U.S. states even allowed execution of minors convicted as adults of murder—making the United States only one of two nations, along with Somalia, not to outlaw capital punishment for children at least in principle. In the United States, nineteen juveniles were executed from 1990 to 2005, more than in any other country.

Americans were still willing to discuss methods of capital punishment. Many states began to give prisoners sedatives to calm them before their execution, although a few critics judged this concession too soft. Reflecting continued uneasiness with administering the death penalties, vigorous debates often surfaced about whether particular methods were humane or cruel. The electric chair, an earlier twentieth-century U.S. innovation designed to minimize suffering and apply modern technology, was still used in some places, but the visible effects it produced, and some painful failures, had brought it into some disrepute. But at the end of the century new questions arose about lethal injections, with many doctors refusing to participate on grounds that victims suffered great, if silent, pain. Several states, including California, suspended the use of injection in 2006, pending investigation as to whether it constituted "cruel and unusual punishment." Critics worried that these discussions concealed larger issues: If one opposed the death penalty, did methodology matter very much? If one favored it, might a bit of pain seem appropriate as part of the larger desire to provide deterrence and retribution? Clearly, however, some Americans were eager to reconcile their acceptance of capital punishment with their reluctance and distaste, by trying to be sure that the death involved was swift and humane.

The more fundamental case—about the death penalty itself, in any form—was not closed, of course. International pressure mounted against U.S. trends, and a variety of domestic reform groups stepped up their efforts. Most mainstream religious organizations vigorously opposed the death penalty. Widely publicized instances where people were executed and later proved innocent created pressure, particularly when, as was often the case, inept defenses had been mounted because the defendants were too poor to afford competent counsel. There was also mounting sentiment against the execution of individuals who were mentally retarded (a practice outlawed by the Supreme Court in 2002, after years of effort by human rights activists). There were even growing doubts about the legitimacy of death in retribution and about how much comfort the penalty provided to grieving families. By 2000, public opinion was evolving once again, in what was clearly an area of both concern and uncertainty. From a high of 80 percent support for capital punishment in 1994, levels had dropped to 64 percent by 2005. An Illinois governor, appalled by executions of people later exonerated, suspended all executions in his state in 2000. Several other states joined in, not abolishing the practice outright but imposing moratoriums. The story continues—again in contrast to western Europe and other regions where, at least by current evidence, the book has been closed.[9]

Other Global Options

The movement against the death penalty, despite the contrariness of some elements in the United States, was increasingly widespread. By 2005, seventy-six countries had abolished capital punishment, and thirty-six more had done so with minor qualifications. The unanimity of the members of the European Union, and of countries like Turkey that aspired to membership, was particularly impressive; Canada also provided an important instance. But Latin American countries had also moved substantially into this camp, in some cases well before the twenty-first century. Revulsion against the executions conducted by authoritarian regimes in the 1960s and 1970s, as in Argentina, contributed to the movement, along with the influence of Western opinion. (Abolition in some Latin American countries was qualified, however, by the fact that extralegal death squads often continued to operate beyond state control, enforcing the wishes of landlords or business by killing leading dissidents.)[10] Eastern Europe surged in the same legal direction after the fall of communism in 1991, and obviously the countries that sought membership in the European Union were particularly alacritous. Russia also abolished the penalty de facto (though not yet in law) in 1999, again a sign of the spread of new standards. A growing number of African countries also began to participate in the ban by the early twenty-first century, including South Africa in its postapartheid constitution of 1995, in part reflecting the greater spread of democracy.

There were notable exceptions to the current, however. Most Islamic nations held back, and executions under Islamic law, for example for crimes such as adultery, continued to occur in some of the more conservative areas. The Taliban regime in Afghanistan, although an atypical extreme, conducted several public executions in soccer stadiums.

China also held out. Criminal executions had long been part of the Chinese commitment to maintain order, and the communist regime, although opening to reforms in the economic sphere, hardly relaxed its hold. China led the world in the number of annual executions in the early twenty-first century, although on a per capita basis, the United States was essentially on par.

India also maintained the death penalty. The Indian Penal Code imposed capital punishment not only for murder, but also for waging war against the government, aiding the suicide of a child or insane person, fabricating evidence in order to convict someone else of a capital crime, kidnapping for ransom and gang robbery that involved murder. Recently the penalty was also extended against terrorism, assistance for *sati*, and certain types of trade in narcotics. As a prominent policewoman put it, "The death penalty is necessary in certain cases to do justice to society's anger against the crime." But debate over capital punishment remains active in India. A number of reformers oppose it outright, arguing among other things that it is most often applied against the poor. And, in part because of hesitations about actually imposing death, rates of conviction for heinous crimes is very low—about 6 percent of all cases brought to trial under this category. On the other hand, some Indians (including some police and some conservative Hindus) who believe in capital punishment continue to take matters into their own hands, bypassing the government and killing offenders privately.[11]

Japan provides another intriguing exception to arguably global trends. Here, too, the death penalty has been maintained. Nationalist pride, after the humiliation of World War II, has caused some resistance to the imposition of international standards in the human rights arena. More important is the deep Japanese revulsion against crime, which contributes to the conclusion that capital punishment remains an essential deterrent. On the other hand, the postwar Japanese constitution severely limited the number of crimes for which the death penalty might apply, reserving only particularly brutal crimes in this category; this was a considerable change from earlier policy, and aligns Japan with international standards to a considerable extent. The government continues to insist that Japanese public opinion opposes full elimination of the penalty, although in fact polls suggest that the Japanese are skeptical about the deterrence value and appeals for full abolition are gaining ground steadily. Amnesty International campaigns in Japan have raised wide support. In fact, low Japanese crime rates also mean that the death penalty is very rarely applied. Even more than in the Indian case, Japan constitutes a partial and perhaps transitional exception to wider trends.[12]

World Opinion

By the 1990s, something like an identifiable world opinion began to be mobilized against the death penalty, in any form. The voice of the Catholic Church was an important component here, as popes and the Catholic hierarchy spoke against the death penalty generally and also intervened in specific cases with appeals for clemency. As early as 1971, the United Nations had passed a nonbinding resolution, urging governments to consider abolition. In 1990, the Organization of American States (of which the United States was a member) adopted the densely titled Protocol to the American Convention on Human Rights to Abolish the Death Penalty. The commitment of leading international NGOs, headed by Amnesty International, was a vital factor. Amnesty, founded in 1961 to oppose human rights violations, fairly quickly turned against capital punishment systematically, leading campaigns in many countries. Amnesty also spoke out in individual cases. Several instances in which women were sentenced to death for sexual crimes in Islamic regions—in one recent Nigerian case, not only death but death by public stoning—prompted widespread petition campaigns, using the Internet, which often induced the governments involved to reverse field. Various units of the United Nations also continued to pass resolutions against the death penalty.

World opinion was of course not uniform. Its mobilizers used regions in which opposition to the death penalty was widespread and claimed a moral urgency that could distract from the fact that many places and many people disagreed. But the sense that the death penalty was uncivilized, along with educational programs showing how often innocent people were wrongly convicted and punished, gained ground widely. Countries responsible for the greatest number of executions—notably, China, the United States, Iran, and Saudi Arabia, where 94 percent of all executions occurred by the late 1990s—received special attention. The United States was a particular target, partly because it was an open society, responsive to world opinion to some degree and with a large public opinion segment internally mobilized against capital punishment, partly because—to the converted—the death penalty seemed a particular anomaly given U.S. human rights ideals more generally. Individual, widely publicized sentences, particularly where minority individuals or people of arguably diminished capacity were involved, drew massive international petition campaigns, aimed at governors of the states in question. And although these rarely succeeded in the cases involved, they did begin to contribute to the new American doubts about the death penalty by the early twenty-first century.

By this point a host of ad hoc groups had formed to press the global cause—in Britain, Canada, France, Denmark, Slovenia, Italy, and elsewhere. A Europe-wide organization was headquartered in Norway, campaigning actively but also contacting condemned prisoners to offer moral and legal support. A Swiss branch even produced hip-hop music composed by U.S. death row inmates. Canadian unions, such as the Union of Public Employees, blasted capital punishment in Texas, particularly in instances where the criminals involved were mentally impaired. Religious organizations (including many in the United States) and prominent individuals such as former Secretary of State Madeleine Albright and South African Bishop Desmond Tutu, joined in as well. Various organizations visited parliamentary delegates in countries where the death penalty was still in effect. A group called Hands Off Cain combined with Italian parliamentarians to press officials in a number of Caribbean countries, in 1999. Proposals surfaced to organize tourist boycotts of places like Texas, or to restrict investment, although these had little echo. Without question, a level and geographic range of moral fervor had developed of the sort that, a century before, had successfully combated remnants of slavery on an international basis. Few other causes roused such widespread passion by the early twenty-first century.

The Death Penalty: A Status Report

Obviously, what passes for world opinion, headed by European nations and institutions like the Catholic Church, has turned against the death penalty over the past several decades. Decisions by coalitions such as the European Union to require renunciation of the death penalty as a condition of membership are truly historic, given the long tradition of capital punishment in virtually all organized societies. In this context, efforts by NGOs, like Amnesty International, against the death penalty generally and against specific applications viewed as particularly unfair, gain great attention and not infrequent success.

At the same time, recent history suggests the possibility of some public volatility on the subject of capital punishment. Although public opinion in places like western Europe has been moving toward rejection of the death penalty for many decades, capping a trend first launched two centuries ago, oscillations have been undeniable, depending a bit on what political party gains power and what the most recent crime statistics suggest. Conversion to full rejection is fairly recent, and only time will test its durability.

Certainly, divisions still complicate the subject. Debate is currently over in the European Union, but there are minorities still hopeful of restoring capital punishment for particular types of crimes. Public controversy remains active in places like the United States that have stood apart from the broader international trends. Several key societies remain so convinced of the need for a death penalty that serious public discussion has not even emerged. Whether divisions will persist or harden is another important question for the future.

Again, changes of great magnitude have occurred, directly associated with the larger reconsiderations of death and its meaning. They seem to be gaining ground particularly in recent decades. Global agreement on the subject remains elusive, however.

A reminder of the passions and divisions over capital punishment in the contemporary world occurred late in 2006, when Saddam Hussein, former ruler of Iraq, was hanged for war crimes. His hanging was recorded on a cell phone, accompanied by cheers and jeers from many Iraqis in attendance. The episode, combined with some sense his trial had not been fair, stirred a major outcry in many parts of the world—that such punishments were wrong, or that they should be accompanied by respect, or that they should be rigorously private—or some combination thereof. In Europe particularly, the hanging spurred efforts to get the United Nations to ban capital punishment altogether. The debate, obviously, continued.

Conclusion: Death Penalty and Abortion

Abortion and the death penalty both provided dramatic political flashpoints by the late 1990s and early 2000s. U.S. elections could be polarized by attempts to portray candidates as "soft" on the death penalty (and, by implication, therefore, lax on crime) or "anti-life" (or anti-woman) on abortion. Societies in Europe and elsewhere were somewhat less roiled; although abortion was a hot-button issue in some Central American and European societies, they obviously developed a more assertive moral identity through their opposition to capital punishment. The new elements in both issues, linked in part to new concerns about death, helped explain the lack of agreement and the difficulty of establishing definitive policies.

Globally, and within individual societies like the United States, the result could be near-gridlock. NGOs hammered against the death penalty worldwide, but societies like China, much of the Islamic world, and some individual U.S. states seemed deaf to these pleas. Similar divisions described attitudes and policies toward abortion. Definitions of appropriate death policy rested at the core of these debates, and this in itself was a new element in international relations. But there seemed no early likelihood of a resolution of impassioned differences.

Obviously, significant changes in attitudes and policies toward both abortion and capital punishment occurred in many parts of the world during the past half century. On the whole, the movement has involved wider criticisms of the death penalty and new openness to abortion, but amid great debate and disagreement. The two topics combined raise, as commentators have often noted, some interesting issues of consistency.

How, an antiabortionist can well argue, can U.S. or European liberals be so passionately opposed to killing even brutal murderers, when they easily countenance the killing of innocent fetuses? The question can be somewhat unfair: Few pro-choice advocates are entirely comfortable with abortion. Europeans, particularly, have worked hard to limit abortion even while maintaining its legality. But some issues remain.

And of course the question can be reversed. How can U.S. antiabortionists fight so hard for their cause while vigorously defending the death penalty and sometimes even urging its extension (and sometimes at an extreme, even countenancing the killing of abortion clinic personnel)?

A few groups struggled for what might seem full consistency. The Catholic hierarchy, most notably, became equally adamant in opposing abortion and the death penalty alike.

Full consistency, however, was rare, for two reasons. First, issues were often highly complicated. Abortion-rights advocates sincerely believed that they were protecting the life and health of mothers, so that their anti-death credentials remained essentially intact. Advocates of the death penalty often contended, equally sincerely, that this punishment was an essential protection against higher levels of murder and other vicious crimes—so that, again, there was consistency at base. Additionally, of course, abortion and death penalty campaigns, for and against, involved issues beyond death itself—issues about sexuality, or race, or feminism that could pull away from exclusive attention on minimizing death.

Notes

1. Lewis Lawes, *Twenty Years in Sing Sing* (New York, 1932), p. 302.

2. Lawes, *Twenty Years*, as above.

3. Mary Jane Brown, *Eradicating This Evil: Women in the American Anti-Lynching Movement* (New York, 2000); and Philip Dray, *At the Hands of Persons Unknown: The Lynching of Black America* (New York, 2002).

4. Victor Bailey, "The Shadow of the Gallows: The Death Penalty and the British Labour Government, 1945-51," *Law and History Review* 18 (1990).

5. James Christoph, "Captial Punishment and British Party Responsibility," *Political Science Quarterly* 77 (1962): 19-35.

6. EU Memorandum on the Death Penalty, http://www.eurunion.org/legislat/deathpenalty/eumemorandum.htm, accessed October 9, 2006.

7. Hazel Erskine, "The Polls: Capital Punishment," *Public Opinion Quarterly* 34 (1970): 290-307; Barbara Norrander, "The Multi-Layered Impact of Public Opinion on Capital Punishment Implementation in the American States," *Political Research Quarterly* 53 (2000): 771-793.

8. David Jacobs and Jason T. Carmichael, "The Political Sociology of the Death Penalty," *American Sociological Review* 67 (2002): 109-131.

9. Amnesty International, *The Death Penalty in America; Study Guide* (2006); Michael Radelet and Marian Borg, "The Changing Nature of Death Penalty Debates," *Annual Review of Sociology* 26 (2000): 43–61.

10. Francisco Panizza, "Human Rights: Global Culture and Social Fragmentation," *Bulletin of Latin American Research* 12 (1993): 205–214.

11. Julia Eckert, "Death and the Nation: State Killing in India," in Austin Sarat and Christian Boulanger, eds., *The Cultural Lives of Capital Punishment* (Stanford, CA, 2005), pp. 195–218.

12. John Peck, "Japan, the United Nations, and Human Rights," *Asian Survey* 32 (1992): 217–229; see also "Public Attention Focuses on Capital Punishment," *Japan Times Weekly*, May 2, 1987, p. 4.

CHAPTER 11

Contemporary War and Contemporary Death

A poll in 2006 asked a national sample how many American lives lost would be tolerable in war. The most common answer was zero. Of those willing to risk a bit, the median response was five hundred. Of course, the poll might have been silly: The war was hypothetical, without indication as to what importance the public would assign to it. And the poll came in the midst of widespread disillusionment with the engagement in Iraq. Still, the response might be interesting: Could a great power, which as a matter of fact had fought frequently from the 1960s onward, continue to maintain its military commitments amid this kind of public hesitation about death?

The growing aversion to death and the desire to limit its reach crashed repeatedly against the realities of twentieth–twenty-first-century warfare. Efforts at consistency can be identified, but they were overwhelmed by unprecedented slaughter. This in turn raised questions about the impact of war on attitudes toward death, for the mixture was complicated. Special issues arose for the United States, one of the leaders in death aversion but also, with a combination of reluctance and zeal, emerging as the world's leading superpower, with the military obligations this status seemed to impose. After 1945, the United States was noticeably more often at war than other major societies, and it struggled to accommodate this role with its considerable aversion to untimely death. Changing attitudes toward death did not shape the history of modern war, but they had a definite impact, particularly where the United States was involved.

There are several strands in this intricate, often repellent, tapestry. Efforts at consistency showed particularly in the growing attempts to improve military medicine, to save lives that once would have been lost to disease or battlefield fatalities. From the mid-nineteenth century onward, as we have seen, Western military efforts were accompanied by growing medical staffs. Florence Nightingale launched a new nursing presence with British troops in the Crimean War. Medical programs associated with the U.S. Civil War showed a similar interest in improved care, although results were mixed. Military medicine improved far more rapidly in the twentieth century, resulting in markedly lower death rates, in the forces of industrialized nations, than would have occurred otherwise. By the time of the U.S. invasion of Iraq, in 2003, advances in surgery and the capacity to airlift badly injured troops to full hospital settings (in Germany, for example) saved many troops from death, despite devastating injuries. The ability to prevent death from head wounds, in particular, showed progress, although often at the cost of a permanently impaired existence thereafter. As in civilian life, questions were raised about the advisability of using some of the medical interventions now possible—but there was no doubt about the consistency with other approaches to contemporary death.

There were also some continuing efforts to regulate warfare through international agreements like the ongoing series of Geneva Conventions. Use of poison gas was banned after World War I. Disarmament programs sought to limit naval weaponry during the 1920s, although with limited effect, and again applied to nuclear armaments and rocket delivery from the 1960s onward, although again with modest gains as the number of nuclear powers continued to expand rapidly.

Consistency showed from another angle as well: Many people in Western countries, especially Great Britain, reacted to the massive slaughter of World War I by becoming pacifists: No cause, in this argument, was worth the devastation and loss of life of contemporary warfare. A similar surge of pacifism affected Japan after the atomic bomb attacks in 1945. Reasons for pacifism went beyond revulsion against death, but the connection was important. Pacifism declined in the West with the rise of Nazi Germany and then the Cold War, but the sentiment persisted. Many west Europeans—and perhaps particularly Germans—welcomed the evolution of their societies after World War II toward more civilian directions, away from massive military commitments, even though in one sense this marked a reduction in world power: It was good, after two major European conflicts in the first half of the century, not to have to worry so much about potential death. Certainly, as we will see, many people became increasingly sensitive to news about military casualties, a clear indication that larger attitudes toward death were being applied to wartime situations.

Globally, however, new death concerns obviously did not govern contemporary military developments. More people were killed by wars and civil wars in the twentieth century, by a massive margin, than had ever been killed before. The partial list shown in Table 11.1 is staggering.

Table 11.1 Death Count: All Sides, Combat and Civilian (Best Estimates)*

War	Military Deaths
World War I	8.5 million
World War II	55 million, including Holocaust-related deaths
Jewish Holocaust	6 million (standard figure disputed by revisionists)
Korean War	5 million; 55,000 Americans
Iran-Iraq War (1979–1988)	1.2 million
Rwanda Genocide	800,000 to 1,071,000 killed between April 6 and mid-July 1994

*These figures do not include wounded, missing in action, or prisoners of war who were never declared dead.[1]

Why, in a century unprecedentedly devoted to death fighting, could all this unfold?

Three or four ingredients combined to make it happen. Most obviously, the technology available to kill people on a massive scale outstripped cultural constraints on death—by a wide margin. The U.S. Civil War had already given some indication of the potential here, when industrial weapons were applied to warfare. Imperialist armies in the later nineteenth century, supplied with artillery or machine guns, could cut down many thousands of native troops, as happened in several battles in Africa. But it was World War I that showed the full potential: Pounding artillery, gas attacks, the use of tanks, the introduction of bombing from airplanes led to huge slaughter. And from this point, the technology arsenal expanded steadily: Air strikes grew in potency during the 1930s, in the ramp-up to World War II both in China and in places like Spain; rockets added to devastation during World War II itself; the addition of nuclear weapons accelerated death-dealing potential as well, although, of course, they have been used only twice thus far. Deployment of gas chambers during the Holocaust applied technology to the perverted slaughter of civilians. The list is long.

Much of the new technology allowed death to be delivered impersonally, which helps explain how soldiers could assimilate the normal modern distaste for death in their personal lives but still deal it out in war. Of course individual reactions varied; some military personnel were untroubled by their role in applying the technology but others—like one of the pilots involved in the first atomic strikes against Japan—suffered lifelong guilt and disorientation.

Additionally, not every society accepted new death concerns in any event. This might have been particularly true when population pressure expanded but a full death revolution—in the sense of significant improvements in normal life expectancy—had yet to occur. The huge death totals in African or Cambodian civil strife in the latter twentieth and early twenty-first centuries—with literally 2 to 3 million death totals in individual conflicts like southern Sudan or the Congo—did not involve terribly sophisticated technologies. Repeating rifles and machetes did most of the damage. Clearly, in the heat of battle, novel concerns about inappropriate death did not apply in cases of this sort.

Still more important, and often involving industrial societies where death attitudes had changed in some respects, was the capacity for hatreds to override death constraints. Here, too, developments built on some of the complexities that had emerged in the nineteenth century, including nationalism and modern forms of racism. Germans, to take the obvious example, had participated strongly in medical advances against death in the nineteenth and early twentieth centuries. They had engaged in some of the reductions of death ceremonialism and in other changes that suggested serious recalculation of traditional attitudes. But, after the searing death experiences of World War I and subsequent dislocations, and under the leadership of an anti-Semitic zealot, many Germans came to the conclusion that normal constraints on death did not apply to Jews. Of course, many did not know precisely what was happening during the Holocaust years, and many who probably did have some idea were careful not to find out too explicitly. But the fact was that not only Nazi leadership, but also some fairly ordinary foot soldiers, became very comfortable leading Jewish civilians, including women and children, to slaughter. Hatred could override.

Passion could operate on smaller scales. Elements of U.S. military forces both in Korea and Vietnam and later in Iraq, under intense pressure from the enemy whom they also saw as racially different, periodically cracked and slaughtered unarmed groups of civilians, out of some mixture of sheer brutality, fear, and retaliation. The exceptions were uncommon; they were against U.S. military policy, which sought to be much more precise, but they could be quite bloody. Hatred, again, could override.

Technology and, often, hatred combined in what was perhaps the most significant countervailing current in contemporary warfare, the blurring of the boundary between military and civilian. This was not, somewhat ironically, a major problem in World War I: There were civilian casualties in places like northern France, and the Germans attacked some civilian shipping, but the killing of civilians was not an explicit goal, and the vast majority of losses were military. But the situation began to change dramatically in the 1930s, in one of the big shifts in contemporary history. Japanese attacks on Chinese civilians and German and Italian bombings of Spanish cities as part of their participation on the fascist side in the civil war made it clear that something was changing, and not just as a result of the new technological capacity for air strikes. Killing many civilians as part of intimidating the enemy began to become standard policy, and this was a huge and fateful change. The fourth Geneva Convention of 1949 responded directly to the change, after two decades of extensive slaughter, but although it relieved the tensions between modern death attitudes and modern war, it proved inadequate to the task.

Obviously, military forces in the past had occasionally deliberately killed civilians. We have seen that imperialist forces pursued this strategy sometimes in Africa, to wear down resistance and express racial hatred; U.S. forces sometimes did the same against Native Americans. Genghis Khan presumably used the slaughter of some urban populations as a means of persuading other cities to back down without a fight in face of his conquering hordes. And the list could be expanded. But the idea of killing civilians deliberately and massively in wars of European against European, or East Asian against East Asian, was an innovation at least in modern times. Further, the technology now involved meant that the scale could become unprecedented.

From 1930s precedents, the policy of civilian slaughter extended in World War II. German attacks on London and other cities were deliberately designed to cow the British through random death and destruction; there was no pretense of particularly military targets. Japanese attacks on civilian centers also continued. At least as important was the fact that allied powers adopted the same policy in retaliation. In 1943 the British Royal Air Force launched Operation Gomorrah against Hamburg, using incendiary bombs "with the aim of wiping Hamburg from the map of Europe." The result was the first firestorm ever caused by bombing, with 45,000 people killed, almost all of them civilians. Winston Churchill, seeing a film of the bombing, asked "Are we animals? Are we taking this too far?" But the air force leadership wanted, and got, more attacks: The later British assault on Dresden, for instance, was a deliberate effort to repay the Germans for bombing the city of Coventry earlier in the war. Overall, it has been estimated that allied bombings killed at least 800,000 civilians in Germany and Japan. U.S. policy in Germany, interestingly, emphasized more precision attacks, seeking military and industrial targets with some limits on random civilian deaths. But in Japan, where anger at the Pearl Harbor attack combined with American racism, the strategy was quite different. Firebombing of Tokyo took out more than 100,000 civilians. The atomic bombs dropped on Hiroshima and Nagasaki were part of this policy. Despite the beliefs of some scientists that a bomb should be exploded harmlessly, to encourage the Japanese to surrender without massive loss of life, President Truman decided that direct action was needed, partly because few bombs were available, and he was reluctant to waste one, partly perhaps to impress the Russians who were just entering the Pacific War. The result, again, was massive and deliberate civilian casualty, with more than 150,000 people lost, some amid great pain. The leaders involved, Truman himself, and the British military concerning Germany, sincerely believed that bombing was "a war-winning weapon," and they were eager to bring conflicts to an end with as little additional loss of military life as possible. The fact was, however, that they innovated massively.[2]

And the blurred boundary has continued, whether or not as a direct consequence of the events of the 1930s and 1940s. Most obviously, contemporary terrorism shifted from targeting individual political leaders (the tactic in the late nineteenth and early twentieth centuries, for example in Russia or the Balkans, albeit sometimes with peripheral civilian loss of life) to massive slaughter of civilians through suicide bombings or the manipulation of aircraft. Arguably—and the point can be debated—certain governments have also continued civilian targeting, as in the massive civilian casualties often associated with Israeli actions against Palestinians or Lebanese-based terrorists. A Pandora's Box has been opened that coexists very badly with the "normal" attitudes toward death in the United States and elsewhere.

This in turn brings us back to the question: How could societies like the United States juggle their aversion to death with the realities of contemporary military and paramilitary life, when simple pacifism or some other separation from military engagement did not seem possible? How could the nation sincerely accept the modern distaste for death and still maintain an aggressive superpower posture? The answer to these more precise questions has several strands and provides a vital, sometimes troubling, way to link American death attitudes with the nation's global role.

When Anti-Death Nations React to War

The problem is quite specific, applying to roughly the past hundred years from 1914 onward: how to combine genuine, and genuinely novel, dislike of death with what happens when contemporary war occurs. Medical efforts to reduce death remain part of the answer, but there is more.

Humanitarian response and, after 1945, changes in bombing policy offer some connections, although they do not get at the heart of the matter.

Death of Others

Tales of wanton slaughter by peoples who presumably have not accepted modern death standards began eliciting moral outrage actually even before World War I. Here, the focus was on other, possibly less "civilized" societies, not one's own, which made outrage easier and less ambivalent. But the reaction is significant nonetheless, extending the humanitarian reactions that had first followed from changes in nineteenth-century death culture.

It was in the mid-1870s that European opinion roused against news of mass killings of Bulgarians by the Ottoman Empire, designed to damp down nationalist agitation. Press accounts claimed 30,000 deaths, although this was greatly exaggerated. Whatever the numbers, the images of many innocent civilians slaughtered galvanized nascent Western public opinion, already hostile to the Ottomans and convinced that this kind of killing must be stopped. Tens of thousands marched and petitioned, causing many officials to claim that they had never seen such intense emotion, with references to "deep and lasting crimes against humanity." Later Ottoman attacks on the Armenians generated similar concern, again along with some possible exaggeration. News of attacks on civilians during the Spanish Civil War prompted widespread public reactions, although they were ineffective.[3]

This kind of outrage could be manipulated, by clever media or by foreign interests eager to mobilize Western support. It could be hollow, as in the Spanish Civil War when Western governments were too paralyzed to do anything to follow up. But it was a genuinely novel reaction that need not be entirely belittled: One way that people (first in the West, then more broadly) tried to reconcile new attitudes toward death with ongoing violence was to voice moral objections and to press their governments to insist that those responsible cease and desist.

The momentum for this kind of reaction revived of course after World War II. Evidence of massive civilian slaughter helped prompt public opinion to galvanize their governments to intervene twice in the Balkans, in the 1990s, to put an end to brutal ethnic cleansing. Evidence of considerable bloodshed—200,000 killed—pushed several nations, headed by Australia, to intervene in East Timor at about the same point. Here, efforts to protect innocent victims of mass violence actually grew some teeth, leading to at least temporarily effective interventions.

Widely publicized Israeli strikes that, although seeking military or political targets, killed numerous civilians, helped turn public opinion against Israel not only in the Arab world, but in Europe and Japan as well. Israel's bombardments in Lebanon in the summer of 2006 exacerbated these reactions.

It was also obvious, of course, that moral outrage was inconsistent and that it hardly prevented the dreadful epidemic of genocides that continued to plague world affairs. Condemnations did not keep pace with reality. The Holocaust had passed largely unnoticed at the time. Belated guilt helped spur greater attention to subsequent genocides, but even this was unpredictable. Most of the great civilian slaughters in Africa drew expressions of anguish but no effective intervention, including the bloody conflict in Rwanda but also later episodes in Sudan, Congo, northern Uganda, and elsewhere. Humanitarian reactions linked changes in private views of death with the world stage, but they hardly reconciled the various forces involved. Millions of people continued to be condemned to die in an "anti-death" century.

Closer to home, the growing immersion in an anti-death culture combined with some rethinking of World War II to generate serious second thoughts about the saturation bombing of civilians. Public majorities did not apologize for what had happened—the American public bitterly protested an effort to present a balanced view of the atomic bombing of Japan—but no conflict arose after 1945 that pushed the Western powers, the United States included, into indiscriminate attacks on civilians. Rather, considerable efforts were devoted to more precise bombing methods that would allow attacks on military targets, even in cities, while limiting civilian casualties. Where wider damage to civilians did occur, as in Vietnam, the result could help undermine a military campaign. By the time of the U.S. invasion of Iraq, bombing, both from airplanes and from rockets, had become impressively refined, and civilian deaths were far more limited than expected during the attack phase of the operation. Exceptions and mistakes were widely noted and produced almost immediate apologies and investigations. Here was a concrete effort, partly successful, to reconcile new attitudes toward death, at least civilian death, with the realities of war—an attempt to harness technology rather than simply to indulge it.

Death of One's Own

But what of deaths to one's own soldiers?—another inescapable feature of any war and, as the two world wars demonstrated, particularly of modern war. How could the massive carnage in the trenches of World War I, where a modest offensive could produce nearly a million dead, be reconciled with the larger changes in attitudes toward death? Here, a twofold evolution occurred, each phase quite revealing.

The first reaction, particularly important in Europe because of World War I death rates, but also applicable in the United States, involved an interesting combination of public stoicism and careful individual remembrance. We have seen that grief was discouraged as undermining the war effort. It was important to praise the courage of the fallen, but not to linger over their deaths. This element in the reaction fed the larger movement to attack nineteenth-century grief levels as excessive. In the case of Britain, war reactions also encouraged the kind of rethinking of death rituals that would ultimately promote greater use of cremation. On the larger scale, the official approach obviously reflected a belief that the war's importance greatly overshadowed any personal affliction.

United States magazines furthered this tone eagerly. People were urged to "efface as far as possible the signs of woe," and the Literary Digest argued more generally that "Death is so familiar a companion in war-time that a revision of our modes of dealing with its immediate presence is pertinent to the relief of human anguish." Similar attitudes dominated the media in World War II.

"Don't wear mourning too long. It expresses no real respect for the dead, and it is depressing to the person who wears it and to friends and family who see it." A few psychologists objected to this stance, worried that grief needed fuller expression for emotional health. But the modernist approach seemed to win out, at least publicly, with its primary focus on good cheer among the living amid a rather cavalier dismissal of death itself. Newspapers did their bit by avoiding massive emphasis on casualty statistics and featuring uplifting stories of heroism and unexpected survivals. Even accounts of bereaved individuals back home stressed their fortitude and their pride in the lost spouse or son. And of course this was a "fight for democracy" against a "treacherous foe," in which some death would be an unwanted but acceptable price to pay. War movies did their bit, finally, either by bypassing death in combat in favor of upbeat camaraderie; or by focusing almost exclusively on deaths administered to the enemy; or by making sure that the actor-soldiers most appealing to the audience did not die.[4]

But this stiff upper lip approach was combined with unprecedented efforts to provide individual burial sites and name-filled memorials to those who fell. Every French town established public lists of its war dead, carved in stone and displayed prominently in a public place; then these lists were expanded, after 1944, to include the World War II dead. Many other regions, including the United States, adopted a similar approach. This reflected, of course, the enhanced record-keeping abilities of modern bureaucracies, but it also followed from a real belief that war death was special and demanded a special kind of rendering. The contrast with more traditional war memorials that featured lusty praise of victories—as in the triumphal columns of Rome or Napoleon—and did not lament for those lost was obvious. The same recollective approach applied to the increasingly systematic—and often expensive—efforts to bury each soldier in a separately marked, and where possible individually labeled, grave site. The burial grounds of World Wars I and II dead in France—even including separate, equally careful treatment for fallen German soldiers—became special places of remembrance. Although there had been hints of this approach in the U.S. Civil War, no wars in history had ever generated such individualized attention, despite or perhaps because of the massive levels of slaughter.

Whether this first approach—the combination of publicly controlled emotion and the individualized honoring of the dead themselves—was satisfactory could be open to question. The carnage of World War I created levels of personal grief and collective shock that had wider ramifications. And the combination itself might have expressed an interesting tension, between the impulse to dismiss death in favor of ongoing goals like the war effort and the sense of the inappropriateness of the loss of young life that supported the burial sites and the war memorials. Ultimately, however, it seems probable that the dismissive part of the equation was simply not compatible with the deeper modernist revulsion against death itself. Attacks on ritual were fine, but they assumed that death itself was under control—and that was not the case in the world wars.

Whatever the evaluation, the fact was that the combination did not hold. The memorializing impulse persisted—the sorrowful list of names that defines the memorial to the Vietnam War in Washington, D.C., is an impressive extension of this modern innovation—but the public control in the face of war casualties was not fully sustained. War death, after all, conflicted directly with the larger goal of beating death back, and acceptance of the casualty levels of the two world wars could not be reconciled with the more general changes in death culture.

For the United States, the shift toward a different approach—combining continued memorialism with a much more concerted resentment of military deaths—began to show up in the reportage of the Korean War, even before television brought war's grimness into every American home. The war began with a tone similar to that of World War II, with little detail about casualties. But then, as the war dragged on, there was a measurable change—associated with growing unpopularity as both cause and effect. Even journalists remarked on the new situation, noting the difference from World War II as "strangely disturbing" amid an increasing sense that "our boys" should not die, U.S. families should not be called upon to face grief.[5]

Mainstream news magazines like *Newsweek* and *Time* greeted the onset of the war without much attention to potential casualties. There were concerns about policy, but little doubt about the superior capacities of U.S. troops to do their job. Early defeats and setbacks were noted, but with no explicit casualty lists. *Newsweek* cited heavy losses in one campaign, under the oddly breezy title "More Bloody Noses," but there were no specifics. A few discussions of wounded GIs emphasized that they would recover. Heroism and ultimate victory were the order of the day, and even an accusation in Congress that the military were covering up loss rates was not followed up in the press.[6]

As greater stalemate developed, however, the mood changed. Pictures began showing soldiers holding dead comrades in their arms, requiring support from others, and readers responded with real emotion. As one letter put it,

> And somewhere, in this great country, there must be a mother, wife, or sister—perhaps all three—who recognizes as her own the stalwart soldier who, amidst the horror ... of war, has the compassion and greatness of soul to comfort in his strong capable arms the lonely, heartbroken lad so shaken by grief for his fallen buddy.[7]

More starkly, half a year into the war, the major magazines launched regular and systematic casualty reports. *Time* noted that, with 2,441 dead, rates were already almost as high as those of the entire North African campaign in World War II. Newsweek simply called the figures "staggering," while warning there were more to come. A few months later still, the same magazines began adding equally regular features, giving personal accounts of soldiers' deaths and coverage of the emotional turmoil of families back home, conveying the episodes in ways designed to elicit wider sympathy and grief. Graphic accounts of soldiers' fear and screaming, amid their wounds, were now appropriate fare. And the numerical specifics became inexorable. Thirty percent of the troops in one operation, or 3,000 men, killed or wounded; "100 dead ... flown out for burial" in another report; a Korean girl placing a flower on the grave of a GI "who will never come home," with wooden crosses stretching endlessly in the distance; the "mangled bodies" of forty-four airmen killed in a crash, with gifts they had bought for loved ones back home strewn around them. Personal involvements and the "rising toll" combined, as the magazines began to make it clear that the equivalent of more than a full army division had already perished. Icons helped back up the numbers: One regular feature involved an army helmet symbol for every 250 casualties. Statements by generals like Douglas MacArthur, that these losses were pretty standard, were reported but increasingly judged unsatisfactory. This war was not going well enough to justify the body count.[8]

Another innovation involved heartrending stories of reactions of the families back home more and more replacing the accounts of pride and fortitude. Personal descriptions of recent marriages or high school football prowess combined with details about the death itself. It was not hard to judge that many of these deaths were senseless. And in a final, revealing sign of the intensification of concern about military deaths, magazines began worrying about the bodies that had not been recovered, blasting the government for not making access to battle sites and identification of U.S. corpses a top priority in truce negotiations. Soon, various reporters began accusing the government of concealing losses themselves, while noting that "already" as many soldiers had died as in all the battles of the Revolutionary War and ten times as many as in the Spanish American War. And for what purpose? Many articles, detailing the gruesomeness of mangled bodies, cited as well soldiers' beliefs that the dead would not be properly remembered. One poignant account featured a soldier paying tribute to "the guy who dies not really knowing why he dies, not willing to die at all, wanting to live and give other guys the same breaks he expects, but dying because he is loyal to his own special ideas and demands, even ugly demands." Pictures, finally, picked up the theme, both in magazines and the daily press: pictures of soldiers walking beside trucks filled with bodies; pictures of helicopters evacuating the dead and wounded; pictures of a river filled with bodies and "tinged with red"; pictures of shrouded American bodies in temporary grave sites; pictures of mothers or wives collapsing at the news of death.[9]

Modern war and reactions to death were on a collision course in the United States.

Many military leaders knew that the Korean War had been something of a turning point. They worried about more than death, of course; they were concerned about wars that seemed to have no clear purpose, that dragged on without decisive outcome. They worried about the withdrawal of civilian support from the military in general. Many of them, on these grounds, resisted the growing involvement of the United States in Vietnam, a decade after Korea had ended.[10]

But it was the Vietnamese war that put the seal on the heightened discomfort Americans felt about deaths of their own in battle. This was a war, initially widely supported, elaborately covered by television, replete with scenes of death and destruction along with the by-then-established routines of frequent body counts. Attacks on Vietnamese villagers were bad enough, but the evidence of mounting U.S. casualties—again, in a conflict that became increasingly uncertain—contributed measurably to growing public disenchantment and dispute over the war itself. The losses became too graphic and too numerous to support.

New levels of anguish at American deaths in war showed in the unprecedented effort to retrieve bodies of the missing. The kind of concern manifest from World War I onward (with precedents even in the Civil War), to make as sure as possible that each dead soldier was properly identified and buried, visibly escalated. The U.S. government expended great effort, and no small expense, on expeditions designed to find additional MIAs (Missing in Action), as they were called. The issue loomed large in negotiations for a peace settlement, and in later interactions with the Vietnamese government, another sign of how serious the symbolism had become. Congressional critics recurrently pressed the administration to do more.

Here, too, the actual intensification began with the Korean War: Pressure to locate all possible bodies increased, and Americans began to insist, in contrast to what had occurred in World War II and all previous wars, that the dead be embalmed and sent home for burial. MIA agitation increased steadily. By the 1970s, with a Joint POW (Prisoner of War)/MIA Accounting Command in Hawaii, with a budget of $100 million a year, the effort was in full swing. As one of the four hundred employees of the office noted, "It's an amazing endeavor. Not many other cultures would go as far as this." Indeed, almost none would. Only Israel (retrieving bodies from Palestinian territory) and Japan (in seeking World War II remains in China) showed comparable zeal. By the 1970s, Americans were sending teams into places like Korea or Vietnam to follow up on rumors, to use the latest technology on sites where contact with aircraft had ceased during the earlier war, to scour places where shells or helicopter wreckage is found, hiring local villagers to supplement U.S. scientific expertise. Physical anthropologists and forensic scientists provide new levels of data analysis; searches take place despite the danger of unexploded shells, so important has it become to reduce the number of traceless dead. The heightened concern partly reflects a widespread sense that Korea and, even more, Vietnam had turned out to be foolish, ineffective wars: it's harder to abandon the dead when the cause is unclear. Groups like the National League of Families developed serious political clout, in representing wider public dismay as well as their own grief at loss. But new discomforts about death are involved as well: It has become so hard to come to terms with military fatalities that a massive investment and visible public effort are essential for public expiation. The result: the largest forensic operation in the world, still identifying about two soldiers a week from past wars. (There were still, however, more than 8,000 missing soldiers from the Korean War alone, so gaps between expectations and results remained.) The result: an unprecedented clause in the Paris treaty that ended the Vietnam War, insisting that "the parties shall help each other to get information about those military personnel and foreign civilians of the two parties missing in action, to determine the location and take care of the traces of the dead so as to facilitate the exhumation and repatriation of the remains, and to take any such other measures as may be required to get information about those still considered missing in action." New death attitudes and the realities of one of the United States' least happy wars did not comfortably coexist.[11]

The overall dilemma was clear: how to combine the kind of muscular foreign policy American great power status seemed to require, including periodic military action, with the seemingly inescapable revulsion against death. Possibly, at some point another war might develop with such overwhelming public support that the dismissiveness of the world wars would revive, but such has not been the case to date, and the prospects, short of direct attack on the nation itself, seem slender.

New Efforts in Limiting Death

Several strategies, often in conjunction, have increasingly emerged to deal with this situation. First and doubtless most important is the use of U.S. airpower to bomb targets into submission before, and in some cases instead of, the commitment of ground troops. High technology, in other words, which is fairly safe in terms of potential American loss of life, might promise to limit the kinds of casualties that most clearly rouse public concern. The strategy had already been suggested by the deployment of nuclear weapons against Japan in World War II: The American public accepted the bombings, after the fact but even today in historical memory, on grounds that U.S. lives were saved. The same strategy cropped up during the Korean War transition to still-greater concern about U.S.

lives. Editorialist David Lawrence contended that "American boys" were being needlessly killed because the government was unwilling to bomb the enemy sufficiently. "It is for us, the living, to remember the 20,915 American boys who can never vote again."[12]

With the experience of public dismay in Korea and Vietnam before them, U.S. military leaders plumped ever more readily for the bombing option. Vietnam itself involved extensive air attacks, in hopes of limiting infantry casualties. Even more clearly, heavy bombing partly substituted for infantry involvement in the Balkans in the 1990s. The same applied to the Gulf War, when infantry deployments were deliberately limited because of casualty fears. In a few cases, air attacks were all that occurred: responses to al Qaeda threats in the 1990s led to rocket launches against Afghanistan and Sudan, and nothing more.

The mastery of the air strategy had some limitations, of course. It did not necessarily work well: The sorties intended to punish al Qaeda had no effect whatsoever, except for some civilian casualties in Sudan. Enemies of the United States increasingly planted military operations near civilian centers, in hopes of reducing U.S. willingness to bomb or, more likely, rouse world opinion when the inevitable casualties occurred. Most obviously, the overall death toll might be higher than it would have been in more orthodox infantry activities. To be sure, increasing precision bombing reduced this problem, but it did not eliminate it. The commitment to air attack to limit American losses was predicated to some extent on a willingness to kill other people, often relatively innocent civilians, though non-Americans, instead. This, too, had potential costs to the United States: It could inflame local opinion; it could antagonize larger world opinion; and it could rouse critics within the United States for whom loss of civilian life, from whatever source, was simply unacceptable. Civilian death tolls in the Vietnam War, and the media coverage surrounding them, played a definite role in mobilizing European publics against the war and in fueling the antiwar movement within the United States. Americans were open to accepting a bargain that pitted reduction of U.S. losses against wider damage to others, but support could fray if the damage mounted too visibly.

All this helped produce a final tactic, informed by the disastrous public outcry that had accompanied the Vietnam conflict: an effort at concealment. Military management of the media markedly increased after the Vietnam War, most obviously in the Gulf War and then the invasion of Iraq. In this last war, media groups were "embedded" within military units, which gave them a front seat view of some of the action but also allowed their movements to be monitored, for safety among other things, and so integrated them into group morale that their objectivity might be compromised. Independent reporting, including on civilian casualties, was discouraged. Television featured dramatic shots of the Baghdad skyline illuminated with bombs and tracers, in both the Iraq wars, but with little opportunity to show the results of the bombing on the ground.

This overall management was supplemented by two other devices. First, the interest in regular reporting on civilian casualties declined. Americans were given almost no information about the number of Iraqis—military or civilian—killed in the Gulf War and the ensuing military embargo on Iraq. Some estimates ranged as high as 100,000, but the public was not informed and, probably, preferred to remain ignorant; there was no big pressure to learn. Even more revealing: although there was no possibility of concealing U.S. casualty counts from the media, the symbolism of death in war was dramatically reduced. Pictures of fallen soldiers became less common. Media coverage of the sorrowful returns of flag-draped coffins was discouraged. Concern persisted: The media did list the names of soldiers killed and often added features on their family life and the disruption that resulted. But, in light of modern sensitivity on the subject, a fairly deliberate effort aimed at keeping emotions within manageable bounds.

In many respects, the 2003 invasion of Iraq was the most carefully calibrated campaign yet to adapt the realities of contemporary war to American attitudes toward death. All the strategic components were assembled. The invasion was prepared by massive bombing raids, designed to reduce U.S. casualties on the ground; but these raids were unprecedentedly precise, amid military claims that civilian losses would be kept to a minimum. A few stray bombings occurred, nevertheless, and were seized on by the Iraqi media, but the bombing phase was short enough—in a campaign billed as "shock and awe"—and the strikes were well enough targeted that the spillover, at least in American public opinion, was limited. The idea was to take out some military targets and scare the Iraqi people more generally; civilian casualties were accepted in this strategy, but there was a hope that they would be limited once the infantry invasion began. Commanders reminded U.S. troops of the rules against attacking innocent civilians, although a number of lapses occurred. Controlled media—the U.S. public was shown vastly different scenes from those displayed to publics in Europe, the Arab world, and elsewhere—helped maintain the image of a relatively sanitary operation. The invasion itself proceeded as swiftly as anyone could imagine, punctuated with a few heroic stories of soldiers (now including women) rescued from the jaws of death. Accounts of civilian casualties, both during the invasion and then in the subsequent civil strife, were limited, for although daily tolls were featured, cumulative figures rarely appeared. Most Americans had no idea of the overall total of Iraqi deaths from the operation, which probably had mounted to 40,000 to 50,000 by 2006 (some estimates ran much higher). Rare appeals for regular reporting went unheeded, which obviously helped preserve the lesser concern for the deaths of others. Finally, amazingly few Americans died; again in 2006, the total was only a bit more than 2,800. This was a tribute to very cautious tactics; to massive protective efforts; and to state-of-the-art medical care (severe injuries mounted to a far more troubling level, with upwards of 45,000 cases, but these were less regularly reported). Finally, though there was no way to prevent the media from listing the U.S. totals and doing human interest stories on the fallen troops, symbolism was kept to a minimum. The government flew the flag-covered coffins back to the United States at night, only rarely allowing pictures of clusters of coffins at the Andrews landing base in Maryland. No one claimed this was a death-free war, but the control effort was sweeping, and it met with considerable success.

There were problems, of course, even aimed at these unprecedented levels of management. If U.S. opinion remained fairly quiet about Iraqi casualties, this was less true in other parts of the world. The war was deeply unpopular in world opinion before it began, in part because of concern about loss of innocent life, and American tactics—apart from the impressive swiftness of the invasion itself—did nothing to conciliate. The second problem was that U.S. strategy did not prove adequate to win a peace. Iraqi resistance mounted steadily, and this, along with the inescapable awareness of casualties to Iraqis and Americans alike, did ultimately turn American opinion itself against the war. In a final irony, some observers contended that the problems in keeping the peace resulted from an original decision to limit the number of U.S. troops put on the ground—a decision that doubtless stemmed from many motives, including cost, but that included a desire to limit the potential for casualties. The constraints posed by U.S. death attitudes—along, of course, with many other factors—could contribute to failure.

The Iraq War, in other words, illustrated the impact of the clear tension between U.S. death attitudes and modern warfare. But it also suggested that a resolution had yet to be found that would keep public opinion calm while also enabling a successful military operation once the fighting had to move from the skies to the ground. What was clear—although whether this was desirable or not could be debated—was that, in the decades after World War II, U.S. death culture, amplified by media coverage, had a decided impact on military strategies. Superpower ambitions continued—the nation did not adopt the conflict-avoidance impulses of countries like postwar Japan or Germany—but the combination remained extremely challenging, the inherent contradictions not yet fully resolved.

There was a final irony. Enemies of the United States became well aware of the national squeamishness about death—at least, American death. This is why they often deliberately encouraged civilian casualties, by planting military operations in center cities, in hopes of provoking U.S. as well as world opinion. This is why they frequently miscalculated U.S. resolve, believing that a few U.S. deaths could cause the public to pull out of a war effort altogether. Although

U.S. military leadership did become cautious about public support, there was no lack of willingness to respond to provocation. U.S. military assertion might seem necessary simply to counter outside efforts to exploit American distaste for death. Complexities abounded, and they could spill over from formal war to terrorism.

Death and Terrorism

Attitudes toward war deaths fed reactions to terrorism by the early twenty-first century, particularly in the United States. Obviously—and it took no particularly refined death culture to predict this aspect—terrorist attacks were widely condemned. They generated exactly the kind of unpredictable, undeserved death that was being opposed with increasing vigor in emergency rooms or birth clinics or war strategy rooms throughout the Western world and beyond. Terrorists, often willing to give up their own lives and certainly willing to strike randomly at civilians, were almost impossible to understand in terms of dominant death attitudes in places like the United States, and this made them all the more frightening.

The impulse to memorialize those struck down ran very strong, a sign of the high emotion and public discomfort with this kind of death. (The impulse went beyond the victims of terrorism; practices of contributing to public displays of flowers as a reaction to mining disasters or even individual accidents like that of Princess Diana began in Britain in the 1980s.) The United States displayed a particularly elaborate need to memorialize. After a domestic terrorist blew up a federal building in Oklahoma City in 1995, the whole block, in the city center, was turned into an elaborate remembrance site. Similar if slightly less spacious plans followed the September 11, 2001, terrorist attacks on New York's World Trade Center and the Pentagon in Washington, D.C. Televised repetitions of the attacks themselves, plus newspaper treatments of the individual victims and their families, generated a level of public emotion greater than that now routinely applied to military casualties. Urged on by the media, and repeated media displays of death and grief, Americans were clearly willing to provide unprecedented support for durable demonstrations of sorrow and outrage. This kind of death should not happen, so it demanded public apology.

The same public culture promoted extensive fear in the face of the terrorist threat, again particularly in the United States. Whereas the Pearl Harbor attack of 1941 had been greeted with fairly calm resolve—along with a desire to retaliate—the 9/11 tragedy produced widespread panic. Polls showed that more than 65 percent of all Americans felt personally afraid. People distant from the attacks, in Minnesota or Texas, reported fears about leaving home and an urgent sense that they might be next to fall victim. Public figures recurrently compared

9/11 to disasters such as the Black Death (which had killed 25 percent of the European population), an exaggeration that revealed how profoundly unsettling terrorism could be in contemporary death culture. It seemed difficult to brush off terrorism as a problem worthy of some attention but—in terms of lives thus far lost—a fairly minor irritant. When it came to military death or similar civilian casualties, numbers were not the main point: It was the inappropriateness that predominated. Americans did not want to have to worry about this kind of death or face the strain of public grief—and so they reacted very strongly, in memorializing, remembering, and seeking every assurance of protection from renewed attack, no matter what the statistical probabilities or the expense.[13]

A number of factors went into the U.S reactions, beyond attitudes toward death. Other groups seemed more prepared to get on with normal life in the face of terrorism, without so much attention to remembrance or reassurance. Both Spaniards and Britons, faced with terrorist bombings of commuter lines, in 2003 and 2005, respectively, deliberately emphasized public demonstrations of calm and defiance, rather than widespread fear—although, admittedly the death levels involved were far lower than in the American 9/11, and the Europeans had the precedent of extensive American anxiety before them. The British deliberately recalled their calm response to German bombings in World War II and explicitly distanced themselves from U.S. innovations such as color-coded terror warnings that almost explicitly appealed to fear. The British, similarly, surrounded their public buildings with far less protective apparatus than Americans developed in their attempt to make sure that inappropriate death would not reoccur. Revealingly, the most anxious public reaction to the 2005 attacks on the London subways came not from Britons, but from commanders of two U.S. military bases that forbade their personnel from traveling to the capital, until reprimanded for their timidity by British authorities.

Fear of inappropriate death did not lead Americans to capitulate in the face of terrorism. It did encourage elaborate countermeasures, including public acceptance of a war on Iraq that was sold in terms of protection from dire threat in terms that later proved misguided. It did encourage openness to political campaigns based on threat. One of the intriguing aspects of the post-9/11 reactions was the widespread sense of personal vulnerability that emerged: The many Americans who said they were afraid were not primarily worried about New Yorkers (although they felt empathic grief) or the fate of the nation; they were worried about themselves and their families. This is why, in the 2004 presidential political campaigns, candidates could successfully persuade people that a vote for their opponents would invite another terrorist attack. Many mothers, particularly, switched their votes to President Bush because they found him more reassuring when it came to their children's safety. As one put it, "I have recently become a soccer mom—and I'm a security mom too. I take the job seriously and

I expect my president to take it seriously. When I tuck my daughter in at night, I want to know that my president is watching my back and keeping me safe." A measurable swing of votes in this group occurred between 2000 and 2004, based on new levels of fear.

No society enjoys loss of life to war or terrorism. Clearly, however, the kinds of death attitudes developed in some regions during the past century have complicated reactions to military commitments. The United States has found the combination of modern resistance to death and great power activities particularly difficult—not unmanageable, but commanding careful attention and shifting specific categories. The combination has also affected the rest of the world, whether the subject is responses to terrorism enhanced by fears and resentments associated with death or military tactics designed to minimize loss of American life even at costs to others. To date, the broader uneasiness with death, developed since the early nineteenth century, has not been unseated by power considerations that can drive toward considerable callousness about losses in the presumed national interest. But the relationship is complicated, encouraging deliberate manipulations as well as uncomfortable distinctions between deaths of others and deaths of one's own.

A final symptom, by no means unique to the United States, involves morbid fascination. The horrors of contemporary warfare, now combined with recurrent terrorism, have become standard media fare, and the coverage is now available around the clock. Quite apart from death scenes omnipresent in entertainment, more death is visible on the evening news than many people, in the days before television, saw in a lifetime. How does this impact death attitudes more generally? Certainly it cautions against glib generalizations about death as taboo—many contemporaries watch death regularly. Does death news confirm discomfort and revulsion? Does it encourage a separation between deaths of others, often in distant places, and the kinds of deaths one really cares about? Personal reactions doubtless vary, but the clash between death's visibility in war and apparent modern standards adds a further complexity to a challenging subject.

Notes

1. Figures extracted from the *World Almanac*, 2006.

2. A. C. Grayking, *Among the Dead Cities: The History and Moral Legacy of the WWII Bombing of Civilians in Germany and Japan* (New York, 2006).

3. Peter N. Stearns, *Global Outrage: The Impact of World Opinion in Modern History* (London, 2005).

4. "The Presence of Death," *New Republic* (May 1917): 45–47; "The Unseemliness of Funerals," *Literary Digest* (April 1917): 1170; M. Weldman, "America Conquers Death," *American Mercury* (February 1927): 216–227; R. Dickerson, "Sorrow Can Be Faced,"

Saturday Evening Post (July 1944): 269–270; L. Holman, "The War Department Report," *Ladies Home Journal* (July 1944): 142; S. Fahs, "When Children Confront Death," *Parents Magazine* (April 1942): 34; W. Bacchus, "The Relationship between Combat and Peace Negotiations: Fighting While Talking in Korea," *Orbis* XVII (1973): 845–874; J. Halliday and B. Cummings, *Korea: The Unknown War* (New York, 1988), p. 159 and *passim*. For general understanding of the "frustration," A. Schlessinger Jr., *The Bitter Heritage: Vietnam and American Democracy* (Boston, 1967), p. 65.

    5. R. Thompson, *Cry Korea* (London, 1951), pp. 39, 42, 54.

    6. *Newsweek* (27 Feb. 1950): 23; (24 July 1950): 11–15; (21 Aug. 1950): 31–32; (18 Sept. 1950): 21–24; (2 Oct. 1950): 25.

    7. *Newsweek* (9 Oct. 1950): 24; (23 Oct. 1950): 6–7, 23.

    8. *Time* (7 Mar. 1951): 47; (1 Apr. 1951): 16–18; (18 June 1951): 25–26; (14 Jan. 1952): 17.

    9. *Saturday Evening Post* (24 May 1952): 38–39; "Atlantic Repartee," *Atlantic Monthly* (Nov. 1950): 25; R. Montague, "A Soldier's Thoughts on Memorial Day," *New York Times Magazine* (27 May 1951): 13–14; *Life* (17 July 1950): 46; (24 July 1950): 21–22; (31 July 1950): 37; (14 Aug. 1950): 22; (4 Sept. 1950): 36; (18 Sept. 1950): 41–47; (25 Oct. 1950): 11; (25 Dec. 1950): 9–14; (21 July 1951): 29; (11 Dec. 1951): 32–43; H. Moffit, "The Situation in a Nutshell," *Life* (6 Jan. 1951): 73.

    10. Bacchus, "The Relationship between Combat and Peace Negotiations": 845–874; Halliday and Cumings, *Korea: The Unknown War*, p. 159 and *passim*.

    11. Rachel Snyder, "Prisoners of War and Missing in Action," *American Heritage* 56 (Feb./Mar. 2005): 30–40.

    12. *U.S. News and World Report* (15 Sept 1950): 14; (20 Oct. 1950): 14–15; (14 May 1951): 20, 23; (11 May 1951): 21; (26 Oct. 1951): 15, 22; (30 Nov. 1951): 102; (8 Feb. 1952): 16, 34; (19 Sept., 1952): 39; (10 Oct. 1952): 108; (17 Oct. 1950): 18.

    13. Peter N. Stearns, *American Fear: The Cause and Consequences of High Anxiety* (New York, 2006).

CHAPTER 12

Conclusion

The modern history of death is a rich topic. It shows how historical analysis can extend to vital but unexpected aspects of the human experience. Death is death up to a point, with elements applicable to all places in all times, but it is hardly a changeless experience. We can understand contemporary death issues—including our wide aversion to the subject—far better if we know their recent history, if we grasp how the present emerged from a fairly complicated past—from tradition, to nineteenth-century innovation, to the emergence of contemporary patterns.

Modern death history also displays an intriguing mixture between cultural elements and material realities. Beliefs matter greatly; sometimes they change in advance of shifts in the physical nature of death and even help cause these shifts; always of course they must also adjust to physical changes.

Further, death history illumines a wider history. Changes and continuities in death shed light on many aspects of culture, political dynamics, war, international versus regional standards—the list is considerable, as understanding the modern evolution of death improves our assessment of topics as wide-ranging as childhood and military policy.

A host of complexities and analytical challenges remain in the history of death, quite apart from the fact that the subject is not as fully treated for some societies as it is for places like the United States (even for Japan, historical work is not as full as one might wish). Obviously, changes in death attitudes and experiences have not produced uniform policy results: Fierce debates over the death penalty, the right to die, or abortion show how groups can draw passionately different conclusions from the current context. Although dispute partly reflects the newness of the contemporary death situation—it is vital to remember that aspects of contemporary death have no prior precedent in human history—it is not clear how the gaps can be closed in the future, although they significantly complicate domestic political agendas and international relations alike. The gulf between death standards and military realities in places like the United States is another open subject of vast importance. There are other anomalies: Why, in societies like the United States or Japan, where the social importance of death has been reduced, is there so much fascination with portraying violent death in movies and in video games? There may be no inconsistency: The portrayals hardly dwell on death itself, in favor of sudden and bloody endings. But some observers wonder if, by downplaying death as an acceptable topic, modern societies encourage some people—particularly, some young people—to develop unhealthy attitudes toward death and violence. The relationship between modern death taboos and rates of suicide and murder, as we have seen, also raises questions that are difficult to resolve.

The modern history of death also illustrates the complexity of American experience in global context. Developments around death help "internationalize" American history, which is a current and quite appropriate new plea among many historians, but they also show that this internationalization is not a simple matter. The United States has shared in many key death trends, cultural as well as physical. It has even influenced global standards in some respects, and it certainly has overlapped with western Europe in many ways. At key points in modern history, one can use death to help illustrate how the United States is part of a larger Western or even modern-industrial framework. But the United States has also been different, and some of the differences have increased in recent decades, moving the nation away from larger convergence. In certain aspects the United States has become surprisingly traditional about death, compared say with western Europe; in others, less surprisingly, it displays unusual religiosity; in still others, it has become clearly neo-imperialist in its willingness to treat the deaths of Americans very differently than the deaths of foreigners. Death history helps show the advantages of comparison; it demonstrates that aspects of what some historians have called "American death" are in fact part of modern death more generally. But U.S. peculiarities stand out as well and must be analyzed and explained. This applies most obviously to the zigs and zags of the U.S. relationship to European patterns in death attitudes and policies alike. Some of the U.S. peculiarities, particularly in military or abortion policy, affect wider contemporary world history, and others help explain the nation's ambivalent position regarding world opinion, where there is hesitation about accepting reigning international standards on death.

Death history, including its comparative features, easily slides into value judgments. It's hard not to rate key elements of the modern pattern of death as "good," particularly when it comes to the vast reduction of traditional mortality rates. And this might already distort our view of advantages of death cultures in the past. More obvious: Whose version of modern death works best? Are greater ritual and larger slices of tradition preferable, or is it better to emphasize a willingness to use rational examination to determine how to ease death? Is it best to control immediate grief, or is death so powerful that this approach will leave huge psychological scars or social deficiencies? And values issues abound when we extend the history of death to deal with abortion, or the death penalty, or euthanasia, or efforts to limit deaths in one's own military by bombing foreign civilian populations. History answers none of these moral dilemmas. But the actual history of death at least clarifies what some of the dilemmas are and how they have emerged. We have different values about death from those of our ancestors; and changes in death have also produced issues that our ancestors could not have identified.

Finally, the modern history of death is a story not yet ended. Many parts of the world are just moving into a modern death framework: How will they handle the cultural issues involved with lower rates of death before later age? Or will some parts of the world continue to exhibit unusually high death rates, so that death continues to serve as a global divider, marking often tragic differences between the prosperous and the poor, the stable societies and societies wracked with war and disorder? Will a more consistent and durable global standard on the death penalty emerge, or will this topic continue to display both division and oscillation?

"Unfinished story" also describes the United States in global perspective. In the 1990s the United States seemed to be moving defiantly away from international standards, most obviously concerning the death penalty. More recent developments, including the Supreme Court's 2005 decision that children should not be put to death for any crime, intentionally move the nation closer to international standards. Americans are less willing than Europeans to consider medically assisted suicide, part of the greater and more conservative reluctance to think about palliatives in the death process generally; but Oregonians are almost as willing to innovate as the Dutch. The comparative case—whether the United States will carve its own modern path or share key trends with other advanced industrial societies—remains open.

Most important, in the United States, but also Japan, Korea, western Europe, and soon other places as well, the modern approaches to death are about to encounter the rapid aging of society. The numbers of people in the age eighty or over category have been increasing faster than any other age group for some time now, thanks to low birthrates and increasing adult longevity. This trend will escalate further, particularly in the United States, when baby boomers reach this level, about twenty years from now. The fact is that even with the longer life expectancies, death rates accelerate rapidly after age eighty, so a growth in this age category will mean an increase in numbers of deaths. Twenty years from now, the United States might begin recording as many as 50 percent more deaths per year than is now the case. What will the inescapable need to deal more often with death do to broad death attitudes? Will it force modifications in the modern tendency not to think about or deal with death too often in society at large and in familial life alike?

Quite possibly the twentieth century, with its tendency to downplay death and related emotional reactions, will prove to be an anomaly, an odd island between periods when death commanded more attention. After all, some experts predict not only an increase in occurrences of death, owing not only to larger old-age segments but also to genetically modified disease strains that will prove more resistant to modern medicine—thus forcing increased attention to death, even in other categories of the population. Again, there are stages in the modern story of death and death culture still to be encountered.

"Yet to be determined" also applies to the issue of consistency. We have seen that important changes in the wider history of death have generated remarkable opportunities for disparities in approach. When new death attitudes first emerged in the nineteenth century, they suggested some interesting connections between new personal reactions and broader policies, particularly concerning the death penalty and abortion. But these connections exploded in the twentieth century, although in different ways in different places: Revulsion against death in one setting often had little to do with deaths directed at others, whether in war, in criminal justice, or concerning the unborn. Societies newly concerned about death at home can be remarkably nonchalant about death elsewhere. People defend the death penalty but resist abortion, and vice versa: The combination might be quite understandable, but it certainly suggests some uncertainties about how to define the appropriate administration of death. More broadly, revulsion against death has vied with increased ability to disseminate death through the new technologies of war. Attitudes to death as a personal or family matter often conflict with broader social policies. Many modern societies, the United States certainly included, are finding it difficult to reconcile social goals of fighting death with what many people actually seem to want when they are dying.

These various inconsistencies reflect the magnitude of modern change, which leaves many loose ends: More-traditional societies had benefited from a longer period of time to work out greater harmony in the various facets of death, albeit around standards many modern people would find deeply objectionable. Will modern societies ultimately work out a more evenhanded approach, or is consistency worth worrying about at all? It can certainly be suggested that divisions over aspects of death form some of the more intense political issues in modern societies and from one society to the next, where international standards are involved. In that sense, it would be useful if greater consensus could be forged, but it is impossible to predict if this will occur.

Questions for the future abound, and there are no clear answers yet. Stay tuned, is the clear message. Modern approaches are still being worked out. But we should use the rich findings of the history of death so far to help refine the questions and assess the further changes as the modern patterns of death continue to unfold.

Suggestions for Further Reading

Historical work on death is rich and provocative, but also quite uneven in terms of times and places. Fairly general overviews (although focused on western Europe) include Philippe Ariès, *Hour of Our Death* (New York, 1981) and *Images of Man and Death* (Cambridge, MA, 1985); Peter Jupp and Glennys Howarth, eds., *The Changing Face of Death: Historical Accounts of Death and Disposal* (New York, 1997); Ellen Badone, *The Appointed Hour: Death, Worldview and Social Change in Britanny* (Berkeley, CA, 1989); Thomas Kselman, *Death and the Afterlife in Modern France* (Princeton, NJ, 1993); Robert Houlbrooke, ed., *Death, Ritual and Bereavement* (London, 1989); Joachim Whaley, ed., *Mirrors of Mortality: Studies in the Social History of Death* (New York, 1982). Arthur Imhof, *Lost Worlds: How Our European Ancestors Coped with Everyday Life and Why Life Is So Hard Today* (Charlottesville, VA, 1996), is a fascinating discussion of death rates and coping strategies over time. See also David Troyanky, "Death," in Peter N. Stearns, ed., *Encyclopedia of European Social History* (New York, 2001), II, pp. 219–233 for a good summary and additional references.

Exceptionally rich historical work applies to early modern Europe: Michelle Vovelle, *La mort en Occident: de 1300 à nos jours* (Paris, 1983); Samuel Cohn, *Death and Property in Siena, 1205–1800: Strategies for the Afterlife* (Baltimore, MD, 1988) and the *Cult of Remembrance and the Black Death: Six Renaissance Cities in Central Italy* (Baltimore, MD, 1992); Sharon Strocchia, *Death and Ritual in Renaissance Florence* (Baltimore, MD, 1992); Ralph Houlbrooke, *Death, Religion and the Family in England, 1480–1750* (Oxford, 1998); Carlos Eire, *From Madrid to Purgatory: The Art and Craft of Dying in Sixteenth-Century Spain* (Cambridge, UK, 1995); John McManners, *Death and the Enlightenment: Changing Attitude to Death among Christians and Unbelievers in Eighteenth-Century France* (Oxford, 1981); David Cressy, *Birth, Marriage, and Death: Ritual, Religion, and the Life-Cycle in Tudor and Stuart England* (Oxford, 1997); Craig Koslofsky, *The Reformation of the Dead: Death and Ritual in Early Modern Germany* (New York, 2000); Margaret Kind, *The Death of the Child Valerio Marcelle* (Chicago, 1994); Mary Dobson, *Contours of Death and Disease in Early Modern England* (Cambridge, 1997).

On the United States, key works include: David Stannard, *The Puritan Way of Death* (New York, 1977) and (ed.) *Death in America* (Philadelphia, 1975); James Farrell, *Inventing the American Way of Death* (Philadelphia, 1980); Robert Wells, *Facing the "King of Terrors": Death and Society in an American Community, 1750–1990* (Cambridge, 2000); Gary Laderman, *Rest in Peace: A Cultural History of Death and the Funeral Home in Twentieth-Century America* (New York, 2003); Richard Meyer, ed., *Ethnicity and the American Cemetery* (Bowling Green, OH, 1993); Robert Haberstein and William Lamers, *The History of American Funeral Directing* (5th ed., Brookfield, WI, 2001); Leo Touchet, *Rejoice When You Die: The New Orleans Jazz Funerals* (Baton Rouge, LA, 1998); Karla Holloway, *Pass On: African American Mourning Stories* (Durham, NC, 2002); Wright Hughes and Wilbur Hughes III, *Lay Down Body: Living History in African American Cemeteries* (Detroit, 1996). On emotional change, Peter N. Stearns, *American Cool: Constructing a Contemporary Emotional Style* (New York, 1994), and Paul Rosenblatt, *Bitter, Bitter Tears* (Minneapolis, MN, 1983).

On abortion: Linda Gordon, *Moral Property of Women: A History of Birth Control Politics in America* (Urbana, IL, 2002) and *Woman's Body, Woman's Right: A Social History of Birth Control in America* (New York, 1976); James Mohr, *Abortion in America, The Origins and Evolution of National Policy* (New York, 1978); John Riddle, *Eve's Herbs: A History of Contraception and Abortion in the West* (Cambridge, MA, 1997); Edward Shorter, *A History of Women's Bodies* (New York, 1982).

On the death penalty: Pieter Spierenburg, *The Spectacle of Suffering: Executions and the Evolution of Repression* (Cambridge, 1984); V. A. C. Gatrell, *The Hanging Tree: Execution and the English People, 1770–1868* (Oxford, 1994); Richard Evans, *Rituals of Retribution: Capital Punishment in Germany 1600–1987* (Oxford, 1996); David Cooper, *The Lesson of the Scaffold: The Public Execution Controversy in Victorian England* (Athens, OH, 1974); Richard van Duelmen, *Theatre of Horror: Crime and Punishment in Early Modern Germany* (Cambridge, 1990); Arlette Farge, *Fragile Lives; Violence, Power and Solidarity in Eighteenth-Century Paris* (Cambridge, MA, 1993).

On death and commemoration: John Gillis, ed., *Commemoration: The Politics of National Identity* (Princeton, NJ, 1994), with some exceptionally rich essays; Sarah Farmer, *Martyred Village: Commemorating the 1944 Massacre at Oradour-sur-Blane* (Berkeley, CA, 1999); Peter N. Stearns, *American Fear: The Causes and Consequences of High Anxiety* (New York, 2006); Adrian Kear and Deborah Steinberg, *Mourning Diana: Nation, Culture and the Performance of Grief* (London, 1999).

On war: Paul Fussell, *The Great War and Modern Mourning* (New York, 1975), and *Wartime: Understanding and Behavior in the Second World War* (New York, 1989).

On suicide: Olive Anderson, *Suicide in Victorian and Edwardian England* (Oxford, 1987); Georges Minois, *History of Suicide: Voluntary Death in Western Culture* (Baltimore, MD, 1999); Howard Kushner, *American Suicide: A Psychocultural Exploration* (New Brunswick, NJ, 1989); Victor Bailey, *This Rash Act: Suicide Across the Life Cycle in the Victorian City* (Stanford, 1998).

Index

About the Author

Peter N. Stearns is Provost and Professor of History at George Mason University. He has taught previously at Harvard, the University of Chicago, Rutgers, and Carnegie Mellon; he was trained at Harvard University. He has published widely both in modern social history, including the history of emotions, and in world history. Representative works in world history include *World History: A Survey, The Industrial Revolution in World History, Gender in World History, Consumerism in World History,* and *Growing Up: The History of Childhood in Global Context.* His publications in social history include *Old Age in Preindustrial Society, Anger: The Struggle for Emotional Control in America's History, Jealousy: The Evolution of an Emotion in American History, American Cool: Developing the Twentieth-Century Emotional Style, Fat History: Bodies and Beauty in Western Society, The Battleground of Desire: The Struggle for Self-Control in Modern America,* and *American Fear: The Causes and Consequences of High Anxiety.* He has also edited encyclopedias of world and social history, and since 1967 has served as editor-in-chief of *The Journal of Social History.*

In most of his research and writing, Peter Stearns has pursued three main goals. First, as a social historian he is eager to explore aspects of the human experience that are not always thought of in historical terms, and with attention to ordinary people as well as elites. Second, building on this, he seeks to use an understanding of historical change and continuity to explore current patterns of behavior and social issues. Finally, he is concerned with connecting new historical research with wider audiences, including classrooms. History must be seen in terms of the expansion of knowledge, not primarily the repetition of familiar topics and materials. As he has worked extensively in world history, Peter Stearns is also eager to promote comparative analysis and the assessment of modern global forces—for their own sake and as they shed light on the American experience and impact. He is deeply interested in using history to illuminate contemporary issues and politics.